LATIN BIOGRAPHY

STUDIES IN LATIN LITERATURE AND ITS INFLUENCE

Editors

D. R. Dudley and T. A. Dorey

CICERO

Chapters by J. P. V. D. Balsdon, M. L. Clarke, T. A. Dorey, A. E. Douglas, R. G. M. Nisbet, H. H. Scullard, G. B. Townend

LUCRETIUS

Chapters by D. R. Dudley, B. Farrington, O. E. Lowenstein, W. S. Maguinness, T. J. B. Spencer, G. B. Townend, D. E. W. Wormell

ROMAN DRAMA

Chapters by W. R. Chalmers, C. D. N. Costa, G. L. Evans, J. A. Hanson, A. Steegman, T. B. L. Webster, T. L. Zinn

LATIN HISTORIANS

Chapters by E. Badian, F. W. Walbank, T. A. Dorey, G. M. Paul, P. G. Walsh, E. A. Thompson, J. Campbell

LATIN BIOGRAPHY

Chapters by Edna Jenkinson, E. I. McQueen, A. J. Gossage, G. B. Townend, A. R. Birley, T. A. Dorey, D. H. Farmer, Rosalind Brooke

LATIN BIOGRAPHY

Chapters by

Edna Jenkinson   E. I. McQueen

A. J. Gossage   G. B. Townend

A. R. Birley   T. A. Dorey

D. H. Farmer   Rosalind Brooke

Edited by

T. A. DOREY

BASIC BOOKS, INC., PUBLISHERS

NEW YORK

To the Mayors and Chairmen of Warwickshire, 1965–66, and their charming Ladies

Contents

Abbreviations

AE	Année Epigraphique
AJA	American Journal of Archaeology
AJP	American Journal of Philology
CIL	Corpus Inscriptionum Latinarum
CQ (NS)	Classical Quarterly (New Series)
EHR	English Historical Review
IG	Inscriptiones Graecae
IGR	Inscriptiones Graecae ad res Romanas pertinentes
Josephus *Ant.*	Josephus, *Jewish Antiquities*
JRS	Journal of Roman Studies
Migne P. L.	Migne, *Patrologia Latina*
Pliny N. H.	Pliny, *Natural History*
RE	Realenzyklopädie (Pauly-Wissowa)
RS	Rolls Series
SHA	*Scriptores Historiae Augustae*

Introduction

THIS volume contains chapters on Nepos, Plutarch, and Suetonius, the three best-known Classical biographers. There are also accounts of the less-familiar works of Q. Curtius Rufus and the author—or authors—of the *Historia Augusta*, while an attempt has been made to trace the development of Latin biography in the Middle Ages.

Biography has always been a popular literary genre—from the point of view of both the reader and the writer. There is something in human nature that makes men more interested in people than in events, and the details of the personal life and habits of eminent men have always fascinated the more ordinary members of the community. For the writer, the span of one man's life forms a compact literary unit, and, in the case of a biography written by a disciple or a protégé, the material will lie ready to hand.

The greatest name in Latin biography is Suetonius. He influenced biographies written at Rome during the next three centuries. The *Historia Augusta*, for example, follows the pattern he laid down, though not his technique. Almost more important was his influence in the Middle Ages. Einhard's *Life of Charlemagne*,[1] which owed much to the *Twelve Caesars*, marks the point where hagiography begins to be replaced by secular biography.[2] Suetonius also affected the historiographical tradition, and it was as a result of his popularity in the Middle Ages that character sketches, descriptions of personal appearance, and examples of various types of behaviour became a feature of many histories written at that period.

The Middle Ages were indebted to Suetonius, Shakespeare to Plutarch, Gibbon to the *Historia Augusta*. Since the Renaissance their methods have gradually been superseded by a more critical and scientific approach, but the ancient biographers can always claim the credit for having established biography as a major form of literature.

NOTES

[1] Cf. ch. IV.
[2] Cf. R. W. Southern, *St. Anselm and his Biographer*.

I

Nepos—An Introduction to Latin Biography

EDNA JENKINSON

WHY spend time on Nepos? The question is a fair one, especially in these days when the Classics base their claim to our attention, at least in part, on offering us the study only of the very best. Cornelius Nepos is not a first-rate author, and it is all too easy to fault him on grounds both of subject-matter and of style, but chance has made him the earliest Latin biographer whose work survives today. Thus he has an interest for us and an importance in the history of Latin literature out of all proportion to his intrinsic literary merit. The man himself is a somewhat shadowy figure (even his *praenomen* is unknown), but it seems that he was born about 99 B.C., perhaps at Ticinum in the Insubrian area of Cisalpine Gaul,[1] the native land of his friend and near contemporary Catullus. His family were wealthy, but not of senatorial rank,[2] and he settled at Rome in early manhood, choosing to devote himself to letters rather than to politics, yet counting among his close friends many of the leading public figures of his age.[3] His was a quiet life, spent in writing and occasional publishing, and he stayed at Rome until his death in 24 B.C. His prolific output suggests that he was far from idle, though he could not rival the indefatigable productiveness or the encyclopaedic knowledge of a Varro. Apart from a single book of love poems,[4] perhaps a mere *jeu d'esprit*, he published only prose. In the dedication to his poems Catullus[5] mentions his *Chronica*, a three-volume outline history of the world in the annalistic tradition, and teases him about it as only a good friend could. We hear, too, of a comprehensive treatise on geography, though later critics castigate it as diffuse in structure and uncritical,[6] so that we need not lament its loss. Most of his other work was biographical in character, and we would give much to possess his full-scale *Life of Cato* or the *Life of Cicero* which he wrote as an act of homage after the orator's death.[7]

Today, however, Nepos must be judged by the surviving portions of the *De Viris Illustribus*. In its complete form in at least sixteen books[8] this work contained biographies of famous men, both foreigners and Romans, from many walks of life. The categories of generals, historians, kings, and poets are certainly established, and there are strong grounds for assuming that orators, statesmen, philosophers, and grammarians were represented, too. This ambitious project was dedicated to Atticus, Cicero's close friend and correspondent, with whom the biographer, too, had been on intimate terms since his return from Greece in 65 B.C., and the complete work first appeared whilst he was still alive. After his death in 32 B.C., Nepos issued a revised edition, and it is to this that all that remains belongs. It is not much—just the book on foreign generals and two complete *Lives* and a few fragments from the book on Latin historians—but on this comparatively slight evidence we must base our study of the origins and early development of biography at Rome.

The impulse to record the lives of famous men sprang, like much else in the literature of Greece and Rome, from a desperate bid to outwit man's last enemy, the grave. Death alone brought the Classical world up sharply against its limitations,[9] representing, as it did, the obliteration of achievement and the annihilation of the human personality. Against these tragedies, it was believed, the pen could in some degree prevail and win a sort of immortality both for the writer and his theme. Hence arose the celebration of the deeds of heroes in Greek epic, and hence, too, the dirges and the funeral eulogies we find from early times in Greece and, quite independently, it seems, at Rome. Cicero[10] mentions the singing of commemorative songs at banquets as an early Roman custom, and elsewhere we read of prose orations delivered at the obsequies of famous men. One of the earliest known examples, that on Brutus by Valerius Publicola, is preserved for us by Dionysius.[11] Such *laudationes* were written down after delivery and kept among the other family archives in the *atrium*.[12] They seem to have been life histories in brief, and it is hard to deny them their place, as Leo does,[13] in the family tree of literary biography at Rome. But the main impetus towards the development of the genre came, as almost always, from the Greeks.

The Sophists, as purveyors of the craft of rhetoric, exerted an influence both potent and profound upon the literature and thought of fifth-century Greece. Oratory had, of course, existed in the past, but first became self-conscious when Gorgias and his successors formulated rules for expression, speech structure and argument, and extended the subject's range to cover political and general, or 'epideictic', as well as purely forensic themes. These new pre-occupations with language and effective argument came just at the time when prose was emerging as a vehicle for expression, and they caused it to change direction. The old concern for simplicity and clarity of narrative, derived from the technique of the epic poets, now suffered an eclipse, but from the poets the rhetoricians imported into prose both embellishments of style and themes which once belonged to poetry alone. Among these last was the *encomium*, once the triumphal song with which a victor in the games was led back in procession to his home. In its new prose form this now became an exercise in epideictic oratory, whereby the merits of a mythological character were celebrated according to a fixed formula, and the surviving examples from the early period all belong to this type.[14] In the fourth century, however, concern with the individual increased, and Greek biography proper may be said to begin in about 365 B.C. with the publication of Isocrates' *Evagoras*. This somewhat florid work claimed to be the first *encomium* on a living person, the head of the ruling house of Cyprian Salamis, and though it still followed the traditional scheme, the possibilities for more sincere appraisals of the lives and characters of real people were now apparent. Soon afterwards there followed the very similar *Agesilaus* of Xenophon, some parts of which were borrowed with very little change from narrative passages and a speech in the *Hellenica*. At the same time what one can call the legend of Socrates was also attracting a literature of its own and giving impetus to the emergence of yet another genre, memoirs.

It was for Aristotle and his successors in the Peripatetic school to develop biography further. The new interest in ethics led to the deeper exploration of the human personality, both of individuals and of types. Here one cannot ignore, though they are not biography as such, the famous *Characters* of Theophrastus, Aristotle's successor, which appeared about 319 B.C. The old view that they were intended as an illustrative appendix to a work of instruction in ethics has now been abandoned, and it seems that they provided materials for rhetorical exercises,[15] or served as a pattern book for the stock figures of the contemporary stage.[16] Theophrastus' rival

Aristoxenus was more concerned with individuals, and his *Bioi Andron*, including *Lives* of Pythagoras, Socrates, and Plato, established the so-called Peripatetic type of biography, in which a man revealed his character through his actions. The practice was not confined to professed Peripatetics, and one of the most famous of this school of writers was the Academic philosopher Antigonus of Carystus, whose style was much admired. Also eminent in their day were Satyrus, who worked mainly at Alexandria and extended the scope of biography to include the *Lives* of men of action as well as thinkers, and Hermippus of Smyrna, the author of a vast work on philosophers, poets, and law-givers. A fragment of Satyrus is preserved among the papyri from Oxyrhynchus and reveals his merits as a stylist, but he was said to be wholly uncritical. Hermippus was important for his influence on Plutarch, but his work, fragments of which are preserved in Diogenes Laertius, shows all the worst faults of the school—scandalmongering, sensationalism, and an almost complete indifference to the truth.

Alexandria produced a rather different type of biography, too. The work of editing Greek texts created a need for biographical introductions not too out of key with the scholarly character of the main body of the work. More attention was paid to chronology and less to character, and there seems to have been a rudimentary attempt to weigh conflicting evidence to try to ascertain the truth. The result, however, can only have been dry and uninspiring, and the main importance of these writers lies in the influence they had upon biographers at Rome. Names can mean little to us, but we hear of Jason, a pupil of Posidonius, as eminent among biographers of this kind.

A third type of biography was based on the *encomium* and was in the tradition of the *Evander* of Isocrates or *Agesilaus* of Xenophon, which have been discussed above. Such *encomia* could be developed at length and have an independent existence, as Polybius' *Life of Philopoemen*, or they could be incorporated into a full-scale history as a character sketch.[17] We have seen that there was precedent for this 'double-purpose' type of composition in Xenophon.

At Rome all these types of Greek biography soon won acceptance. They appealed to the strong native commemorative instinct to which we have already referred, and we find experiments in Latin biography made from an early date. The first writer to produce the form was that 'most learned of the Romans', as Quintilian calls him,

M. Terentius Varro. Jerome,[18] at least, quotes Suetonius' authority in naming him as founder of the genre, but nothing of Varro's in this line survives. Wo do hear, however, of a strange work called the *Hebdomades* (through its preoccupation with the number seven) or *Imagines*. This was a collection in fifteen books of character sketches of Greeks and Romans, seven hundred in all, accompanied by a portrait and an epigram in every case. It was perhaps the earliest illustrated book produced at Rome. It was also the first work setting the personalities of Greeks and Romans side by side; the reader would be invited to draw his own comparisons, and so, one suspects, a new way developed of enhancing the glory of the rising power of Rome. After Varro, Jerome mentions Santra and Hyginus, of whom we know but little,[19] and so we come to consider Cornelius Nepos himself. At last we get our feet on solid ground, and turn to the study of a substantial and readily accessible text.[20]

Nepos followed the Peripatetic tradition in the main, and thought of himself as a popularizer, writing to entertain and to give moral uplift of a general kind, not factual information more suited to history:

> Pelopidas Thebanus, magis historicis quam vulgo notus. cuius de virtutibus dubito quem ad modum exponam, *quod vereor, si res explicare incipiam, ne non vitam eius enarrare, sed historiam videar scribere*; sin tantummodo summas attigero, ne rudibus Graecarum litterarum minus dilucide appareat quantus fuerit ille vir. itaque utrique rei occurram, quantum potuero, et medebor cum satietati tum ignorantiae lectorum. (xvi. 1.1)
>
> The Theban Pelopidas is better known to historians than to the general public. I am uncertain how to expound his merits; *for I am afraid that I may appear to be writing history rather than giving an account of his life if I embark upon a systematic account of his achievements*; but if I merely touch on the high spots, I am afraid that to those unacquainted with Greek literature it will not be clear beyond all doubt how great a man he was. So I shall face up to both these difficulties as best I can, bearing in mind how much my readers can take and how little they know.

He was well aware that biography lacked the dignity of history, and this explains his defensive manner in the preface:

> non dubito fore plerosque, Attice, qui hoc genus scripturae leve et non satis dignum summorum virorum personis iudicent. (*Praef. 1*)
>
> I am well aware, Atticus, that a great many people will look upon

5

this kind of writing as trivial and unworthy of the roles played in life by men of eminence.

Nepos goes on to explain that many of the trivia he records are included to open the eyes of his compatriots to the different usages of other nations, notably the Greeks; he might have added that they were designed to entertain the reader, and not primarily to instruct at all.

What were Nepos' sources? Principally, it seems,[21] the lost biographers who preceded him, both Greek and Roman, but he quotes freely from historians, too, though it is doubtful if he had first-hand knowledge of the works of the many writers whose names he drops so knowledgeably. Nepos does not mention Herodotus, but Thucydides is referred to several times: in the *Life of Themistocles*,[22] for instance, his evidence is preferred to that of later writers on the grounds that he was a near contemporary of the politician and a native of the same city. Nepos twice translates passages from the Greek historian,[23] once with an error so glaring[24] that one would assume he had before him a different text from ours, were it not for his gross carelessness in other ways elsewhere. Several later Greek writers get direct references,[25] though how much this really means is uncertain, and in at least one case their relative merits are compared. Of writers of the Roman period he mentions Polybius, Sulpicius Blitho, an annalist of the Punic War era,[26] Hannibal himself, and his own friend Atticus.

In a superficial sense, at least, Nepos was a Romanizer, perhaps because he saw this as a way to help his readers to accept strange customs. We can stomach a temple of Minerva at Sparta,[27] since English writers followed the same practice until the present century, but Hamilcar's offering to Jupiter Optimus Maximus instead of Baal is less convincing.[28] Sometimes, too, but not consistently, Roman political terms obtrude into Greek contexts: thus on occasion we find the Gerousia at Sparta has become the Senate and the ephors *magistratus*. Again, in military contexts the familiar can replace the unfamiliar, and in the siege of Paros by Miltiades *vinea* and *testudines* oust the Greek μηχανήματα.

The Peripatetic biography, which we see in its classic form in the *Parallel Lives* of Plutarch in a later age, followed a fixed formula: the subject's birth, youth and character, achievements and death were narrated, all to an *obbligato* accompaniment of ethical reflection, and

6

diversified by anecdotes whose purpose was solely to entertain. Nepos' tentative flirtation with the form produced less uniform results, and there is great variation, particularly in length and wealth of detail, between the different *Lives*. Aristides, for instance, is dismissed in three brief chapters, but the *Life* is typically Peripatetic in the way the subject's virtues are shown up by his deeds:

> neque aliud est ullum huius in re militari illustre factum quam huius imperii memoria, iustitiae vero et *aequitatis* et innocentiae multa, in primis quod eius *aequitate* factum est, cum in communi classe esset Graeciae simul cum Pausania, quo duce Mardonius erat fugatus, ut summa imperii maritimi ab Lacedaemoniis transferretur ad Athenienses. (iii. 2.2)
>
> Though there is no other brilliant exploit in his military career except the memory of this command (at Plataea),[29] there are many instances of his justice, *equity* and integrity; in particular it was due to his *equity* when he was serving in the combined Greek fleet with Pausanias, the general who had routed Mardonius, that the control of the sea passed from the Lacedaemonians to the Athenians.

In contrast, the Machiavellian character of Alcibiades caught Nepos' imagination, and here we have a detailed and clear picture of this spoilt favourite of fortune, who could be a force for evil as well as good;[30] his fatal charm drew all men's eyes upon him,[31] and 'wherever he lived he held the limelight, as well as being greatly loved'.[32]

It is usual to say[33] that Nepos attempted also the Alexandrian-philological type of *Life*, and *Cimon, Conon, Iphicrates, Chabrias*, and *Timotheus* are quoted as examples of the briefer, more factual style. In practice it is hard to draw a firm line between these biographies and those we have surveyed already. The *Life of Cimon* shows the same progression from the cradle to the grave and has its share of trivial anecdote to illumine character:

> He was so generous that, having estates and gardens in numerous places, he never set a watchman in them to protect the fruit, since he did not wish to prevent anyone from enjoying any part of his property that he chose. Pages also followed him with money, so that if anyone needed his help he might have something immediately available to give, fearing to seem to refuse if he delayed. (v. 4.1–2)[34]

Nothing could be more in the Peripatetic tradition than this. Conon, too, was 'like the rest of mankind in showing less wisdom in good fortune than in bad'.[35] In the account which follows his downfall is traced back to his *hybris*; facts are once more linked with attitudes of mind.

Three biographies, however, in some sense stand apart from the rest. The *Epaminondas* and *Agesilaus* are eulogies, the first somewhat like the conventional form taught in the schools of rhetoric, the second an imitation, in the event not close, of Xenophon's work of the same name. Both, like Nepos' other *Lives*, also seem to owe something to the native commemorative oration, and it is difficult to submit them to systematic analysis. The *Epaminondas* is unique in having a formal introduction:

> cum autem exprimere imaginem consuetudinis atque vitae velimus Epaminondae, nihil videmur debere praetermittere, quod pertineat ad eam declarandam. quare dicemus primum de genere eius, deinde quibus disciplinis et a quibus sit eruditus, tum de moribus ingeniique facultatibus et si qua alia memoria digna erunt, postremo de rebus gestis, quae a plurimis animi anteponuntur virtutibus. (XV. 1.3–4)
> Since, then, I wish to portray the life and habits of Epaminondas, it seems to me that I ought to omit nothing conducive to that end. Therefore I shall begin by speaking of his family, then of the subjects he studied and who taught him, and next go on to discuss his character, his natural qualities and anything else that seems worth recording. Finally I shall give an account of his exploits, which most writers think more important than intellectual qualities.

There is also an attempt at an epigrammatic ending:

> ex quo intellegi potest *unum virum pluris quam civitatem fuisse.*
> (*Ibid.* 10.4)

But, in spite of evidence of greater care in composition, the main body of these two *Lives* is very little different in style and content from the rest.

The *Life of Atticus* is more distinctive, as Nepos' only extant biography of a contemporary he had known well and admired. As we have already seen, it was first issued within the subject's lifetime, but we possess the revision published shortly after his death. In form it, too, is a eulogy, but it has a unique freshness and immediacy of appeal that come from first-hand knowledge of the subject. It is Nepos' only *Life* which we can seriously consider as an historical source for its period, and it serves as a useful background against which to read Cicero's one-sided correspondence with Atticus. It is also interesting as Nepos' only voyage on the troubled waters of contemporary politics (he would have used the metaphor himself),[36] and his own quietism and love of compromise is everywhere apparent in his approval of these attitudes in Atticus. In commenting on the fact that Atticus achieved the difficult feat of admiring Cicero and Quintus Hortensius, those great rivals for the first rank in eloquence, exactly equally, he remarks:

> et, id quod erat dificillimum, efficiebat ut inter quos tantae laudis esset aemulatio, nulla intercederet obtrectatio essetque talium virorum copula. (xxv. 5.4)
> He even accomplished the difficult task of preventing any ill-feeling between those rivals for a position of such glory, and served as a bond of union between those two great men.

In politics, too, Atticus commended himself to Nepos by his caution:

> in re publica ita est versatus, ut semper optimarum partium et esset et existimaretur, neque se tamen civilibus fluctibus committeret, quod non magis eos in sua potestate existimabat esse qui se his dedissent, quam qui maritimis iactarentur. (*Ibid.* 6.1)
> In political life he conducted himself in such a way that he always was and appeared to be a member of the 'best party', yet he did not launch himself upon the waves of civil strife, since he thought that those who had wholly surrendered themselves to them had no more control of themselves than those who were tossed on the billows of the sea.

His neutrality in the Civil War, which must have seemed to his enemies suspiciously like fence-sitting, is equally approved, not least because it paid off afterwards:

> Atticus' neutrality (*quies*) was so acceptable to Caesar that when he had won his victory and was making written demands for monetary contributions from private individuals, he not only left Atticus untroubled but also yielded to his entreaties and pardoned his nephew and Quintus Cicero, both of whom had served Pompey. Thus by the long-established habit of his life he escaped the new dangers. (*Ibid.* 7.3)

In the epilogue added to the second edition Nepos applauds similar tact in his subject's relations with Caesar (Octavian) and Antony; commenting on the fact that Antony and Atticus carried on a correspondence across the world, he adds:

The importance of this can more readily be understood by one who can judge what great tact it requires to retain the intimacy and good-will of persons who were not only rivals in most important matters, but also such enemies as Caesar and Antony inevitably became, since each desired to be the ruler, not just of the city of Rome, but of the world. (*Ibid.* 20.5)

Nepos obviously preached the gospel of non-involvement and stood in marked contrast to his near contemporary Sallust, who followed an active career in politics by a decade or so devoted to writing which shows equal partisanship.[37]

All the *Lives* afford a happy hunting-ground for those in quest of historical errors. The book on great non-Roman generals claims to be comprehensive, in that it has in the second edition a somewhat pedantic section on kings who were also generals and were to be dealt with more fully as kings elsewhere; yet it omits Brasidas, surely a general who can hold up his head beside any of those included. The *Life of Miltiades* begins by confusing the great Miltiades of Marathon with his lesser-known uncle, and it per-petuates the error throughout the first two chapters. Even the battle of Marathon is not correctly described, and the numbers of Athenians and Plataeans on the Greek side are stated wrongly.[38] The *Life of Themistocles* shows the same fine indifference to dates, times and distances; for instance, in chapter 5, in telling the story of how Xerxes heard that a plan was afoot to cut off his retreat to Asia by destroying the bridge over the Hellespont, Nepos states that the Persian king had taken six months to make the outward journey, but completed his return in thirty days. These figures not only con-flict with those given in our Greek sources; they are also at variance with those Nepos himself gives in another place.[39] I suspect, how-ever, that these discrepancies would not have worried him at all.

On the whole the lives of Carthaginians and Romans are less in-accurate than those of the Greeks, but even here the standard is somewhat low, and there are plenty of instances of carelessness and exaggeration. When he praises a man, especially, Nepos loses all sense of proportion, and exposes himself to ridicule: thus in the *Life of Atticus* Cicero's foresight is described as 'almost like divina-tion'. Such expressions can be paralleled from Cicero himself, of course, but Nepos continues:

He not only predicted the events which actually happened during his lifetime, but also, like a prophet, foretold those things which are now being experienced. (xxv. 16.4)

This surely is too much!

Nepos' style is very uneven, and shows that he has not complete mastery over his medium, the Latin tongue. He is at his best when he expresses himself in the short, simple sentences which are most appropriate to his unpretentious subject-matter. An excellent example of his narrative style is the vivid account of Alcibiades' return to Athens in 408 B.C.:

> All the city went down to the Piraeus to meet them; but so keen was the desire everyone felt to see Alcibiades that the people thronged round his trireme exactly as if he had come alone. For they were firmly convinced that both their reverses in the past and their successes in the present were to be ascribed to him. Therefore they blamed themselves for the loss of Sicily and for the victories won by the Lacedaemonians because they had banished so great a man from the state. And indeed it seemed that they had reason to hold this view; for as soon as he had assumed control of the army the enemy had at once met their match on both land and sea. When Alcibiades disembarked it was him alone that the populace escorted, though Thrasybulus and Theramenes had shared in the command and had come with him to the Piraeus; crowns of gold and bronze were showered upon him from every side, a thing which had never happened before save to Olympic victors. He received these tokens of the devotion of his fellow-citizens with tears in his eyes as he recalled their harsh treatment of him in the past.
>
> As soon as he arrived in the city the public assembly was called and he spoke in such a way that none was so hard-hearted as not to weep for his fate and show the anger they felt towards those who had caused his exile—just as if this were a completely different people, and as if those who were then shedding tears for him were not the self-same men who had condemned him for impiety. (vii. 6.1–4)

This same *Life*, one of Nepos' most successful, also shows him rivalling the great Roman historians of later ages in the delineation of character:

> natus in amplissima civitate summo genere, omnium aetatis suae multo formosissimus; ad omnes res aptus consiliique plenus— namque imperator fuit summus et mari et terra; disertus, ut in primis dicendo valeret, quod tanta erat commendatio oris atque orationis,

ut nemo ei [dicendo] posset resistere; dives; cum tempus posceret,
laboriosus, patiens; liberalis, splendidus non minus in vita quam
victu; affabilis, blandus, temporibus callidissime serviens: idem
simul ac se remiserat neque causa suberat quare animi laborem per-
ferret, luxuriosus, dissolutus, libidinosus, intemperans reperiebatur,
ut omnes admirarentur in uno homine tantam esse dissimilitudinem
tamque diversam naturam. (*Ibid.* 1.2–4)

This passage stands comparison with Livy on Hannibal, but Nepos
cannot sustain the level of achievement.

Sometimes, and especially in the eulogies *Epaminondas*, *Agesilaus*,
and *Atticus*, he attempts mild flights of rhetoric, and, as we have
seen, the use of a highly wrought style on such occasions had
honourable ancestry both in the Greek *encomium* and the native
laudatio. Long before the advent of Greek rhetoric to Rome the
funeral orations were highly 'oratorical' in style. There was a
rhetorical element in the native genius of the Latin tongue which
important occasions could bring forth. As Quintilian wrote in a
later age, 'Even peasants and the uneducated use lively, emphatic
and exaggerated language, for no one is content with the un-
embellished truth.' Soon, however, such national tendencies were
further stimulated by the systematic study of the art of public
speaking.

Greek and (after some initial difficulties) Latin teachers of rhetoric
were settled at Rome by the end of the second century B.C. By the
time of Nepos' youth the pattern of their training would have been
standardized to some extent, though never into anything like
the orderly curriculum we read of later in Quintilian. Among the
exercises Nepos would certainly have practised in the schools the
'praise and blame of famous men' was most appropriate for his
future craft. At this time rhetoric was still, at least in theory, the
handmaid of oratory, and the teacher would have in mind his pupil's
need to convince an opponent; hence both sides of every case were
argued out (*argumentatio in utramque partem*). If one side only was
put, it was put with overemphasis, to silence the opposition before
it became vocal. To this training we can trace the exaggerations in
Nepos' eulogies: he sets out to convince a potential adversary and
'protests too much'.

Nepos on occasion attempts the periodic style, but cannot sustain
it, and the result is often bathos. Indeed, even his simplest sentences
are often unevenly balanced and end abruptly:

hoc loco libet interponere, etsi seiunctum ab re proposita est, nimia fiducia quantae calamitati soleat esse. (xvi. 3.1)

The verbs at the end do not counterbalance the sentence's pretentious start, and one feels the thought, not just the language, is inadequate. Such examples could be multiplied many times. Again, he is overfond of antithesis, often with strained effect:

at ille post non multo sua sponte ad exercitum rediit et ibi *non callida sed dementi ratione* cogitata patefecit. (iv. 3.1)
But not long afterwards Pausanias returned to the army on his own account, and there revealed his plans in a manner *inane rather than adroit*.

His love of alliteration is almost childish (*tam turbido tempore*, for instance), and he is fond of collocations of liquid consonants.[40] In syntax he uses the present participle freely, in a way not acceptable in later Latin prose:

at Alcibiades, victis Atheniensibus non satis tuta eadem loca sibi *arbitrans*, penitus in Threciam se supra Propontidem abdidit, *sperans* ibi facillime suam fortunam occuli posse. (vii. 9.1)[41]

In vocabulary he is more limited than later writers, but in my view he has been overcriticized, and his style is lively, on the whole, and well able to convey his meaning. There are some colloquialisms, a few archaisms and some words which are not found again in prose until much later. He keeps some Greek words without attempting to find Latin equivalents,[42] but as we have seen he Romanizes customs and institutions on occasion, too. He can be repetitious, and is overfond of *nam* and *enim* and of the demonstrative pronoun *hic*. This Leo traces to the influence of the Alexandrian-philological type of Greek biography,[43] but I am inclined to disagree.

However, with these reservations, and especially when he does not try too hard, Nepos is a pleasant if unexciting writer, well suited to the fate which soon befell him, that of becoming a school book for more junior pupils, valuable both for his easy, lucid Latin and the interest of his subject-matter. Syme, indeed, in his book on Sallust,[44] suggests that Nepos even wrote with this end in view, but he quotes no evidence to support his theory. Be that as it may, Nepos formed part of the curriculum in English and Scottish grammar schools from early in the eighteenth century.[45] Construes and paraphrases were made of him which enjoyed a wide circulation, and he gave many British schoolboys their first (albeit inexact) acquaintance with the history of Greece. He could well be used more often in the 'O' Level book rota today. More interesting, at least to girls, than isolated books of Caesar or of Livy, he serves as an admirable introduction to the ancient world. For the mature student, however, his work may well appear somewhat dull in itself, and his main importance will be seen to lie rather in the influence he had on the biographers who followed and in every case surpassed him—Plutarch, who brought the Peripatetic type of *Life* to perfection, and Suetonius and Tacitus among the Romans. How their work evolved it is for others in this book to examine and record.

NOTES

[1] Pliny, *N.H.* iii. 127.

[2] Pliny, *Epistles* v. 3.6.

[3] e.g. Cicero (Suetonius, *Divus Iulius* 55; Gellius xv. 28.1; Macrobius, *Sat.* ii. 1.14) and Atticus (v. infr.).

[4] Pliny, *Ep.* v. 3.1 ff.

[5] Catullus I. 5–7.

[6] e.g. Pliny, *N.H.* v. 4.

[7] Gellius xv. 28.2. (It seems to have been quite critical in parts.)

[8] Charisius i. 141.13 Keil, cites the sixteenth book.

[9] Sophocles, *Antigone* 361.

[10] Cicero, *Tusc. Disp.* iv. 3.

[11] Dionysius, *Rom. Ant.* v. 17.

[12] Cicero, *Cato Maior* 12.

[13] F. Leo, *Die Griechisch-Römische Biographie* (Leipzig, 1901), pp. 226 ff. Cf. D. R. Stuart, *Epochs of Greek and Roman Biography* (Berkeley, California, 1928), ch. 7 and 8.

[14] e.g. Gorgias' (?) *Helen*. (The lost *Praise of Death* and the *Praise of Naïs* of Alcidamas were of this type.)

[15] Latin rhetoric schools, at least, practised such sketches, and we may assume Theophrastan influence on them: 'illa in scholis ἤθη—quibus plerumque rusticos, superstitiosos, avaros, timidos secundum condicionem propositionum effingimus' (Quintilian, *Inst. Orat.* vi. 2.17).

[16] *v.* R. G. Ussher, *The Characters of Theophrastus* (1960), Intr., pp. 11–12.

[17] e.g. Polybius x. 2.

[18] Jerome, Migne, *P.L.* xxiii. 821, *prolog. ad Dextrum in librum de illustribus*; cf. Suetonius, *Reliquiae*, ed. Reifferscheid, p. 3.

[19] Suetonius, *Gram.* 14 and *Poet.* 4; cf. Gellius 1.14.1 and Asconius, *Pis.* 12.

[20] e.g. Oxford Classical Text, ed. E. O. Winstedt (1904); Loeb edition, ed. and trans. J. C. Rolfe (London and Cambridge, Mass., 1929).

[21] *v.* e.g., xv. 4.6.

[22] ii. 9.1.

[23] ii. 9.2–4; cf. *ibid.* 1.4.

[24] ii. 9.4; *tuam petens amicitiam* = διὰ τὴν σὴν φιλίαν.

[25] e.g. Theopompus, Dinon and Timaeus; vii. 11.i; ix. 5.4.

[26] xxiii. 13.1.

[27] iv. 5.2.

[28] xxiii. 2.3.

[29] Aristides also fought at Marathon, and later against the Persians in Cyprus and on the Hellespont.

[30] vii. 3.5.

[31] *Ibid.*

[32] *Ibid.* 11.6.

[33] e.g. Rolfe, *op. cit., Intro.*, p. 360; cf. Leo, *op. cit.*, p. 210.

[34] Cf. the rest of the chapter.

[35] ix. 5.1.

[36] xxv. 6.1; cf. 10.6.

[37] R. Syme compares the two in his Sather Lectures on Sallust (University of California Press, 1964).

[38] i. 5.1–2.

[39] Cf. xvii. 4.4.

[40] e.g. Epaminondas a Thebanis morte multatus est (xv. 8.3); animi magnitudinem admirans (ii. 10.1).

[41] Cf. *ibid.* vii.4 (*existimans*); ii. 10.1 (*admirans cupiensque*).

[42] e.g. xxv. 14.1 (*anagnosten*); but sometimes he does produce a Latin equivalent, as *clava* for the σκυτάλη, the Spartan ephors' special staff (iv. 3.4); cf. also p. 6 *supra*.

[43] Leo, *op. cit.*, p. 217; cf. Rolfe, *op. cit.*, p. 361.

[44] *Op. cit.*

[45] M. L. Clarke, *Classical Education in Britain* (1959), pp. 51, 138, 194–5.

II

Quintus Curtius Rufus

E. I. McQUEEN

THE inclusion in a volume devoted to Latin biography of a chapter on Quintus Curtius, leaving as it does unanswered the question, 'Is Curtius writing biography or is he writing history?' or rather creating a strong presumption in favour of the former, may give rise to serious objections. Nevertheless in a survey of Roman literature some definite decision must be taken, and for the inclusion of this chapter in the biography volume rather than in the volume on the Roman historians I am not myself responsible. It may therefore be not entirely inappropriate to say a few words on this topic as an introduction to my subject.

In our present age, any discussion on the type of literature to which Curtius' work belongs may be largely an academic question, but a Roman, living at a time when the various literary genres were sharply distinguished one from another, would have given the matter more serious consideration. The distinction between history and biography was for the most part clear cut, and the most celebrated of ancient biographers within the full meaning of the word, Cornelius Nepos and Plutarch, inform us categorically that they are writing *Lives*, not *Histories*.[1] Of these, the former writes:

> Pelopidas Thebanus, magis historicis quam vulgo notus. Cuius de virtutibus dubito quem ad modum exponam, quod vereor, si res explicare incipiam, ne non vitam eius enarrare sed historiam videar scribere.
>
> Pelopidas of Thebes is better known to historians than to the general reader. With regard to his virtues, I am in doubt as how best to set them forth, because of a fear that if I begin to describe his exploits, I shall seem to be writing not his biography but history.

Plutarch makes the distinction between the two even clearer:

I am writing the lives of Alexander . . . and Caesar . . . because of the number of their deeds to be treated, I shall make no other preliminary statement than to beg my readers not to criticise me if I do not describe everything or narrate fully any of their celebrated exploits in each case, and if instead I curtail most of these. For I am writing biography, not history, and in the most famous deeds there is not always a revelation of virtue or vice, but often a trifling matter like a saying or a joke affords a greater indication of character than battles in which thousands are killed and the greatest armaments and sieges of cities. Accordingly just as painters obtain their likenesses from the face and the expression of the eyes and regard the remaining parts of the body as of little consideration, so it must be permitted me to penetrate to the signs of the soul and through these to represent the life of each, leaving their mighty exploits and struggles as a theme for others.

The purpose of both Nepos and Plutarch is to attempt a differentiation between the two literary genres, and both take roughly the same line, namely that whereas history describes in detail what its personages *do*, biography is more concerned with revealing what sort of person they *are*, and with this aim in view does not attempt a comprehensive survey of their deeds, but prefers rather to dwell on anecdotes and such activities as contribute towards an illumination of character, any straightforward narrative that occurs being entirely selective.

Now, when we apply this criterion to Curtius' work we find a large number of passages which would be unexpected in a biography —detailed accounts of battles (3.9–13; 4.12–16; 8.13–14) and of sieges (4.2–4; 4.6; 7.11; 8.11), or formal and highly elaborate set speeches (3.10; 5.8; 6.3; 7.1.18 ff; 7.8.12 ff; 9.6.17 ff; 10.2.15 ff; 10.3.7 ff), sometimes in pairs (4.14; 6.9–10; 8.7–8; 9.2–3), quite apart from numerous smaller snatches of conversation scattered about the work. We also find lengthy geographical and ethnological descriptions of the various areas traversed by Alexander (3.1.11–13; 3.4.6–10; 4.7.16–21; 5.1.11–16 and 25–35; 5.3.1–3; 6.4.4–7 and 15–22; 6.5.13–15; 7.3.5–22; 7.4.26–31; 7.7.2–4; 7.10.2–3; 7.11.1–3; 8.9; 9.1.4–5, 9–13), and in addition a considerable number of passages where Alexander is not personally at the centre of affairs and which are of little relevance in a biography pure and simple (3.2–3, 3.8.1–15, 3.8.24–3.9.6, activities of Darius; 3.13, Parmenio at Damascus; 4.1.17–20, activities of Amyntas, of Darius' generals, and of Agis; 4.5.13–22, Alexander's generals and admirals; 4.9.1–10, 4.10.25–11.1, 4.11.5–13, 4.13.11–14, 4.14.8, 5.1.1–9, 5.8–12, activities of Darius; 6.1, the Megalopolis campaign; 7.2.18–34, Parmenio at Ecbatana; 7.4.1–12, 7.5.19–26, activities of Bessus; 7.4.33–40, the duel in Areia; 9.7.1–11, unrest in the Greek settlements in Bactria; 10.6–10, the political situation after Alexander's death). All passages of this sort, though appropriate in history, are not normally, at any rate in such profusion and wealth of detail, present in biography.[2] In other words, Curtius, unlike Nepos and Plutarch, does attempt a comprehensive survey of his hero's activities, together with much else, and must therefore have considered himself to be writing history, not biography.

At the same time, however, we must be careful to observe the inclusion of material that is strictly speaking biographical: 3.1.14–18, the Gordian knot; 3.6, the story of the Acarnanian doctor; 3.12, Alexander's visit to Darius' captured family; 4.10.18 ff, the story of Tyriotes; 5.2.13–22, the anecdote of Darius' footstool and of Sisygambis and the wool; 6.2.6–9, the story of Ochus' granddaughter; 7.4.9–12, the story of Alexander and the skins of water; 7.7.8 ff, Aristander and the unfavourable omen; 7.10.4–9, the anecdote of the Sogdian nobles; 8.4.15–17, the private soldier resting on Alexander's throne; 8.5.22–24, Polyperchon mocking the prostration ceremony. Now all these sections are historically irrelevant and as such would have been ignored by a Thucydides or by a Polybius, but since they contribute towards an understanding of Alexander's character, they may be taken as examples of the biographical material present in Curtius' narrative.

It may be of relevance at this point to consider the normal practice of Roman rhetoricians in composing *encomia* in epideictic oratory, for although Curtius was not an epideictic orator, he was a rhetorical historian and came very much under the influence of this sort of thing; his *History*, though not an *encomium*, has certain affinities with this type of work. Our best evidence for the rhetorical treatment of such themes is provided by Quintilian, who mentions firstly the events preceding the subject's birth (country, ancestors and parentage, omens and prophecies, etc., 3.7.10), and goes on to suggest that one way of handling the topic is to describe the subject's life in strict chronological order, including both his deeds and his sayings:

Namque alias aetatis gradus gestarumque rerum ordinem sequi

speciosius fuit, ut in primis annis laudaretur indoles, tum disciplinae, post hoc operum, id est factorum dictorumque contextus. (3.7.15) For at times it has been more plausible to adhere to the various stages of his life, and to the due sequence of his achievments, in order to praise in his earliest years his natural talents, then the course of his education, and afterwards of his exploits, both in word and deed.

Lastly, Quintilian's advice is that in some cases certain events after the subject's death, such as divine and posthumous honours, are worthy of mention (3.7.17).

Despite our inability to discover whether Curtius obeyed the injunctions advocated by Quintilian in regard to the events preceding Alexander's birth, owing to the loss of the first two books of his *History*, the remainder of Quintilian's advice—doubtless a fresh exposition of current practice—is scrupulously observed: in addition to describing Alexander's deeds in the narrative, Curtius narrates many of his sayings in the anecdotes, and the last four chapters of the book, relating the events between his death and funeral, may perhaps serve to enhance his reputation by showing how his empire could not survive him. Chronological difficulties make it improbable that Curtius ever read Quintilian's work, but Quintilian was doing no more than write up ideas current in his day, and there is no reason to doubt that Curtius was familiar with these ideas.

Curtius further approximates himself to the biographical style in his frequent comments on Alexander's character (3.12.18–20; 4.6.26 and 29; 4.7.29; 5.4.3; 5.7.1; 6.1.18; 6.2.1–5 and 8; 6.6.1–3 and 9; 8.4.2 and 4–5; 8.5.5–7, and especially 10.5.26–37). The last of these examples no doubt recalls the conventional 'obituary notice' frequently inserted by rhetorical historians at appropriate places in the narrative, but this particular instance is remarkable for its length and for the detailed analysis of character.

Accordingly we must say that while Curtius is attempting consciously to write history, the biographical element is very strong, and his work may be looked upon as being in some sense a fusion of both genres. This is, of course, to some extent true also of the other surviving full-scale work on Alexander, Arrian's *Anabasis*, as well as of the Seventeenth Book of Diodorus, and this fusion of biography and history provides a clear indication of the extent of Alexander's domination over the events of his own lifetime: contemporary history and Alexander's life, in fact, were to all intents and purposes virtually synonymous.

This examination of the type of literature to which Curtius' work belongs leads us to consider his date and social status. Normally we derive our knowledge of the lives of Roman authors from two distinct sources—external information supplied by contemporaries and later writers of the Roman period, and internal information supplied from the author's own work. Now, surprising as it may seem, there is not one single mention of Curtius or his work throughout Classical antiquity and his name appears for the first time at the heading of the earliest surviving manuscript of his *History* in the Ninth Century. Quintilian's failure to include him in his survey of Roman literature (10.1.46 ff) has been cited as proof that he must have written subsequent to the Flavian period, but Quintilian makes no pretence to be drawing up an exhaustive list of writers,[3] and in any case he may have regarded Curtius not as an historian but as a writer of biography, a genre which he ignores completely. The silence of Rome on Curtius may be explained in large measure through his choice of subject, for, unlike the other great Roman historians who discussed foreign affairs only when they were bound up with the history of their own city, Curtius chose as his theme a non-Roman topic, a choice that at once diverts him from the mainstream of Latin historiography. Furthermore, even on this theme there was an abundance of earlier works in existence, to which readers desirous of obtaining information on Alexander would turn —Callisthenes, Aristobulus, Onesicritus, and Clitarchus to name but a few, and readers who knew no Greek would doubtless have found the less-detailed account in Trogus sufficient for their purpose.

For the rest we are dependent entirely on the evidence contained within the work, and of this there is very little, as a work on what was to the Romans both foreign and ancient history afforded its author little opportunity to mention contemporary events. We are further handicapped by the loss of the first two books of which the Preface at least might have been expected to yield a few clues. The upper date limit for the work must be the date of publication of all or part of Livy's *History*, as Curtius' complete familiarity with and absorption of Livy's style and phraseology[4] makes clear; the lower limit is the date of the overthrow of the Parthian empire by the Sassanidae in A.D. 224, since there are several passages in the work alluding to it as contemporary: the Parthians control Parthyaea (4.2.11), Persepolis (5.7.9), Ecbatana (5.8.1), Mesopotamia and beyond (6.2.12), and, apparently, Margiane (7.10.16).

To help us narrow down this lengthy period of two centuries, there are two further passages which may provide clues, though neither is specific. The first of these is the famous passage 10.9.1–6, which is of such importance that it deserves to be quoted in full:

Sed iam fatis admovebantur Macedonum genti bella civilia; nam et insociabile est regnum et a pluribus expetebatur. Primum ergo collisere vires, deinde disperserunt; et cum pluribus corpus quam capiebat <capitibus> onerassent, cetera membra deficere coeperunt, quodque imperium sub uno stare potuisset, dum a pluribus sustinetur, ruit. Proinde iure meritoque populus Romanus salutem se principi suo debere profitetur, qui noctis quam paene supremam habuimus novum sidus illuxit. Huius, hercule, non solis ortus lucem caliganti reddidit mundo, cum sine suo capite discordia membra trepidarent. Quot ille tum exstinxit faces! quot condidit gladios! quantam tempestatem subita serenitate discussit! Non ergo revirescit solum, sed etiam floret imperium. Absit modo invidia, excipiet huius saeculi tempora eiusdem domus utinam perpetua, certe diuturna posteritas.

By now the Fates were bringing civil wars upon the Macedonian nation; for monarchy can have no equal partner and was being sought after by many. Firstly, therefore, they made their forces collide, then split them apart, and when they had burdened the body with more heads than it could carry, the remaining parts began to give way, and an empire that could have survived under the control of one individual collapsed while it was being supported by many. Wherefore justly and rightly the Roman people admits that it owes salvation to its prince who shone out like a new star on the night which we believed to be our last. It was the rising not of the sun but of this star that brought back daylight to a world plunged into darkness, since the various limbs, deprived of their leader, were in the prey of discord. How many torches did he then extinguish, how many swords did he return to their scabbard! How great a storm did he scatter in a sudden tranquillity! And so our empire is not only reborn but also flourishes. And if only the ill-will of the gods be absent, the posterity of the same house will prolong the times of the present age, we may wish everlastingly, but at least for a period of long duration.

In this passage Curtius is comparing the situation in the empire immediately after Alexander's death to the situation which he himself witnessed at Rome shortly before the time of writing. However, the parallel should not be pressed too far, and the only safe inferences are that Curtius witnessed a time of trouble, possibly but not certainly civil war, following the death of an emperor and resulting in the emergence of several aspirants to the succession, of whom one was able to save the city and restore peace, and who was the member of a dynasty.

The identity of this new emperor has been hotly debated by scholars,[5] but it seems to me that there are only three possible candidates who meet the requirements—Claudius, Vespasian, and Septimius Severus. Of the other possibilities, Augustus may be excluded, because Curtius evidently wrote after Livy, Caligula, Nerva, Trajan, and Severus Alexander, because of the absence of any rival claimants, and Hadrian by the use of words like *caliganti*, *faces*, *gladios*, and *tempestatem*, which, when applied to the situation of 117, would put some strain on Curtius' language, and would involve the twisting of his sentences to produce the meaning that Hadrian's timely accession saved Rome from any civil war that might have arisen through the lack of any obvious successor. We are left, then, with a choice between Claudius, Vespasian, and Septimius Severus, all three of whom restored peace after a time of trouble. In the case of Claudius, the *discordia membra* are the people and the praetorians on the one hand and the 'republican' senate on the other, with the very senate divided into genuine republicans and 'monarchists' of whom at least some, like Annius Vinicianus, Valerius Asiaticus, Furius Camillus Scribonianus, and Servius Sulpicius Galba, saw themselves as potential emperors, and the *posteritas* would be a reference to Britannicus, born twenty days before Claudius' accession, and any possible grandchildren through his daughters Antonia and Octavia. In the case of Vespasian, the *discordia membra* would be the senate, the praetorians, and the various legions who proclaimed respectively the successive emperors Galba, Otho, and Vitellius, together with the legions commanded by men like Fonteius Capito and Clodius Macer, who were not without imperial designs themselves, and the *posteritas* would allude to Vespasian's sons Titus and Domitian. Similarly in the case of Septimius Severus the allusion would be to the events of 193, involving the deaths and quick succession of the emperors and imperial pretenders Pertinax, Didius Julianus, Pescennius Niger and Albinus, the nominees of the *discordia membra* who would again be the senate, the praetorians and the various legions: the *posteritas* in this case would be Severus' sons Caracalla and Geta.

Of the three possibilities, Severus is the least probable, when we take into consideration the remarks made by Curtius on the subject of Tyre at 4.4.21:

> Multis ergo casibus defuncta et post excidium renata nunc tandem longa pace cuncta refovente sub tutela Romanae mansuetudinis adquiescit.
>
> Accordingly having suffered many calamities and having been born again after its downfall, at the present time now that a long period of peace is reviving it, it at last rests beneath the protection of Roman clemency.

This chance remark, in fact, fits only two periods of Tyrian history. Firstly there is the time between Pompey's Eastern settlement in 63 and the visit of Augustus in 20 B.C., when Tyre was deprived of its autonomy,[6] during which period the city might well be said to rest 'sub tutela Romanae mansuetudinis', and even Antony on the occasion of the famous 'Donations of Alexandria' expressly secured for Tyre and its neighbour Sidon their ancient freedom.[7] The second period to which Curtius' description is applicable is that between the unknown date of Tyre's recovery of autonomy to A.D. 198, when the city became a Roman colony under the title of *Colonia Septimia Severa Metropolis*:[8] as a colony it could no longer properly be described as 'sub tutela Romanae mansuetudinis'. It is unfortunate that the date of the recovery is unknown, but it was certainly prior to 174, since an inscription of this year refers to the city as 'the sacred, inviolable and independent metropolis',[9] and in all probability prior to the reign of Hadrian, who granted it the title of 'metropolis'.[10] Even if we assume that Curtius was writing at the very beginning of Severus' reign, before its conversion into a colony, the term 'longa pace cuncta refovente' is nonsensical, since in 193 Tyre was sacked by Pescennius Niger in his struggle with Severus for the 'principate'.[11] From this passage, then, we may safely rule out Severus as the 'princeps' of 10.9, and by a process of elimination we are left with Claudius and Vespasian as the only two possible candidates.[12] Beyond this it would be most unwise to proceed, as we have no further evidence.

It remains to be seen whether our historian can be identified with any known Roman of this time. Nothing whatever is known of any Curtii Rufi under Vespasian, but for the reign of Claudius there are two possible identifications. One is with the rhetorician Quintus Curtius Rufus known only from the index to Suetonius' work *De Grammaticis et Rhetoribus*, where he appears between M. Porcius Latro and L. Valerius Primanus. The chronological arrangement of the names affords us some indication of this particular Curtius' date: Latro we know from Jerome to have died in 4 B.C.,[13] and though Primanus' *floruit* is unknown, his name appears in its turn next to that of Verginius Flavus, the teacher of Persius, who may be dated to the Claudian and Neronian period. We thus have some grounds for supposing this particular Curtius to have lived under Augustus and Tiberius. That the rhetorician lived into the reign of Claudius and wrote his *History* in his old age is possible, but the rhetorical nature of our historian's work is not in itself a sufficient reason for identifying him with an otherwise unknown rhetorician who merely happens to have the same name. Our Curtius is not simply a rhetorician but an historian, and one would not expect a writer of considerable literary merit to be classed with rhetoricians and grammarians, the authors of works of a more technical nature.

The second possible identification is with the distinguished politician and soldier Curtius Rufus, whose career lasted from the principate of Tiberius to that of Nero, and whose background is described by Tacitus in a digression on the occasion of his receipt of triumphal insignia.[14] This Curtius was a man of humble origin who rose to be consul in 47 and governor of Africa under Nero. Tacitus' failure to mention any literary activity is not in itself enough to disprove the suggestion that he wrote the *History of Alexander*, as Tacitus is equally silent on the writings of Petronius and of Frontinus,[15] but the charge of 'disagreeable flattery towards his superiors' ('adversus superiores tristi adulatione') seems inconsistent with our Curtius' frequent censures of flattery in the strongest possible terms,[16] and with their corollary, the praise of free speech.[17] Of course, one must beware of believing that Curtius always practised what he preached, but his attacks on flattery are so bitter that he would have exposed himself to the ridicule of his contemporaries had he himself been a flatterer of the worst possible kind. Furthermore, Tacitus' Curtius saw a fair amount of military experience, whereas our historian, though claiming to be an expert on the psychology of the common soldier (3.6.19; 6.2.15; 9.4.22), describes battles and tactics in so defective and sketchy a manner that he can have had little or no acquaintance with war.

Accordingly, the equation of the historian with the consul should not be pressed, and though the evidence is not sufficient to enable us to say for certain that our Curtius cannot possibly be identified with either of his two namesakes, there is a strong presumption against the validity of such an identification. Though we are obliged to concede that Curtius must remain a completely unknown figure, a study of his work reveals his prejudices quite clearly. He shows a typically Roman contempt for foreigners, be they Greeks (4.5.12; 8.5.8), Egyptians (4.1.30) or Orientals (3.10.10; 7.8.10; 8.13.7) and an intolerance of their customs (4.3.23; 5.1.36–39): he is equally contemptuous of the mob (4.10.7; 9.4.22; 10.2.6) and of the *novus homo* (6.11.1). These latter passages may suggest that their author was a man of substance, possibly even a senator, though too much should not be read into these and similar casual remarks.

From Curtius the man we must now turn to Curtius the man of letters, and in this field I propose to select what seem to me to be the most striking features of his work. The first of these is the choice and arrangement of material, and in this respect he parts company not only with his Roman predecessors but also with the other surviving Alexander-historians. As an historian of Alexander, he is obliged to write a competent military narrative, including an account of the activities of Alexander's enemies and subordinates, together with a mention of specific figures indicating time and distance, as, for instance, the dimensions of such natural objects as rivers, rocks, etc., named in the course of his work, as well as details of factual matter like the composition and size of forces sent out on special missions, the arrival of reinforcements and the various appointments to and dismissals from high military and administrative offices made by Alexander in the course of his campaigns. Aware of the need for any historian worthy of the name to include some material of this sort, Curtius has no hesitation about admitting such details into his work, and in a fair number of cases is our sole authority for such information.[18]

However, this was not the kind of information that interested Curtius, nor indeed did he see fit to linger over it. Instead, we find that, though he is careful not to omit factual details, he preferred to concentrate on certain episodes of Alexander's career and to build his narrative round these. Accordingly, we find in each book a series of 'showpieces' which he builds up at the expense of other incidents, and on which he lavishes all his powers. A list of the episodes selected for this treatment will reveal clearly the sort of theme that attracted him.

In Book III, the narrative revolves round three incidents elaborated at length—the numbering of the Persian army and a description of the royal procession (chapters 2–3), the story of Philip the Acarnanian doctor (chapters 5–6), and the battle of Issus (chapters 8–13), which between them occupy ten chapters out of thirteen. Of the remainder of the book, chapter 1 contains only nine sections of narrative pure and simple, and the rest is given over to geographical descriptions and the episode of the Gordian Knot. In Book IV, attention is concentrated on the siege of Tyre (chapters 2–4), the consultation of the oracle at Ammon (chapter 7 and part of 8), and the battle of Gaugamela (chapters 12–16), which together occupy nine chapters out of sixteen, and for the rest, the book is largely devoted to the Abdalonymus episode (much of chapter 1), the siege of Gaza (chapter 6), and the death of Darius' wife and the peace proposal that follows directly upon it (much of chapters 10 and 11). In Book V, one episode alone predominates, the account of the last days of Darius, to which Curtius assigns six whole chapters (8–13), but other incidents treated at length are Alexander's arrival at Babylon and a description of the city (much of chapter 1), anecdotes relating to his visit to Susa (a large part of chapter 2), the meeting with the mutilated Greeks (chapter 5), and the looting of Persepolis and the Thais episode (chapter 6). Book VI is built around the Hecatompylus mutiny (chapter 3, and much of 2), the meeting with the Amazons and Alexander's enervation (chapters 5 and 6), and the Philotas affair (chapters 7–11), while considerable prominence is also given to a description of the Caspian Sea (part of chapter 4), and of the Mardi (part of chapter 5). Book VII focuses attention on the trial of Amyntas (chapter 1 and part of 2), the death of Parmenio (the rest of 2), the description of the Paropamisadae (much of chapter 3), the banquet of Bessus (most of chapter 4), the terrible march through the Sogdian desert (chapter 5), and the Scythian embassy (chapter 8, with part of 9). Book VIII has for its highlights the murder of Clitus (chapter 1, with part of 2), the Callisthenes–Hermolaus conspiracy (chapters 5–8), and the battle on the Hydaspes (chapters 13–14), with the murder of Spitamenes, Alexander's marriage to Roxane, and the description of India as minor showpieces. In Book IX, we have the Hyphasis mutiny (chapters 2–3), Alexander's heroism in the city of the Sudracae

27

(chapters 5–6), the Corratas-Dioxippus duel (chapter 7) and the struggle with the tide and the march through the Gedrosian desert (chapters 9–10).

In some books, notably IV and VIII, the amount of space given to these incidents is justified because of their importance in the story of Alexander, in others (e.g. Books III, V, and VII) Curtius' choice of subjects for elaboration is less sensible and detrimental to the value of the work as history or biography. Nevertheless, whether selected sensibly or not, all such episodes were carefully developed for what seemed to be their own intrinsic interest, and for the greater scope they afforded for him to display his literary and rhetorical powers, in that they are characterized by elements of the picturesque, the spectacular, the sensational, the emotive, the pathetic, and the exotic, all of which Curtius exploits to the best of his ability.

If we add up the space devoted to such passages, we obtain a figure of just under 70 per cent of the total, and from this can be seen the extent to which the concentration of Curtius' powers on these episodes is detrimental to the narrative. Factual details are curtailed to a bare minimum and many important items are dealt with in a few lines, though in this way the losses to the work from an historical point of view are compensated by gains on the literary side. Curtius' treatment of the passages that interest him is in most cases impressive, and while many of the speeches contained in such episodes are merely exercises in rhetoric, the majority of the episodes as a whole succeed in holding the reader's attention and in making the events described come to life in a highly dramatic manner. Such is Curtius' emotive power that the reader is on the verge of tears at the fate of Darius, and becomes almost an eyewitness of horrors like the torturing of Philotas and the tribulations of the march through the Gedrosian desert.

In particular, he shows skill in developing 'emotional' scenes, scenes in which he loses no opportunity to portray and analyse the feelings of Alexander, of Darius, of the Macedonian nobles, and of the army itself, and to describe their reactions to a given situation.[19] Great care is likewise given to book-endings, and Curtius prefers to conclude with as memorable an incident as possible, often but not invariably one which depicts the human actors on the stage in the grip of some strong emotion. In Book III we have Parmenio's capture of Damascus, together with the flight of the Persian governor (panic); in Book IV an assessment of Alexander's general-ship; in Book V the moving saga of the events leading up to the death of Darius (pathos); in Book VI the execution of Philotas (cruelty on the part of Alexander and his intimate circle, com-passion on the part of the army); in Book VII the spectacular capture of Ariamazes' Rock; in Book VIII the excitement of the battle on the Hydaspes, and in Book IX the Bacchanalian frenzy of the procession through Carmania.

By emphasizing so powerfully the end of his books, Curtius shows a preference for a sharp break in this position. Elsewhere, however, he is so preoccupied in the idea of continuity and such is his dislike of abrupt changes of theme or locality that he resorts to the composition of 'transition formulae' to bridge the gap. In some cases these links are harmless,[20] but at times he is so concerned with effecting a smooth transition between incidents that he resorts to the invention of statements designed for the purpose. Thus, at 3.7.1, when he has just finished describing Alexander's illness and wants to move on to the activities of Darius, he effects the transition by writing: 'Darius, having heard a report of Alexander's bad health', although it is clear from our other authorities[21] that Darius was unaware of Alexander's illness. Again, when he wishes to pass from Artabazus' retirement from the satrapy of Bactria into private life to a description of the Clitus episode, he does so by inventing the statement that Artabazus' province was to be assigned to Clitus (8.1.20).[22] Indulgence in such factual distortions is disastrous to Curtius' reputation as an historian, but the literary effects are less reprehensible and serve to cushion the reader against the abrupt change.

From the spectacular and sensational we may turn to consider yet another distinguishing factor between Curtius and other Roman historians and biographers, namely his fondness for moralizing. All ancient historians to a greater or lesser extent indulged in this, but nowhere is it carried to such lengths as in Curtius' work. In passage after passage he drags in one moral maxim after another, even at the slightest excuse, and while at first the reader is inclined to admire his cleverness, he soon wearies of his constant exposure to such maxims, and once he has reached saturation-point his admiration turns to disgust.

Passages of moralizing take different forms, according to the context in which they occur. In speeches, they are introduced in one of two ways: either the speaker reinforces the point he is making by expressing the same idea in a different turn of phrase or, as an alternative, the sentiment follows naturally upon the speaker's words and is introduced in order to elucidate his argument. Thus, of the former device we have an instance at 6.3.7, where Alexander, in attempting to suppress the Hecatompylus mutiny by pointing out that time is needed for barbarians to lose their savageness and become acquiescent in accepting Macedonian rule, reinforces his argument by introducing an analogy from horticulture and explains that the fruits of the earth, too, become mild only at their appointed time. An example of the latter device occurs at 6.10.14, where Philotas, in attempting to defend himself from a charge of treason by drawing attention to the deep sleep into which he had fallen at the time of arrest, adds the perfectly natural generalization that the wicked cannot sleep because of the qualms of conscience. It is in one of these two forms that Curtius' rhetorical moralizing usually manifests itself, for, though he is not averse to expressing himself in similes whether from biology (4.14.3), surgery (6.3.11) or agriculture (9.2.26), simile is for the most part replaced by metaphor and analogy.

In the narrative, Curtius' moralizing tendency, which leads him to interpret the particular in terms of the universal, usually takes the form of a comment which he deduces from the behaviour of a character in a given situation and which he holds to be applicable to human nature in general. Examples of this practice are numerous,[23] and only a few need be mentioned here. At 4.1.29 he records how Amyntas on his flight from Issus reached Egypt and persuaded his troops to make themselves masters of the country, and cannot resist adding the psychological observation that when men's hopes have been ruined by Fortune the future always looks brighter than the present; at 5.10.13, after describing how Bessus feigned veneration for the king he was intending to put in fetters, he adds, 'so ready is deceit in the human heart', and at 8.14.20, when the Indians are so panic-stricken that they disobey their king's orders, Curtius chooses this very moment to proclaim the universality of the principle that fear is a more powerful master than any monarch. In such passages as these, one cannot help suspecting that the moralist has taken precedence over the biographer-historian, or at least that for Curtius the two conceptions were inseparable.

Linked inextricably with the moralist and the biographer is the rhetorician. This side of his work is demonstrated amply by the long set speeches often written in pairs to give opposing points of view. So thorough is his handling of his subject that to look for fresh arguments on either side is usually futile: the rhetorician in Curtius can see both sides of a situation and provide plausible defences of each. Thus on the occasion of the Conspiracy of the Pages, the speech of Hermolaus (8.7) is in effect an attack on Alexander's policies and an effective one at that, but once Curtius has achieved his aim of showing how much of a monster Alexander was, he launches in the next chapter into a defence that is equally plausible. Even more remarkable are the contrasting speeches of Euctemon and Theaetetus, the spokesmen of the mutilated Greeks (5.5.10 ff), the one haranguing convincingly on the need to remain in Asia, the other on the reasons for returning to Greece. Perhaps nowhere else in the work does Curtius exhibit rhetorical influences more clearly: the strangeness of the subject-matter and the stylistic differences between the two speeches make the passage unique in Latin literature, but it is not till we submit it to a critical examination that we realize that the entire episode is pure rhetoric and nothing more.

Akin to the set speech are passages depicting the emotions of the various characters on the scene, to which attention has already been drawn. In particular we know that the hesitations of Alexander and the feelings of his soldiers were favourite themes of the Roman rhetoricians,[24] and it is not surprising that Curtius should have represented Alexander as engaged in inward mental conflicts as he pondered over the advantages and disadvantages of pursuing a certain line of action. Noteworthy are 3.6.5–7, which could be entitled 'Deliberat Alexander an Philippo medico se mandet'; 9.2.8–11, 'Deliberat Alexander Magnus an Hyphasin transeat', and 9.4.17–18, 'Deliberat Alexandri exercitus an in ulteriorem Indiam progrediatur'. Above all, there is a strong resemblance between the language of Curtius in this last passage and that of the elder Seneca in his *Suasoria* 'Deliberat Alexander an Oceano naviget'.

CURTIUS IX.4.18. Trahi extra sidera et solem cogique adire quae mortalium oculis Natura subduxerat . . . caliginem ac tenebras et perpetuam noctem profundo incubantem mari,	SENECA SUAS.I.I. Stat immotum mare quasi deficientis in suo fine naturae pigra moles; novae ac terribiles figurae, magna etiam Oceani portenta quae profunda ista vastitas nutrit,

repletum immanium beluarum	circumfusa lux alta caligine et
gregibus fretum, immobiles	interceptus tenebris dies, ipsum
undas, in quibus emoriens	vero grave et defixum mare et
natura defecerit.	aut nulla aut ignota sidera.

Whether Curtius is here drawing on Seneca or whether both are indebted to an earlier treatment of the subject cannot be determined, but the influence of the rhetorical schools is here clearly discernible.

The third and last category of 'rhetorical' passages in the work is the character sketch, usually in the form of an 'obituary notice', whether of Alexander (10.9.26–37), Parmenio (7.2.33–34) or Callisthenes (8.8.21–22), and such notices are even written for cities.[25] This third type shares in common with speeches and passages of a deliberative or emotional character a flagrant disregard for truth in the interests of effect. All three kinds abound in exaggerations and statements that are at variance with the narrative. Thus at 6.3.16, where Alexander in his speech at Hecatompylus claims that only a four days' march will bring the army to the bounds of the Persian empire, he makes a claim so outrageous that even Curtius must have been aware of its falsity, and at 7.2.13, in his obituary note on Parmenio, he makes the remarkable assertion, 'multa sine rege prospere, rex sine illo nihil magnae rei gessit', a statement difficult to reconcile with his account of Parmenio's activities elsewhere.[26] In these and similar passages,[27] Curtius knowingly and quite intentionally substitutes rhetoric for fact, but only in places where he feels exaggeration and inaccuracy to be acceptable, even appropriate. In other words, there is a sharp distinction between the narrative and passages of the sort I have outlined, where the biographer and historian is overcome by the rhetorician.

From Curtius the orator, the moralist, and the rhetorician, we must now proceed to examine Curtius the philosopher. Was Curtius a student of philosophy, and if so, to what school did he attach himself? Like the majority of Romans, he undoubtedly had an interest in Stoicism, and there is a certain amount of Stoic influence in his work. Like the Stoics, Curtius affects to believe that life is guided by Destiny,[28] he has a healthy respect for the institution of kingship,[29] he approves of the principles of *gravitas*[30] and of the equality of high and low,[31] he regards death as the ultimate release,[32] and is concerned with obedience to the *ius gentium*.[33]

There are, however, a fair number of passages where he appears to reject the Stoic View out of hand. In particular, he shares the Academic and Epicurean scepticism in regard to oracles,[34] and to divination, whether from eclipses[35] or entrails,[36] and he is open minded on the interpretation of dreams[37] and of portents,[38] while his attacks on superstition are especially severe.[39] Furthermore, the words put into Darius' mouth at 5.12.11 suggest that Curtius did not consider suicide to be a commendable or glorious death, and even one of his two allusions to the *ius gentium* looks like an echo of Livy.[40] It is clear therefore that though there is undoubtedly some Stoic influence on Curtius his Stoicism is almost entirely superficial.

There is, however, one philosophical idea to which he adheres consistently all through his work, the concept of *Fortuna* as a guardian deity watching over Alexander throughout his career. At 3.5.11, Fortune catches Alexander off his guard; it attends him everywhere (3.6.17); it keeps the enemy away till Alexander crosses the Tigris (4.9.22); at Gaugamela, it piles up the events of one generation into a single day (4.16.10); it helps Alexander to overcome the Mardi (5.6.19); it gives him a plan for capturing a rock (6.6.28); it makes a success of all his foolish counsels (7.2.38); it never wearies of indulging him (8.3.1); it saves his life on the occasion of the Conspiracy of the Pages (8.6.14); it helps him by converting the disgraceful Bacchanalian procession to glory (9.10.28). Similarly Alexander himself marvels at his good Fortune (3.4.11); he fears Fortune (3.8.21); he finds his Fortune at a standstill (5.3.22); he has confidence in his Fortune even when things look black (7.7.27); he is corrupted by the excessive indulgence of Fortune (8.6.14); he is the darling of Fortune on the occasion of the capture of the town of the Sudracae (9.5.4).[41] In such passages as these Curtius is influenced not so much by any definite philosophical system as by the contemporary conception of *Fortuna* as a tutelary deity whether over Rome,[42] over the Roman people[43] or over individual Romans, like Caesar,[44] Augustus,[45] or, above all, Sulla.[46] From the above paragraphs, we may conclude that Curtius is not particularly interested in philosophy, and the philosopher in him is generally content to play a subordinate role.

There remains to consider the picture of Alexander painted by Curtius, and it is surely on this that his reputation must stand or fall, at any rate if we choose to classify him among the biographers of the ancient world. Do we see his Alexander as a real flesh and blood character who comes to life as we turn the pages of Curtius' work or does he remain a lifeless individual devoid of personality? If we grant, as we certainly must, that in Alexander Curtius had one of the most fascinating, the most brilliant, the most enigmatic characters of history, any interpretation that fails to do justice to at least some aspects of this powerful personality must be reckoned a failure, and though no biography can ever hope to convey the fascination exercised by Alexander in its entirety, any work which is incapable of communicating even some measure of this fascination cannot be considered a success.

Does Curtius' History satisfy this requirement? As a preliminary it will be necessary to examine the 'favourable' and 'unfavourable' interpretations of Alexander's character, as presented by our surviving authorities on the subject—Diodorus in the Seventeenth Book of his *Universal History*, Arrian in his *Anabasis*, and Justin in the Eleventh and Twelfth Books of his Epitome of Pompeius Trogus.[47] Arrian's work, based as it is on the 'official' tradition of Ptolemy and Aristobulus, where the bad in Alexander's character is either toned down or reinterpreted in accordance with the apologetic tendencies of these writers, may be classed as 'favourable', Justin's as 'unfavourable',[48] while the writer followed by Diodorus XVII seems to have attempted to raise Alexander's acts to the heroic plane: like Dionysus, Alexander traversed the whole of Asia, celebrating Dionysiac revels (17.72.4; 17.106.1), like Achilles he visited Troy (17.17.2), fought with a river (17.97.3) and encountered the Amazons (17.77), and, like the more important epic heroes, space was found for his *aristeia* when he engaged in combat (17.20.3–21.3; 17.34.1–4; 17.60.1; 17.98.5–99.4). If it was the intention of Diodorus' source to portray Alexander on a heroic level, it follows that many of the incidents in the latter's career that strike us as being unfavourable were not intended as such by the writer, for, if Alexander was something more than a man, allowance had to be made for the more discreditable elements in his character. For his heavy drinking, there was the parallel of Heracles, and for his promiscuous sexual habits not only Heracles but also the Achaemenids, of whom our tradition regards Cyrus at least,[49] and possibly also Xerxes,[50] as not unworthy of imitation in other fields: Alexander may therefore be presented simply as copying their sex life also, and, as a hero in whom excess is a virtue, he must be endowed with a heroic sexual appetite. Again, just as Heracles' murder of his wife and children could be blamed upon Hera,[51] so could Alexander's murder of Clitus be ascribed to the wrath of Dionysus (17 *Perioche* 2, 27), and for Alexander's massacres (17 *Perioche* 2.20; 17.84.1–2) there is the parallel, for instance, of the blood-bath committed by Achilles by the banks of the Scamander.[52]

So, too, in Curtius, who drew to a large extent on the same writer as Diodorus, Alexander appears as heroic. His *aristeiai* are dwelt upon at considerable length (3.7.9; 4.4.11; 9.4.30–9.5.18), he fights with a river (9.4.14), he imitates the triumphal processions of Dionysus (3.12.18; 9.10.24), incurs his wrath (8.2.4), and follows in the footsteps not only of this hero (7.9.15; 8.10.1 and 11; 9.2.29; 9.4.21; 9.8.5) but in those of Hercules (8.10.1; 8.11.2; 9.2.29; 9.4.2 and 21), of Cyrus (3.4.1; 7.3.1; 7.6.11; 7.6.20), and of Semiramis (7.6.20; 9.6.23). Accordingly, when Curtius is using the same source as Diodorus, his portrait of Alexander cannot be regarded as either favourable or unfavourable, and the heroic colouring cast over the whole makes him appear as a glorifier of Alexander, even in his vices.

Such is the picture inherited by Curtius from his principal source, but he is the master, not the slave of his authorities, and, aware that some of Alexander's virtues and vices were only too human, these he attempts to summarize in his 'obituary notice' at 10.10.26–36. The reappearance, with slight variations, of this character sketch, together with its division into virtues and vices and the ascription of the latter to Alexander's fortune and youth, in Arrian,[53] and to a large part also in Plutarch,[54] suggests that this analysis, too, is based on the analysis of some predecessor, for, although it is just possible that Arrian may have based his sketch on Curtius, Plutarch, with his relative unfamiliarity with Latin literature, is less likely to have read the work of a Roman writer for information on the past history of his own nation. The impossibility of combining these two conceptions of Alexander into a harmonious whole leaves Curtius open to charges of inconsistency, and he makes no attempt, for instance, to reconcile the picture of the Alexander endowed with a heroic sexual appetite with the Alexander endowed with a *modus immodicarum cupiditatum* and with a *veneris intra naturale desiderium usus*.

Curtius himself, in so far as he had a personal opinion, seems to regard Alexander as a young man of a noble and generous disposition who in the course of his career became more and more debased by the excessive indulgence of Fortune, and at length became so corrupted that he took to imitation of the customs of the nations he had conquered. This view is pressed home in several passages, notably 3.12.18–20 (Issus), 4.6.29 (Gaza), 4.7.29 (Ammon), 6.2.1–5 (death of Darius), and 6.6.1–8 (Parthyaea). The change is timed to coincide with Alexander's adoption of Persian customs in Parthyaea, although Curtius foresees earlier occasions on which he betrayed an indication of what was to come. Here Curtius may possibly have been influenced by the picture of Alexander presented by Trogus, who appears to have had plenty to say of his deterioration at Ammon,[55] and to have dated the beginning of this process to Issus.[56] In formulating his view, Curtius very reasonably decides that there is much in Alexander's later career to support the idea of progressive deterioration, but in identifying this deterioration to a large extent with his adoption of Persian customs he went astray.

Of course, here he is following the virtual unanimous tendency of antiquity to censure Alexander, to which even the basically 'favourable' historian Arrian subscribes.[57] No surviving Alexander historian sympathizes with Alexander's desire to conciliate his new Iranian subjects and render himself acceptable to them as their ruler, and none attempts to excuse him in this way. Yet Curtius is acutely aware of the dilemma facing him, and permits him to defend his actions on these grounds:

> 'I came to Asia not to destroy nations utterly nor to make a desert of half the earth, but that those whom I had conquered in war might not be sorry at my victory.' (viii. 10.10)
> 'Wherefore I united to myself in marriage Roxane daughter of Persian Oxyartes, not disdaining to bring up children born from a captive. Soon afterwards, when I wished to spread the stock of my race more widely, I married a daughter of Darius, and caused the closest of my friends to beget children from captives, in order that by this sacred alliance I might remove all distinction between conquered and conqueror.' (x. 3.11)

For these remarks Curtius deserves some credit. Yet, however prepared he may be to put his rhetorical powers at Alexander's service, he has himself little sympathy with these ideals, and in his own comments on Alexander's marriage to Roxane, he makes little attempt to conceal his disapproval and contempt:

> 'Roxane, though she had entered among a select group, attracted the eyes of everyone, especially the king, who was by now less in control of his passions amid the indulgence of Fortune, against

whom no mortal sufficiently bewares. Accordingly the man who had looked with no feeling other than a father's upon the wife and two maiden daughters of Darius, to whom no woman other than Roxane could be compared in beauty, was so carried away with love of this little maiden, humble in origin compared with royal stock, that he said it was in the interest of the consolidation of his empire that Persian and Macedonian should be united in marriage, for in this way alone could shame be taken from the vanquished and arrogance from the victors: Achilles too, from whom he traced his descent, had united with a captive; lest the conquered should think some crime was being committed against them, he was willing to be united in lawful marriage.' (viii. 4.24–6)

If Curtius' equation of Alexander's deterioration with his 'medism' is only partially correct, his dating of this deterioration must be equally faulty. Yet it is one of Curtius' merits as a biographer that he does not distort the facts to sustain his thesis: incidents presenting Alexander in a bad light before the change[58] are narrated as scrupulously as those offering a favourable picture after the change,[59] and no attempt is made to gloss them over. This, too, exposes Curtius to charges of inconsistency, but it is surely preferable to allow a rather inaccurate theory to be discarded than to support such a theory by manipulation of the evidence.

Curtius' portrait of Alexander further differs from those of Arrian and Diodorus in its presentation of a greater number of 'unfavourable' incidents. Of the 'official' tradition and Diodorus' source each in its own way wrote in a generally sympathetic tone; Curtius seeks a more balanced picture by incorporating elements which he has in common with Trogus, his only Latin predecessor on the subject. Consequently we find passages in his work which seem intended to present Alexander as a sinister, unscrupulous tyrant, with a fair amount of space given over to the distortion of facts intended originally to glorify him (e.g. the looting of Persepolis, 5.7.11; the Branchidae massacre, 7.5.28–35), and to sensational incidents like the punishment of Betis (4.6.26–29) and the Bagoas–Orsines episode (10.1.22–42).[60] These and similar incidents conflict with the picture of Alexander given in the character sketch,[61] but the explanation is not so much 'carelessness' or 'lack of interest', as a deliberate attempt to sketch both sides of Alexander's character with the aid of different and largely irreconcilable sources. The inconsistency is also to be accounted for to some extent by the rhetorical nature of the character sketch, where the rhetorician overcomes the historian and constrains him to express himself in generalizations written for the sake of effect, without reference to the narrative.

Nor must we lay the blame for inconsistency entirely on the shoulders of Curtius, since the subject of his biography was himself equally inconsistent in his behaviour. Alexander's character is to the scholars of today, just as it was to his contemporaries, with the possible exception of Hephaestion, something of an enigma. The man who showed such conspicuous bravery in the city of the Malli (9.4.30–9.5.18), who inspired the admiration and affection of his friends and of the entire army (3.6.17–20; 7.4.1; 9.5.19; 9.6.5–16), who showed such exemplary devotion towards the gods (3.7.3; 3.12.27; 4.2.2; 4.8.16, etc.), who was so concerned for the welfare of the common soldier (7.5.9–12; 8.4.15–17) was the very same person who reproached the gods when things started to go wrong (7.7.7), who crucified 2,000 Tyrians at the capture of the city (4.4.17), who treacherously encompassed the death of his most celebrated general (7.2.11 ff), who massacred Iranians who had surrendered under a pledge of safe conduct (7.11.26 f), who murdered one of his best friends in cold blood at a banquet (8.1.43–8.2.10). In no other ancient work do we see such a devastatingly fearful presentation of the uncontrollable bursts of rage and frenzy to which Alexander was undoubtedly subject, and the transition from *ira* to *rabies* is a subject which attracted Curtius' interest on three separate occasions (4.4.17; 4.6.29; 10.4.2; cf. 8.1.43 and 49). Curtius' achievement in passages of this sort, whether 'favourable' or 'unfavourable', is to create a personality who, without quite being the Alexander of history, nevertheless attains the stature of the real Alexander, and on these passages the mind tends to linger, long after the work has been laid aside. At the same time, however, he is too absorbed in the moral side of Alexander, which he communicates to us in his comments on the several episodes of his career (3.12.8; 3.12.21; 4.2.5; 5.7.1; 5.7.16; 6.2.5; 6.6.1; 8.4.46, etc.), and Alexander's aims, his vast plans, his motives for conquest, his political thought, his desire for a cultural fusion of his subjects, his moments of mysticism, his failure to understand the force of Iranian nationalism and many other important aspects largely escape him, if indeed he ever pondered to consider them. Yet despite these faults, Curtius' conception of Alexander will live on in his brilliant series of contrasting pictures so long as his theme continues to fascinate mankind, and it is one of his highest merits that we are aware through his work that, when Alexander died, the world lost one of its greatest men, the man who had within him at least something of the superman.

In the field of Alexander history, Curtius is significant as the creator of the finest of the three surviving works from the point of view of literary merit: Diodorus was neither a man of letters nor an historian, nor indeed did he claim to be one, and Arrian, though by far the best historian of the three, can lay little claim to literary distinction. Arrian's work, important as it is to the student of history, is of little interest to his more literary-minded colleague, and seen through his eyes, emerges as a rather dull work where the amount of fine writing is meagre in the extreme. Curtius alone has produced a literary work worthy of the greatness of his subject.

His place in Latin literature is less easy to determine, as his choice of theme has virtually set him apart from the main stream of Roman writers. He is certainly of importance as the only extant Latin author to combine full-scale historical and biographical elements within the confines of a single work, and his attempt is on the whole successful, though his influence on succeeding generations was minimal.[62] He may indeed have exercised some small amount of influence on Seneca, Lucan, and Tacitus, but the presence of matter common to these writers and Curtius may equally mean that all were drawing on a common source. We have, in fact, no definite proof that Curtius, for all his literary powers, exercised any influence on subsequent Latin literature, and, though he was known to a few scholars of the Middle Ages,[63] it was not till the Renaissance that he fully came into his own.

NOTES

[1] Nepos, *Pelopidas* 1; Plutarch, *Alexander* 1.2.

[2] Such passages appear also in Tacitus' *Agricola*, it is true, but the *Agricola* is by no means pure biography. Cf. H. Furneaux and J. G. C. Anderson, *Corneli Taciti de Vita Agricolae*, 2nd ed. (Oxford, 1922), Introduction, Section III, pp. xxi–xxviii.

[3] Quintilian X. 1.104, sunt et alii scriptores boni, sed nos genera degustamus non bibliothecas excutimus, 'There are also other good writers, but we are sipping from the various literary genres, not compiling libraries.'

[4] See A. Dosson, *Etude sur Quinte-Curce* (Paris, 1887), p. 34 and p. 276, note 5; R. B. Steele, 'Quintus Curtius Rufus', *American Journal of Philology* (1919), pp. 40–46; H. Bardon, 'La Valeur Littéraire de Quinte-Curce', *Les Etudes Classiques* (1947), pp. 214–15.

⁵ See, e.g., W. W. Tarn, *Alexander the Great*, Vol. II (Cambridge, 1949), pp. 111–16; D. Korzeniewski, *Die Zeit des Quintus Curtius Rufus*, Diss. (Köln, 1959) (Augustus); R. Zimmerman, 'Die Zeit des Geschichtsschreibers Curtius Rufus', *Rheinisches Museum für Philologie* (79) (1930), pp. 381 ff (Caligula); L. Hermann, 'La Date de l'Historie de Quinte-Curce', *Révue des Etudes Anciennes* (1929), pp. 217–24; H. Dahlmann, 'Studien zu Senecas Consolatio ad Polybium', *Hermes* 72 (1937), pp. 315–16; K. Glaso, 'Curtius und Claudius', *Wiener Studier* (1942), pp. 87–92; I. Lana, 'Dell' epoca in cui visse Quinte Curzeo Rufo', *Rivista di Filologia Classica* (1949), pp. 48–70; G. V. Sumner, 'Curtius Rufus and the Historiae Alexandri', *Journal of the Australasian Universities Language and Literature Association* (1961), pp. 30–39 (Claudius); J. Stroux, 'Die Zeit des Curtius, *Philologus* 83 (1928), pp. 233–51, and H. U. Istinsky, 'Zur Kontroverse um die Datierung des Curtius Rufus', *Hermes* 90 (1962), pp. 379–83 (Vespasian); F. Altheim, *Literatur und Gesellschaft des ausgehenden Altertums* (Halle, 1948), pp. 153–65 (Septimius Severus); R. B. Steele, 'Quintus Curtius Rufus', *American Journal of Philology* (1915), pp. 412–33 (Severus Alexander).

⁶ Dio Cassius LIV. 7.6.

⁷ Josephus, *Ant. Iud.* XV. 4.1.

⁸ Ulpian, *Digest* L. 15.1.

⁹ C I L X. 1601.

¹⁰ C I G 58531. For Tyre in Roman times, see O. Eissfelt s.v. *Tyros*, R E VIII, pp. 1898–1900.

¹¹ Herodian III. 3 3 ff.

¹² If Tyre and Sidon were in any way parallel to Cyzicus, the other city which lost its autonomy in 20 B.C., and for the same reasons of unruly behaviour and civil strife, they were not penalized for long: Cyzicus, in fact, recovered its autonomy from Agrippa during his eastern tour five years later (Dio Cassius LIV. 23.7; IGR IV. 146).

¹³ Jerome, *Chron.* 16.8.

¹⁴ Tacitus, *Annals* XI. 20.1. He is also mentioned by Pliny, Ep. VII. 27.

¹⁵ For Tacitus on Petronius see *Annals XVI* 18; on Frontinus see *Agricola* 17.3 and *Histories* IV 39 1–3.

¹⁶ 3.2.10; 7.4.9; 8.8.21; and especially 8.5.6 *perniciosa adulatio, perpetuum malum regum.*

¹⁷ 3.2.18; 4.7.31; 8.8.22. Cf. praise of Callisthenes for *gravitas et prompta libertas* (8.5.13), and note especially 6.6.11. *sed opinor liberis pretium servitutis ingratum est.*

¹⁸ Instances when Curtius preserves valuable information of this sort are too numerous to list, but especially worthy of mention are 4.1.34–7; 4.5.9–22; 4.8.9–11; 5.7.12; 6.1.20; 6.6.35–36; 7.5.27; 8.1.3 ff; 8.5.2; 8.13.2; 9.10.21.

¹⁹ Examples include 3.1.17; 3.3.2; 3.5.5–16; 3.6.5–7; 3.8.20–21; 4.10.3; 4.13.16–24; 5.3.21–22; 5.7.10; 5.9.14; 5.12.8–13; 6.9.25–27; 7.1.1–3; 7.6.6–8; 7.8.1–2; 8.2.1; 9.2.8–12, 31; 9.3.1–3, 16–17; 9.5.29–30; 10.3.1–5; 10.5.7–25.

²⁰ 3.1.19; 4.8.4; 4.8.10; 5.7.12; 8.9.9.

²¹ Plutarch, *Alexander* 19.1; Diodorus XVII. 31.2.

²² Other instances of this device are found at 4.3.11; 4.6.6;5. 1.39; 9.7.15, and 9.8.10.

²³ Other examples worthy of mention include 4.1.20, the reason for many

men's poverty is their honesty; 4.3.7, no one is willing to accept responsibility when things go wrong; 4.3.24 necessity is more inventive than any art; 4.10.7, nothing sways the mob more than superstition; 5.4.31, necessity spurs on cowardice, despair is often a cause for hope; 6.6.11, the price of slavery is odious to free men; 7.7.8, superstition is a mocker of the minds of men; 8.5–6, flattery is a constant evil in attendance on kings; 8.9.1, idleness is prone to spread rumours; 9.4.7 war turns upside down even the laws of nature; 9.10.30, cruelty is no obstacle to luxury, nor luxury to cruelty.

24 Seneca, *Suasoria* 1, Deliberat Alexander an Oceanum naviget; id., *Suasoria* 4, Deliberat Alexander Magnus an Babylonia intret. Cf. Quintilian III. 8, 16, an Alexander terras ultra Oceanum sit inventurus, and cf. also Auct. ad Herrenium 22.31.

25 Curtius 4.4.19–21 (Tyre); 5.7.8–9 (Persepolis).

26 Curtius 3.11.14; 4.11.10 ff; 4.16.1–4.

27 Other noteworthy examples (the 'rhetorical' passage is mentioned first) are 4.14.11 as against 3.13.12–14 on the one hand and 4.11.13 and 5.9.5 on the other; 8.7.5 as against 8.1.50–52; 8.8.6 as against 7.1.8 and 10.1.40; 9.2.2 as against 9.3.8; 9.6.10 as against 9.4.26.

28 Inevitabile est fatum, 3.6.18. If at 5.11.10 we read, with Vogel, 'eludant me (vide, codd.) licet quibus forte temere humana negotia volvi agique persuasum est < nec serie> nexuque causarum latentium et multo ante destinatum suum quemque ordinem immutabili lege percurrere', we make Curtius a definite upholder of the Stoic conception of Fate. If, on the other hand, we retain the text offered by the manuscripts with the substitution of Jeep's *nexuve* for *nexuque*, we make Curtius reject both the Stoic and the Epicurean views of divine government. Uncertainty as to the correct text makes the passage useless for any discussion of Curtius' philosophical outlook.

29 Curtius 3.6.18.

30 Curtius 8.5.13.

31 Curtius 7.6.11. Cf. the anecdotes bringing Alexander into contact with ordinary soldiers (7.3.7; 7.5.9 ff; 8.4.15 ff).

32 Curtius 8.7.14–15.

33 Curtius 4.2.15; 6.11.15.

34 Curtius 4.7.9.

35 Curtius 4.10.5.

36 Curtius 7.7.8.

37 Curtius 3.3.2, 'sive illas aegritudo, sive divinatio animi praesagientis accersiit'.

38 Curtius 4.15.26, with reference to the appearance of the eagle at Gaugamela, 'sive ludibrium oculorum sive vera species fuit'. Both here and in the passage quoted in the last note Curtius offers an alternative and more rationalistic interpretation.

39 Curtius 4.6.12; 4.10.7; 5.4.1; 7.7.8.

40 At 4.2.15, Curtius records how the Tyrians put to death Alexander's heralds *contra ius gentium*. This seems to be a reminiscence of Livy's phrase 'ne a legatis quidem, qui iure gentium sancti sunt, violandis abstinere' (XXXIX. 25.10).

41 Other examples of the role of *Fortuna* are given at 3.8.2; 3.11.23; 3.13.13;

4.1.4; 4.5.2; 4.14.19; 4.15.11; 5.2.10; 5.8.15; 5.9.4; 5.13.22; 6.1.9; 7.2.33; 7.8.25; 8.10.10; 8.13.22; 10.3.9.

[42] Plutarch, *Moralia* 325 B.

[43] Livy I. 46.5; II. 40.13.

[44] Plutarch, *Moralia* 391 C. Cf. W. Warde Fowler, *Caesar's Conception of Fortuna*, Classical Review (1903), pp. 155 ff.

[45] Plutarch, *Moralia* 391 E.

[46] Plutarch, *Sulla* 34; Frontinus, *Strategemeta* I. 11, 11. Cf. J. P. V. D. Balsdon, *Sulla Felix*, Journal of Roman Studies XLI (1952), pp. 1–10.

[47] Plutarch's 'Life of Alexander' does not readily attach itself to either category, and must be omitted from the discussion.

[48] Tarn (*Alexander the Great*, Cambridge, 1947, Part II, p. 97) claims that Justin's Alexander was bad from the start, but this is disproved by Justin's dating of his deterioration from the moment of the victory at Issus (XI. 10.1), accelerated subsequently after Ammon (XI. 11, 11). Certainly Justin provides a whole series of malicious distortions of the facts as presented by the other historians (XI. 2, 1; XI. 11.7; XI. 11, 11; XII. 3.1; XII. 3.9; XII. 4.2; XII. 5.1; XII. 6.4; XII. 10.9–10; XII. 12.11; XIII. 1.7.

[49] Nearchus, Fragment 3 (Jacoby); Strabo XI. 11.41; Pliny, *Nat. Hist.* VI. 49.

[50] Arrian, *Anabasis* I. 11.6.

[51] Euripides, *Heracles* 827 ff.

[52] Homer, *Iliad* XXI. 1–199.

[53] Arrian, *Anabasis* VII. 28–29.

[54] Plutarch, *Moralia* 332 C–D, 337 B–C, 343 A–B.

[55] Justin XI. 11, 11.

[56] Justin XI. 10, 1.

[57] Arrian, *Anabasis* IV. 7.4 ff., cf. VII. 6, 1, and VII. 8.2. Cf. also Diodorus XVII. 77, 4–7; Justin XII. 3.8 ff.

[58] Curtius 3.1.18; 3.6.5–7; 3.8.20; 4.3.11; 4.4.1; 4.4.17; 4.6.26–29; 4.12.21; 4.16.3.

[59] Curtius 6.2.6–9; 6.6.27;. 4.3.17; 7.5.10–12; 7.5–16; 7.10.9; 8.2.18– 8.2.35; 8.4.9–10; 8.4.15–17; 8.10.29–30; 8.14.41 ff; 9.1.22; 9.2.8.

[60] Tarn (*op. cit.*, pp. 96–97) believes these hostile passages, together with the idea that Alexander's character deteriorated after the death of Darius through the excessive indulgence of Fortuna, to represent the 'Peripatetic' portrait of Alexander which came to be incorporated into full-length history for the first time by Curtius. This belief cannot stand in face of the criticisms directed against it recently by E. Badian, 'The Eunuch Bagoas', *Classical Quarterly* VIII (1958), pp. 144 ff, and by E. Mensching, 'Peripatetiker über Alexander', *Historia* XII (July 1963), pp. 274–82.

[61] There are many other inconsistencies between the generalized portrait painted by Curtius in his obituary note and Alexander's behaviour in the narrative. His *vis incredibilis animi* is non-existent at 3.6.5–7, 3.8.20, 4.4.1, and 4.12.21; his *clementia in devictos* at 4.4.17, 4.6.26, 7.5.35, and 7.11.28; his *pietas erga parentes* at 8.1.23–26 and 8.7.13; his *in omnes fere amicos benignitas* (apart from the Clitus episode) at 4.11.4, 4.16.3, 6.1.18, 6.8.16, 7.24.6, 8.1.14–16, 8.5.13, 8.5.32–35, 8.6.7, and 8.8.21; his *erga milites benevolentia* at 4.12.22, 4.16.8, 7.2.36–38,

7.7.39, and 10.4.2; his *modicus immodicarum cupiditatum* at 4.4.17, 4.6.29, and 10.4.2.

[62] See A. Dosson, *Etude sur Quinte-Curce*, pp. 31 ff; R. Pichon, *Les Sources de Lucain* (Paris, 1912), pp. 252 ff; R. B. Steele, 'Quintus Curtius Rufus', *American Journal of Philology* (1915), pp. 402 ff; F. Wilhelm, *Curtius und der jüngere Seneca* (Paderborn, 1928).

[63] See H. Bardon, 'Quinte-Curce', *Les Etudes Classiques* (1947), pp. 1 ff.

III
Plutarch

A. J. GOSSAGE

'proponamus laudanda, inuenietur imitator.'—Seneca

ALTHOUGH this volume is nominally devoted to studies of Roman biography, a place must be found for the Greek Plutarch, 'prince of ancient biographers', as James Boswell called him. In the first place, he represents the culmination of an established tradition of biographical writing among the Greeks, and the same tradition influenced certain Roman writers (e.g. Nepos and Suetonius) to some extent. Secondly, Plutarch interested himself as much as any Greek of his age in the political life of the Romans and was a keen student of Roman history and antiquities. Thirdly, he was a prolific writer, whose works made a profound impression on later ages and contributed much to the medieval concept of biography. In this respect he must be regarded as a central figure in the long development of the main biographical tradition from the fourth century B.C. to the Middle Ages.

Plutarch himself was born in the small and unimportant Boeotian town of Chaeronea, whose fame rested solely on two battles fought in its neighbourhood, the first in 338 B.C. when Philip of Macedon defeated the Athenians and Thebans, and the second in 86 B.C., when Sulla won a decisive victory over the forces of Mithridates. His dates are uncertain,[1] but he was born between A.D. 45 and 50 and lived until some time about 120. His main literary activity, therefore, belongs to the Flavian era and the reigns of Nerva and Trajan. As a young man he went to Athens and became a pupil of Ammonius, the Academic philosopher,[2] whose influence on his thought and outlook must have been powerful and lasting. Although he spent the greater part of his adult life in Chaeronea, he travelled from time to time in Greece and Italy, and while still fairly young he was sent by his native city to Rome on a political mission. In Rome he met a number of influential people with whom he became friendly, and he returned to the capital, perhaps more than once, between about A.D. 75 and 90. His business there was partly political, and he also lectured—presumably on a variety of philosophical or rhetorical subjects. It must have been during this period of his life that he collected information concerning famous Romans of the past and Roman political and religious customs that he quotes so frequently to illustrate points in many of his writings. And yet he never properly mastered the Latin language, as he himself confesses, and as is clear from misunderstandings of his Roman sources in certain of the Roman *Lives*.[3]

Generally speaking, Plutarch felt a deep respect for the achievements of great Romans of the past and acknowledged the greatness of Roman power in his own day; but his main sympathies, like those of any other educated Greek, were with his own great countrymen of the past, of whose cultural legacy he was a proud heir. His attitude is best studied in the *Political Precepts*, a work written as a guide to a young friend, Menemachus, entering on a public career in a Greek city-state. In one place, for example, he says:

> Nowadays, when the affairs of our cities do not admit of military commands or the overthrowing of tyrannies or joint actions with allies, how might a young man begin a distinguished and brilliant public career? There are still public lawsuits and embassies to the Emperor, demanding a man of ardent disposition but at the same time one of courage and good sense . . .

and elsewhere:

> When a man enters on any public office, he must not only keep in mind the considerations of which Pericles reminded himself when he assumed the general's cloak—'Be careful, Pericles; you are ruling free men, you are ruling Greeks, Athenian citizens'—but he must also say to himself: 'Although you are ruling you are a subject, and the city you rule is under the control of proconsuls, the procurators of Caesar.'[4]

The spirit in which these words were written was one of cooperation, and it was this same spirit and good sense in many other leading Greeks, as well as the general respect of educated Romans for the great intellectual achievements of the Greeks in earlier ages, that created the fusion of cultures in the early empire and made possible the amalgam which can truly be called Graeco-Roman. Symbolic of this, again, is the way in which Plutarch draws his examples, in the *Political Precepts*, from both Greek and Roman political life, just as Greeks and Romans alike are quoted or discussed in close conjunction by Seneca in his *Letters* and *Moral Essays*.[5]

Plutarch's extant biographical writings comprise twenty-two pairs of *Parallel Lives* (one of which is a double pair, containing Tiberius and Gaius Gracchus and two Spartan kings of the third century B.C., Agis IV and Cleomenes III),[6] and single *Lives* of Aratus, Artaxerxes II (Mnemon), Galba and Otho. The first pair of *Parallel Lives* that he composed, the *Epaminondas* and *Scipio*, has unfortunately been lost, and so have several other single *Lives*, whose titles are known from the so-called 'Lamprias Catalogue'. These included Augustus, Tiberius, Scipio Africanus (Minor?), Claudius, Nero, Gaius, Vitellius, Heracles, Hesiod, Pindar, Crates, Daïphantes, Aristomenes and Aratus (probably the poet of that name). Plutarch refers also (*Marius* 29.8) to a projected *Life of Metellus*, but there is no evidence of his ever having published or even completed this. The *Lives of the Ten Orators* contained in the manuscripts of the *Moralia* are generally regarded as the work of another author.

Biography as a conscious literary genre had first developed among the Greeks in the early Hellenistic period. Already in its earliest developments two main tendencies can be distinguished: in the first place, individual *Lives* were composed under the influence of rhetorical techniques of encomium or, perhaps less frequently, censure, which were evolved for the purpose of commemorating favourably or unfavourably the careers of individual statesmen or other famous persons; and secondly, Peripatetic interests in encyclopaedic inquiry led to the publication of collections of *Lives* in various fields—for example, *Lives* of philosophers, of painters, of musicians, of flute-players. In this latter class the interest had been primarily technical, and it was the development of an art that was studied through the careers and personalities of its main exponents. Suetonius' *Lives of Eminent Grammarians*, for example, belongs to this branch of the biographical tradition. It is not always possible, of course, to keep the two tendencies distinct, and in the case of *Lives of Famous Men* it would be difficult to know whether an author's initial intention was to deal separately with each of a series of famous characters or to treat them all as members of a class possessing some common characteristic, in the manner of the technical biographer. Plutarch, at all events, appears to have followed both tendencies to some extent, since individual characters are discussed by him both as individuals and as having features in common with others. This grouping of persons into classes, however, is limited by Plutarch in the extant *Lives* to groups of two, except for Agis, Cleomenes, and the Gracchi, who form a group of four and are all discussed together in the formal *synkrisis* (comparison) which follows the account of their several careers. The *Lives* of Galba and Otho, on the other hand, relate a continuous historical narrative, and the other *Lives* of emperors that he composed may have been intended to form a historical series with these.

The first pair of *Lives* that Plutarch composed, the *Epaminondas* and *Scipio*, was prefaced, no doubt, by introductory remarks explaining his purpose and his plan of writing, and it is particularly for this reason that the loss of these *Lives* is to be regretted. His main purpose in writing biographies, however, was clearly a moral one, as can be seen from his treatment of biographical material in general and from explicit statements which he occasionally makes. By the time he wrote the *Pericles* and *Fabius Maximus*, which formed the tenth pair of *Lives* in chronological order of composition, his experience of this type of writing was sufficient to enable him to reflect on its potentialities as a medium for studying moral action and expressing moral judgements. In the first chapter of the *Pericles* he says:

> A colour whose brightness and charm refresh and stimulate our sight is beneficial to the eye; similarly, we must apply our understanding to objects which, when contemplated by the mind, give it delight and inspire it to aim at its own proper good. These objects consist of virtuous deeds; when a man has learnt about them he is filled with an eager desire to imitate them.

Plutarch points out that in other spheres of activity, such as the skilled trades and the arts,

> admiration for a product or accomplishment is not immediately followed by an impulse to do the thing oneself . . . But virtuous action immediately so disposes a man that he admires the deeds and at the same time emulates those who have performed them . . . For moral beauty initiates an activity towards itself and immediately creates an active impulse in the spectator. This moulds

his character, not simply through his particular imitation, but because his examination of its effect enables him to acquire a moral principle.[7]

Such considerations made Plutarch decide to continue his biographical writing. It was a genre in which he could satisfy his own deep interest in ethical matters, and at the same time it had a valuable practical purpose. The 'imitation' (*mimesis*) of noble examples, however, as he makes clear in the last passage quoted, is not simply a blind or unthinking repetition of acts performed by some great man in the past. Under the conditions of the Roman empire men were no longer free to show political initiative, except in a restricted sphere and to a limited extent, and Plutarch knew as well as anyone that it was impossible for another Pericles to arise. That is the main point of his remarks in the *Political Precepts*, quoted earlier in this chapter,[8] where he contrasts the political conditions of Periclean Athens with those of Greece in his own day. Nevertheless, 'imitation' in another sense was possible: a man might learn from great examples of the past the way in which to order his life, and thus, without necessarily performing the same actions, he might emulate the virtues of great men, by carefully observing their actions and using them as a pattern for building up his own moral principles. Consequently, when Plutarch says in the *Aratus* (1.3–4) that he is dedicating this *Life* to his friend Polycrates, who was a descendant and compatriot of Aratus, in order that Polycrates' sons, by hearing and reading about 'examples' in their own family, should be trained in these 'examples', which they would do well to 'imitate', he does not mean that the young men should take up arms and attempt to restore the Achaean confederacy, of which their ancestor had been the great champion, but rather that they should reproduce his virtues.

Plutarch tells the reader something of his purpose again in the first chapter of the *Aemilius Paulus*,[9] where he says:

> I began writing the *Lives* for the sake of other people, but now I take delight in continuing them for my own sake. Using history as a mirror, I try in one way or another to order my own life and to fashion it in accordance with the virtues of those lives.

He speaks of his study of great men of the past as a daily association with them, as though he were entertaining them in turn, like guests, and examining their characters, selecting particularly those traits which were 'more efficacious for moral improvement'.

> Through my study of history [he continues], and my practice of writing about it, I constantly entertain a mental record of the best and most reputable characters. Thus I accustom myself to repel and put away any base, malicious or ignoble thoughts that arise from my necessary dealings with people by turning my mind cheerfully and dispassionately to the finest of my examples.

Finally, what Plutarch says about the avoidance of bad examples, in the introduction to *Demetrius* (1.3–6), contains another explicit statement of his moral purpose. He observes that the arts and technical skills,[10] such as medicine and music, employ reason for selecting and adopting what is appropriate for their proper function and rejecting what is not, and that this procedure involves studying undesirable as well as desirable objects. Medicine, for example, studies the nature of disease and music that of cacophony in order to produce their opposites.

> The most perfect of all the arts [he says], namely self-control, justice and prudence, distinguish not only what is good and just and expedient but also what is harmful and disgraceful and unjust. They do not praise guilelessness which takes pride in its inexperience of evil, but they regard it as foolishness and as ignorance of things which men who are going to lead upright lives ought particularly to know . . . Perhaps I may as well introduce one or two pairs of characters of a worse type into my *Lives*, not to diversify my writing, of course, for the pleasure and entertainment of my readers, but with the same purpose as that of Ismenias, the Theban teacher of the flute, who used to point out both good and bad flute-players to his pupils and say, 'You must play like this', or 'You must not play like this' . . . In this way, it seems to me, we too shall be more eager to watch and imitate the better lives if we also study the bad and the blameworthy.

What is immediately noticeable in all these passages is that Plutarch professes to base his study of historical characters on definite moral concepts. When Tacitus apostrophizes the spirit of Agricola, his moralization is brief and it includes a typically Roman exhortation to honour Agricola's memory and to imitate his virtues as far as one can.[11] But the exhortation, like the moralization, is brief and simple, and it appears as only a secondary motif, the first being to honour the deceased. It is not based on any philosophical

theory like that of Plutarch, but it reflects rather the age-long
Roman practice, in the *laudatio funebris*, of honouring with praise a
dead man's deeds and virtues and evaluating them as an example to
his younger kinsmen. It has well been observed that 'among the
Romans . . . the personal example of virtue, the concrete precedents, which it was the immediate business of the biographer and
of the psychological historian to set forth, but which a Horace found
as germane to his purpose as did a Nepos and a Tacitus to theirs,
were more esteemed as guides to living than were the abstractions
of philosophical speculations'.[12] Plutarch's heroes, unlike Agricola,
had been dead for many years, and in some cases centuries, before
he wrote about them, and his praise or blame is the result of philosophical reflection and analysis of character rather than the com-
memoration of someone recently loved and admired. What the
Lives lose in immediacy of affective remembrance, however, they
gain in their solid foundation on philosophic principles. The main
influence on Plutarch's outlook in moral philosophy was ultimately
Platonic and Aristotelian,[13] but his frequent reference to praise and
blame when speaking of desirable or undesirable characters and
actions is reminiscent of the emphasis given to encomium and
censure by the schools of rhetoric, and the use of 'examples' as a
means of moral instruction had become common to most of the
schools of rhetoric and philosophy by his time.[14]

Little need be said here about Plutarch's sources for the historical
material of the *Lives*. Their range is wide and includes official documents, reliable historians like Thucydides and Polybius (as well as a
large number of less reliable ones), memoirs of famous men such as
Sulla and Aratus, authors like Stesimbrotus of Thasos, who wrote
biographies of famous Athenians and introduced details of their
private lives, including some scandal, into his works, philosophers,
poets and dramatists, such as Plato, Ion of Chios, and Aristophanes,
who could provide occasional information about their contemporaries and sometimes offered the sort of criticisms that would
appeal to a moralist, and even traditional, almost legendary stories
that collected round the names of great men and were preserved as
'examples' to elaborate a theme or illustrate a principle in the schools
of rhetoric and philosophy.[15] For the Roman *Lives*, Plutarch had
read a fair amount of Latin, in particular Nepos, Livy, Cicero and
Caesar.[16] In addition to written sources, he drew on local oral
traditions for certain details.[17] He studied public monuments, votive

offerings, tombs and statues of famous men,[18] when he could learn from them anything of relevance to his purpose, and he had visited for himself the sites of certain battles.[19]

From time to time Plutarch gives hints about his method of working. He acknowledges[20] the need for a historical writer to read widely and to have access to works which may not be obtainable in his own country. Consequently, such a writer should live in a great city which is favourable to learning and research and also provides him with the essential facilities. Furthermore, in this city, if it is at the centre of political affairs, he can learn historical details which have not been mentioned by other writers, but have lived on in local traditions. In this way a writer might hope to avoid the most obvious deficiencies in his work. Plutarch himself, to judge from the wide range of authors whom he quotes and from his interest in local traditions, would no doubt have liked, if it had been possible, to work under such conditions, and he probably did as much as he could to collect material when he was in Italy or visiting other places in Greece, especially Athens; but he felt that it was his duty to live in Chaeronea, and when he was in Italy he had little time to devote to his own research, or even to learning the Latin language thoroughly, because of his official duties and his occupation with students of philosophy. One may infer from this confession that his method of working fell short of his own ideal standard. He must have made many notes, however, to take back to Chaeronea with him, and in certain cases he probably relied on his memory for a particular detail or for a quotation which he had mentally excerpted many years before he used it in his writings.[21] For well-known historical events there was no need for him to specify his sources; but the vagueness of some of his references, especially when there were alternative or conflicting versions of an incident,[22] show that he had no ready means of quoting by book and chapter or even of verifying the identity of the authors from whom he had originally drawn his material. On the other hand, he must have had copies of some at least of the works of the most important Greek writers in his own library. In any case, the variety of his sources and his apparent intellectual honesty in reporting what writers before him had written make it probable that he himself had read many, if not most, of the sources that he quotes, and that his biographies were fresh and original in their composition rather than copies or recollections of earlier biographies on the same subjects.[23]

Plutarch's methods of biographical composition are stated in the first chapter of the *Alexander*. There he says:

In this book I am writing the lives of king Alexander and Caesar the vanquisher of Pompey. In view of the great number of deeds forming the subject-matter, I shall say no more by way of introduction than to beg my readers not to raise trivial complaints if I epitomize for the most part instead of relating all the famous actions of these men and dealing exhaustively with separate actions in detail. I am not writing history but biography, and there is not always a complete proof of virtue or vice even in the most illustrious deeds. In fact, a small matter such as a saying or a jest often reveals a character more clearly than battles in which thousands of men are killed, or the greatest assemblies of troops, or sieges of cities. Therefore, just as painters reproduce likenesses from the face and the expressions of the eyes, in which the character is revealed, and do not concentrate so much on the other parts, so must I be allowed to dwell on the signs of a man's soul and by their means to present a life in its true characterization, leaving to others the description of great battles.

This freedom to select his materials in accordance with his purpose is always noticeable in the *Lives*, and Plutarch himself reminds his readers of it on more than one occasion. In the *Fabius Maximus* (15–16), for example, the battle of Cannae is briefly described; as one of Rome's greatest disasters in the second Punic War, and indeed in the whole of Fabius' lifetime, it could hardly have been omitted, but it is included as much to illustrate Fabius' relations with the consuls and the results of abandoning his strategy as for its own sake, and it contains no digressions and very few unnecessary details. At one point (16.4) Plutarch quotes a saying attributed to Hannibal regarding a certain incident in the battle and then adds the brief comment: 'But these matters have been related by the writers of detailed histories.' Then he returns immediately to his narrative of the battle, selecting especially the fate of Aemilius Paulus and his last message to Fabius, with its implicit commendation of Fabius' military strategy. In the same *Life* the departure of Hannibal from Italy, historically an important event, is mentioned only in passing (26.5; 27.1) and in relation to Fabius and his general policy, and the recovery of Capua is not mentioned in the *Life* at all, but only in the *Comparison of Pericles and Fabius* (2.1). Again, in the *Alcibiades* (17.2) Plutarch says that the Sicilian expedition was undertaken on a large scale mainly at the instigation of Alcibiades; but after Alcibiades' withdrawal from the expedition he mentions it only twice: in 24.1 he writes 'After the Athenian disaster in Sicily . . .' as a convenient point in time for dating other events, and in 32.4 he says that when the Athenians received Alcibiades back at Piraeus (in 408 B.C.) it was felt that the Sicilian disaster would have been avoided if he had been left in command at the time. The Sicilian disaster is admittedly described in the *Life of Nicias*, and its details were relevant to the career of Nicias rather than that of Alcibiades, but its omission from the *Life of Alcibiades* is a striking example of Plutarch's method of selecting his historical material.

More is said concerning Nicias and the Sicilian expedition in *Nicias* 1.1 ff. Here Plutarch is conscious of the fact that Nicias' part in the expedition has already been described 'inimitably' by Thucydides, and he is unwilling to try to outshine Thucydides as Timaeus had done. On the other hand,

> I cannot [he says], pass over the actions narrated by Thucydides and Philistus, because the temper and disposition of Nicias, hidden under his many great sufferings, are involved in them. I have touched on them briefly, relating only the bare essentials, in order not to appear completely careless and lazy. But I have tried to collect other details which have escaped most writers, or have been mentioned only by some here and there, or are found in ancient votive offerings or public decrees. In doing this I am not gathering a mass of useless information but passing on the means of observing a man's character and temperament.

Similar remarks are made in *Pompey* 8.6: here Plutarch is careful not to give a disproportionate amount of space to Pompey's early achievements, because he realizes the importance of his later actions and experiences, 'which were the greatest and showed the man's character most clearly'; and in *Galba* 2.3 he leaves the precise narration of details to formal history, but claims not to pass over what is worth mention in the actions and experiences of the emperors.

Plutarch is fond of comparing his biographies to portrait-painting,[24] and his general interest in statuary and portraiture is clear from a number of passages where he describes the physical appearances of his heroes as they were represented in works of art.[25] One passage (*Cimon* 2.3–5), however, is of special importance for the way in which it illustrates his general outlook on biography and his principle of selection. Lucullus had been honoured with a statue by the citizens of Chaeronea for interposing on their behalf in an affair which had come before the governor of Macedonia for judgement. Mention of this statue leads Plutarch to the following reflections:

> I believe that a portrait which reveals a man's character and temperament is much finer than one which represents only his physical appearance, and I shall therefore recount the actions of Lucullus and incorporate a true account of them in my *Parallel Lives*. It will be a sufficient favour to him if I recall them. But he himself would not have regarded a false or fictitious account of his life as a fitting recompense for the truthful testimony which he gave (i.e. in defence of the Chaeroneans). When an artist paints a portrait of someone beautiful who has great charm we ask him neither to omit entirely any slight blemish that the person may show nor yet to reproduce it exactly, because the exact reproduction makes the appearance ugly and the omission prevents the likeness from being a true one. In a similar way, since it is difficult, if not impossible, to represent a man's life as blameless and pure, we must fill out the truth in the noble parts as though it were a likeness of him. If, on the other hand, we find errors and faults in men's careers, arising from some emotion or political necessity, we must regard them as shortcomings in a particular virtue rather than the evil that comes of moral baseness, and we must not point them out too readily or abundantly in our history but show respect for human nature, which produces no character perfectly good and indisputably disposed towards virtue.[26]

Generally speaking, Plutarch's characters are described in accordance with this principle, that 'human nature produces no character perfectly good'. Most of them are basically noble, but many of them have some personal weakness: e.g. the haughtiness of Pericles, the superstition of Nicias, the lax and luxurious way of living of both Cimon and Lucullus, the contentiousness of Philopoemen, the surliness of Dion, the rashness of Pelopidas and Marcellus. In no case is the particular weakness exaggerated; it is admitted and occasional references to it are made so that a character appears to be human in this respect. Sometimes it is given a more prominent place, if it affected a person's career (as did rashness in the case of Pelopidas and Marcellus), but without destroying the proper balance of a total characterization. On the other hand, it is rare for any character to be described with more than one such weakness, unless the weaknesses are closely interrelated, like contentiousness and irascibility, or superstition and hesitancy. There are cases where Plutarch rejects the evidence of his authorities for no other reason, it seems, than that it would attribute a fault to a character whom he regards as otherwise free from that fault. This occurs especially in the *Lives* of men who lived many centuries before his time, concerning whose careers it was difficult to determine the trustworthiness of his sources. He rejects, for example, stories told about Pericles by Ion of Chios and Stesimbrotus, which speak of Pericles' arrogance and his alleged adultery with his daughter-in-law, not from any clearly defined principle of historical criticism but simply on the grounds of moral improbability. 'We may ignore Ion,' he says, 'because he expects virtue, like the tragic drama, to have an accompanying satyric element'; and his criticism of Stesimbrotus turns on the distortion of truth by envy and flattery.[27]

A different kind of example occurs in *Coriolanus* (26.2), where Plutarch reports that 'some say' that Coriolanus used deceitful means to embitter the Volscians against Rome. He does not appear to adopt this version of the incident he is describing, possibly because to suggest that Coriolanus practised deceit would throw discredit on his hero;[28] but in the *Comparison of Alcibiades and Coriolanus* (2.1 ff.) he says that Coriolanus was understood to be an upright character, but used deceit to stir up war between the Romans and the Volscians. Here Plutarch accepts the story and names his source as Dionysius of Halicarnassus. This apparent change in his attitude becomes clear and comprehensible in the comparison that he makes between the character of Alcibiades and that of Coriolanus. Alcibiades had earned considerable disrepute for his deceit towards the Lacedaemonian ambassadors in Athens, and a similar detail about Coriolanus, although of no great importance in the *Life*, becomes immediately significant in the *Comparison*. Coriolanus' deceit, Plutarch now says, was the worse because he was influenced not by ambition but by anger. Then there follows a comparison of Coriolanus' anger with that of Alcibiades and a survey of the suffering caused by their respective angers. Here, then, are the 'faults arising from emotion' that Plutarch has spoken of; Coriolanus' deceit arises from anger, and it is not, presumably, to be regarded as moral baseness but as a 'shortcoming in a particular virtue'. It becomes relevant to Plutarch's immediate purpose in the *Comparison*, whereas in the *Life* it is deliberately understated.

Elsewhere, Plutarch is more clearly concerned to present a character in a good light and to reject evidence suggestive of blemishes. One of the most remarkable examples of this procedure is the *Life of Lycurgus*. Plutarch begins (1.1) by saying that among the sources in general there is no agreement concerning the life, travels, and death of Lycurgus, or concerning his political actions and his laws. Yet in spite of this lack of certainty regarding what was almost a legendary figure, he is careful to present Lycurgus as a just and peace-loving man, dear to the gods and comparable to Numa as a good ruler.[29] It is wholly because of this concept of him that he rejects the evidence of the sophist Hippias (23.1), that Lycurgus took part in many campaigns, and accepts that of Demetrius of Phalerum, that he undertook no military actions. Again, he says (28.1 and 6) that, judging from the character of Lycurgus, he cannot ascribe to him the introduction of the *krypteia*, the secret service designed to kill off Helots from time to time, even though this view conflicted with the evidence of Plato and Aristotle. In this case the 'blemish' would have been too ugly a feature to include in the noble nature of Lycurgus.

German scholars have distinguished two main elements in Greek and Roman biography, which they have called respectively *Chronologie* and *Eidologie*.[30] If these terms are to have any meaningful application in the analysis of the form of a biographical work such as those of Plutarch, they must be understood in the widest possible sense. *Chronologie*, broadly speaking, is the narrative account of a man's career, containing his accomplishments in peace and war, in a chronological sequence, while *Eidologie* is the classified account of deeds, incidents, habits, and sayings illustrative of his character without any chronological relation to each other. Within this scheme there may be considerable overlapping, since a man's character could be illustrated by his achievements equally well whether they were narrated chronologically or given as classified examples of this or that characteristic. Moreover, an *Eidologie* might occur, according to the author's judgement or inclination, at almost any point in a *Life*, whether near the beginning or the end of a man's career or even at its height, and it might describe him as he was at that particular point or without any particular chronological significance.[31] Plutarch usually narrates chronologically in the course of a *Life*, beginning with a man's ancestry, parentage, boyhood, and education, and continuing through his career to his death, and he suspends the chronological narrative from time to time to concentrate on the illustration of his hero's character by various means.

In this way the *Lives* differ considerably from the *Agricola* of Tacitus, for example, which is written almost entirely as a chronological narrative, and resemble rather Suetonius' *Lives of the Caesars*. The form of a particular *Life* by Plutarch, however, differs from that of one by Suetonius in its arrangement of materials. In the *Augustus* (9.1), for example, Suetonius says that he has given a short summary of the life of Augustus and will now discuss various details, classified according to their nature (i.e. 'eidologically', not 'chronologically') for the sake of clarity. First he enumerates the wars which Augustus fought. Even these are not all given in chronological sequence, but are subdivided into civil wars and external wars. Then follow his various undertakings and measures, again classified according to their several spheres, but allowing an occasional glimpse of his character (e.g. his clemency, in chapter 51). At the beginning of chapter 61, Suetonius turns from the public aspect of Augustus' life, civil and military, to describe his private and domestic affairs from his early youth to his death. These details follow a general pattern of classification; sometimes they are related to a particular point in his career, but as often as not there is no chronological indication.[32] Plutarch's purpose of 'presenting a life in its true characterization'[33] could not be vividly or convincingly achieved in this way. His concentration upon character delineation, and perhaps also his sense of artistry, prevented him from adhering too rigidly to a system of classification like that of Suetonius, and although observations on a character break his chronological narrative at frequent intervals, most of his illustrative details are fairly well integrated with the narrative.

Plutarch's *Eidologie* is presented by various means. Most frequently he illustrates his characterization or moral observation with relevant incidents selected from a man's career, or with anecdotes such as the stories told about Alcibiades' boyhood or Agesilaus' love of children and his habit of joining in their games.[34] The sayings of famous men were another traditional feature of biography, and Plutarch, as was seen above in a passage quoted from the *Alexander*,[35] appreciates the importance of sayings for illustrating character. In the *Cato Major* he completes an *Eidologie* with two chapters (8–9) of such sayings, which he introduces with the remark: 'I shall record a few of his famous sayings, in the belief that men's characters are revealed by their speech much more than by their appearance, as some people think.' In certain other *Lives*[36] collections of sayings are formally introduced as part of the character description and a chapter or two devoted to them, as in the *Cato Major*, without any chronological indications; but more often the sayings are quoted singly in a historical and chronological context to illustrate a man's reaction to some event or situation. They appear more naturally, of course, when they are reproduced in this way. Some of the *Lives* contain few sayings, but others, and in particular those of Phocion and Cicero, are rich in them. In the *Phocion* (5.4) Plutarch remarks that 'a mere word or a nod from a good man has quite as much weight as innumerable arguments expressed in elaborate sentences', and the *Life* lavishly illustrates this principle. In the case of Cicero, it was his eloquence and wit, as an important aspect of his character, which interested Plutarch. On the whole, however, the sayings in any *Life* are limited to a reasonable number. In this, as with his many digressions, Plutarch observes moderation. After recording some of the sayings of Demosthenes, for example, he suddenly says: 'But I am going to stop here, although I have still more to say about these things, because it is appropriate that I should examine other aspects of his character from his actions and his policy.'[37]

Besides collections of sayings and separate *obiter dicta* occurring at appropriate places in the chronological narrative, there are many reported conversations illustrating men's wisdom and other characteristics, such as those between Solon and Thales, Aristides and Themistocles, Agesilaus and Lysander, Pyrrhus and Cineas, Brutus and Cassius, and others. The sayings themselves can be classified roughly into (i) gnomic or proverbial generalizations, e.g. 'It is impossible to escape what is fated' (*Pyrrhus* 16.9); (ii) repartee and witticisms, e.g. Cicero's remark on the sphinx of Hortensius (*Cicero* 7.6); and (iii) remarks strictly relevant to a particular political or military situation, either moralizing on the lessons to be drawn or illustrating a man's prudence in handling the situation. Remarks of this last type are often elaborated into short speeches[38] or form part of discussions with other persons.

Plutarch also uses other means of presenting character in an *Eidologie*, such as descriptions of the entertainments that men gave, or the frugality of their daily life,[39] the lavishness of their gifts,[40] their style of writing,[41] or their 'hobbies'. In this last respect there is an especially interesting passage[42] in which Plutarch contrasts the slighter, but significant, diversions that other kings indulged in with the building of war engines and experimental ships on a vast scale by Demetrius Poliorcetes.

One of the main features of Plutarch's *Lives* which distinguishes them formally from other extant biographical writings of the ancient world is the fact that they are, with four exceptions, 'parallel'. This formal pairing of characters for comparison was not a new departure. It can be seen as early as the *Frogs* of Aristophanes, for example, when the rival claims of Aeschylus and Euripides to be taken back to the world of the living are examined. As was not unnatural in a culture which owed much to Greek originals, Roman writers had consciously emulated their Greek counterparts for many years before Quintilian made his famous comparisons of Greek and Roman literary figures in the various genres. Thus Catullus occasionally liked to think of Callimachus as his model.[43] Virgil had Hesiod in mind when composing the *Georgics*,[44] Horace modelled himself partly on Archilochus and the lyric poets of Lesbos,[45] and Propertius regarded himself as the Roman Callimachus or Philetas[46] and was ready to compare Virgil, as the poet of the *Aeneid*, and Ponticus, who was writing a *Thebaid*, to Homer.[47] It was in this spirit that Cornelius Nepos, possibly following a practice already established by Varro in his *Imagines*, wrote a biographical work *de Viris Illustribus*, comparing Romans and distinguished foreigners.[48] At first it is likely, as in the literary examples just mentioned, that Rome wished to display to the Greek world her worth in thought and action, but by Quintilian's time there was no longer much need to impress the Greeks, and such comparisons were made in the schools of rhetoric for purposes of instruction:

> hinc illa quoque exercitatio subit comparationis, uter melior uterue deterior; quae quamquam uersatur in ratione simili, tamen et duplicat materiam et uirtutum uitiorumque non tantum naturam sed etiam modum tractat.[49]

Plutarch's purpose in following this practice of composing biographies in pairs and concluding with a *Comparison* was doubtless stated in the lost *Epaminondas and Scipio*, the first of the *Parallel Lives* to be written, but it can be seen from certain of the *Lives* themselves and from the extant *Comparisons* that his main purpose was a moral one. He also probably wished, at least to begin with, to show that in the past Greece had produced men in every way equal to the great men of Rome. This can be seen from his procedure in selecting a famous Roman and then casting round for a Greek with whom to compare him.[50] The moral value of comparison is suggested in the *Phocion* (3.4), where, after speaking of the virtue of the younger Cato, he says,

> I am comparing the virtue of Phocion with that of Cato as good men and statesmen, not for their general resemblances. There is, of course, a difference between one man's courage and another's, for example between that of Alcibiades and that of Epaminondas, and between the prudence of a Themistocles and an Aristides, and between the justice of a Numa and an Agesilaus.

The *Comparisons* not only compare similar features in two characters or two careers; they also point out important contrasts, so that a characteristic of one is seen in clearer perspective from its different appearance in the other. One example will suffice: in the *Comparison of Lycurgus and Numa* (1.2) one of the points of contrast between the two men is that Numa accepted a kingdom which was offered to him without his asking for it, whereas Lycurgus voluntarily resigned that which he already had. Plutarch reflects on the contrast thus:

> It is a noble thing to obtain a kingdom through one's justice; it is also a noble thing to prefer one's justice to one's kingdom. Virtue made the one so famous that he was thought worthy of a kingdom and the other so great that he despised a kingdom.

This is typical of the way in which one man's virtue or situation is contrasted with another's in these *Comparisons*. By going over some of the material already dealt with in the *Lives* and discussing it from various new angles in comparison or contrast, Plutarch is enabled to gain a clearer perception and a more exact definition of individual moral qualities. This, presumably, is what Quintilian meant when he described the function of *comparatio*: 'et duplicat materiam et uirtutum uitiorumque non tantum naturam sed etiam modum tractat.'[51]

The basis for a particular comparison is explicitly stated in the introductory chapters of many of the *Lives*, and where it is not it usually becomes clear from the *Comparisons* themselves. Theseus, for example, is compared with Romulus on the grounds of their obscure parentage, their renown as warriors, their power and wisdom and various circumstances in which their careers were similar. Cimon is compared with Lucullus because both men won brilliant victories against barbarians, both were humane in their politics, both lived luxuriously and entertained lavishly, and there were various points of general resemblance in their careers. Plutarch is aware that he may have omitted other resemblances in this summary, but he says that they will be seen in the course of the narrative.[52] Besides the comparison of similar virtues, Plutarch is clearly interested in resemblances in external details of men's careers, and part of the basis of comparison consists in many cases of such details as successes in war, exile, the treatment of a famous man by his native city, various fortuitous circumstances in a man's rise to power, and, in general, the effects on men's careers of the incalculable element in human life which the Greeks called *tyche* and the Romans *fortuna*. Plutarch's interest in this aspect of human life is seen in his essays *de fortuna Romanorum* and *de Alexandri magni fortuna aut uirtute*, in which he discusses the contribution of 'fortune' and 'virtue' to the successful career of a nation or a great ruler; and he refers in many places to the 'fortune' of the men whose lives he is describing, whether individually[53] or in comparison with others.[54] Most of the *Comparisons* also contain judgements on the characters compared, expressed in terms of praise or censure, and a series of preferences for the one character in certain respects and for the other in other respects. Thus, for example, Lysander is said to have been more humane in his attempt to make changes in the Spartan constitution than Sulla was in usurping power and reforming the constitution at Rome; but Sulla's military victories were far greater than those of Lysander.[55] This is the general pattern of the *Comparisons*. Most of them express no final preference, but a few end with a brief summary containing a partial preference: e.g.

> The reader will perceive, from what has been said, the difference between these men. But if I must declare my opinion of them individually, I make Tiberius the first in virtue, whereas the young king Agis committed the fewest errors, and Gaius was far inferior to Cleomenes in achievement and courage.[56]

Plutarch's outlook and purpose, his method of composition and the form of his biographies have made him vulnerable to modern criticism. Life at Chaeronea, even for one engaged in local administration, must have been far more leisurely than was possible in most other parts of the Roman empire, and Plutarch felt that he had the time to pursue his various intellectual interests even when composing the *Lives*. His style is discursive and unhurried, and he digresses on the slightest pretext. The most significant remark in this respect is one that he makes in the *Timoleon* (15.6) after a digression on the sayings of Dionysius II in exile at Corinth: 'these details, then, will not, I think, seem foreign to the composition of the *Lives* nor without use[57] to readers who are not in a hurry or otherwise occupied'. His digressions cover a wide variety of topics, more suitable to miscellaneous essays, perhaps, than to biography: they include discussions of religious festivals and rites, both Greek and Roman, philological inquiries and attempted etymologies of Greek and Latin words, discussions of meteors and shooting stars, of the causes of *boulimia*, of Greek and Roman months, of Roman divorce, of underground water channels, of the 'Atlantic islands', of the volume and power of the human voice, of the temple of Jupiter Capitolinus, of ghosts, of miracles and portents, of Archimedes and the history of mechanics, of the introduction of wine among the Gauls, and other topics. The digressions are kept within reasonable limits and occasionally Plutarch either tries to justify them or says that a more detailed discussion belongs to another kind of writing.[58]

More serious charges, however, are brought against Plutarch both as a historian and as a biographer.[59] It has been seen that he took some trouble in collecting the material for his work and was alive to the significance of details such as portrait statues, inscriptions, etc.;[60] but on the whole he was unable to evaluate his sources as a writer should if he wishes to present a true historical account. Admittedly, he finds fault with writers like Stesimbrotus and Ion, but this is rather for moral than for valid historical reasons.[61] He follows up his criticism of Stesimbrotus with this reflection:

> Thus it seems that truth is altogether difficult to attain and hard for research to track down, since those who live at a later date find that the lapse of time obstructs their investigation of events, while contemporary accounts of men's actions and lives, either through jealousy and hostility or through gratification and flattery, twist and do violence to the truth.[62]

Although this shows that Plutarch sought the truth, it does not prove that he could recognize it or its opposite, and, in fact, he has no good criterion by which to test the reliability of his sources. He tends to accept the majority opinion or else that which, to his own reasoned view, seems 'probable'. The fact that he is ready to regard both Theseus and Romulus as historical characters is not to his credit, even if he tries, as he says, to 'purify mythology and give it the appearance of history'. He seems to be aware that his success will be limited in this respect and he hopes for indulgent readers if he cannot give his account an admixture of 'probability'.[63] It may perhaps seem not quite fair to judge Plutarch merely from the *Theseus* and the *Romulus*, but these *Lives* show very clearly how far he fell short of acquiring even a genuine historical outlook. The intellectual judgement of many writers in antiquity was clouded by the concept of τὸ εἰκός, which was often no more than *a priori* likelihood, and the extent to which it affected Plutarch's attitude to his sources is seen in what he says about the foundation of Rome:

> Although most of these details are told by Fabius and by Diocles of Peparethos, who appears to have been the first to publish a work on the foundation of Rome, some people are suspicious of them because of the legendary and fictitious character of their works; but we ought not to be incredulous, seeing the things of which fortune is the creator, and reflecting that the Roman state would not have advanced to such power if it had not had some divine origin, attended by great wonders.[64]

Other criticisms made of Plutarch are that he had no clear sense of chronology and little understanding of the political conditions of earlier ages, and that he does not relate a man's career to its historical background with any care or show the lasting effects of a man's policies. These defects, naturally, are regretted most by historians.[65] Plutarch does show a chronological awareness and he even complains of Hippias and Stesimbrotus[66] for their unreliability in this respect; and at least the careers of the men whose *Lives* he is writing are narrated after a chronological scheme. In this he shows a better historical sense than Suetonius, for example. But in his characterizations, which occur frequently in the course of the chronological narrative, as has been seen above,[67] the classifier-collector has the better of the historian, and chronology is lost in anecdote. The other defects should probably be explained by a certain lack of historical imagination and insufficient study or appreciation of the available sources. It requires an effort of imagination and a thorough appreciation of the political conditions in other ages to see the people of those ages in their true setting and to be able to assess the causes of a man's rise to power or the effects of his actions and policies on his contemporaries and on posterity. In the *Tiberius Gracchus* (8), for example, Plutarch states the immediate reasons for Tiberius' agrarian policy, just as he states those for Agis' reforms at Sparta (*Agis* 3.1; 5.1 ff), but there is no indication that he had any proper understanding of the actual conditions or of their underlying causes in either case, and consequently neither Gracchus nor Agis is seen as a product of his age. Similarly, there is no reference to the repercussions of the Gracchan legislation in Rome and Italy, or of the attempted reforms of Agis and Cleomenes affecting Sparta and the Peloponnese. Even when Plutarch says, regarding the death of Tiberius Gracchus, that 'this is said to have been the first civil disturbance in Rome since the expulsion of the kings to end in bloodshed and the death of citizens' (*Tiberius* 20.1), he does not add, as well he might, that it set a new trend in Roman politics; he is interested in emphasizing the importance of the event only as a climax to the career of Tiberius and not as a sinister historical precedent.[68]

Again, some criticism may be made of the presentation of the characters themselves. Since Plutarch's main interest in composing the *Lives* was a moral one, it was natural that he should concentrate on this aspect of the presentation, and to some extent it is true that the presentation is often affected, if not actually distorted, by the emphasis of otherwise trivial or unimportant details and the omission of historically more important ones. He began, as can be seen from the introductory chapters of many of the *Lives*, with a moral concept and then described his heroes in accordance with the concept as far as possible. Aristides, for example, was the just man *par excellence*, whereas Themistocles was ambitious and a lover of glory; and their political differences are seen ultimately as an opposition of moral tendencies in their respective natures.[69] Their *Lives*, in fact, are built up so closely on this pattern of opposition that when the two men are found acting in concert during the Persian War, Plutarch finds it necessary to give special prominence to an interview between them, initiated, of course, by Aristides as the juster man, in which they agree to lay aside their personal contentions for the sake of their country.[70] Similarly, Pelopidas and Marcellus are seen as noble characters marred by rashness in exposing their lives to danger, Philopoemen and Flamininus as contentious rivals, Alcibiades and Coriolanus as irascible characters,[71] and Pericles and

Fabius Maximus as men able to control both their own passions and those of their countrymen. The consequence of this is that the moral contrasts are unnaturally strong. On the other hand, it would not be fair to say that Plutarch's characters are nothing more than character types. Although they do illustrate moral concepts, there is usually sufficient complexity within a single *Life* to prevent this. Again, it is much more likely that if Plutarch had chosen the traditional method of presentation that can be seen in the *Caesar* and *Augustus* of Suetonius,[72] his *Eidologie* and the moral emphasis that he gives would have resulted in a series of character types. He was too much of an artist to allow this to happen.[73]

A further criticism is that there is no real development of character in the *Lives*. The portrayal of character development in ancient biography is in any case a rare phenomenon, and the main cause of this appears to have been the way in which writers approached the task of describing character. If the *Eidologie* is separated from the *Chronologie*, the character cannot be examined in its chronological development, but only as a fixed constituent in a *Life*. Furthermore, the stratification of the ingredients of character themselves, as they are presented by Suetonius, for example, with his classified system of describing wars, constitutional acts, legal reforms, social reforms, public spectacles, provincial regulations, sayings, benefactions and gifts, friendships, domestic relationships, scandalous stories—whether true or false—personal appearance, illnesses, style of writing, etc., makes any hint of character development impossible, except perhaps in a very primitive way.[74] Plutarch is not free from this stratification. He, too, can 'collect' if he feels inclined, whether lists of sayings, of royal hobbies, or of famous one-eyed generals.[75] The disposition of his material, however, is on the whole such that the reader is presented with a chronological progress, through which the characterization of a hero is gradually unfolded. He has conceived the character as a complete product from the beginning, and hence he is not fully aware of development; what develops is not so much the character but rather the characterization in the course of the descriptive process.

For all his faults, Plutarch remains, nevertheless, a most readable biographer. Like Rembrandt, he portrays men in the style and habit of his day and according to his own personal vision, with something of the same exaggeration of light and shade. He is intelligent, but not a true scholar; he is a moralist and an artist. His philanthropic outlook, his moderation, his variety of interests, and his leisurely manner of writing have had a wide civilizing influence on subsequent ages.[76]

Plutarch was not unknown in England before the first English translation of the *Lives* appeared, but the publication of North's memorable translation from the French of Amyot in 1579 brought him immediately to the notice of the educated classes in this country. Shakespeare's indebtedness to this version of the *Lives* is so well known that it needs only a brief mention here.[77] Plutarch's *Coriolanus, Brutus, Julius Caesar*, and *Antony* are followed or drawn upon, sometimes in close detail, in the Roman plays *Coriolanus, Julius Caesar*, and *Antony and Cleopatra*. Besides these, *Timon of Athens* is based on chapter 70 of the *Antony*.[78] There are many references to Caesar, Brutus, Alexander, and other heroes of Plutarch in the plays, and it is likely that most of them reflect Shakespeare's knowledge of the *Lives*. There is even a burlesque comparison between Harry of Monmouth and Alexander in *King Henry V*, Act iv, sc. 7, where fortuitous similarities of circumstance in the two men's lives and contrasts of their characters are made after the style of Plutarch, but with such forced artificiality that they are quite absurd; and yet the burlesque makes it clear that Shakespeare was closely familiar with Plutarch's manner of writing. A more detailed examination of the ways in which Shakespeare's thought, outlook, and concept of moral character were influenced by North's Plutarch is beyond the scope of the present chapter, but it should be mentioned here, more generally, that echoes of Plutarch, even without close verbal similarity, are not hard to find in the plays.[79]

One of Plutarch's greatest and most sincere admirers was John Dryden. The temper of English society and culture had undergone profound changes in the hundred years that had passed since the middle of Queen Elizabeth's reign, when North's translation first appeared, and it was no doubt felt in many quarters that a more modern English version of Plutarch was required. Dryden,

> that great man, who is never to be mentioned without pity and admiration, was prevailed upon, by his necessities, to head a company of translators, and to lend the sanction of his glorious name to a translation of Plutarch, written, as he himself acknowledges, by almost as many hands as there were lives.[80]

This translation appeared in the years 1683–6. Dryden himself did no more than supply a *Preface* and a *Life of Plutarch*, but the work has been generally known by his name. Despite its many defects, it was the standard English translation of the *Lives* for nearly a century, undergoing periodical revision by various hands. Dryden expressed great admiration for Plutarch and acknowledged his skill as a biographer; and his tragedy *Cleomenes the Spartan Hero* owes much to Plutarch's *Life* of Cleomenes.

The eighteenth century in particular appreciated Plutarch. It was an age of enlightenment and cultural assimilation, and in Plutarch it found an author of congenial taste and outlook, from whom much moral good could be learnt.[81] Pope, for example, who knew the *Moralia* as well as the *Lives*, was full of praise for his moral qualities and his 'good nature'.[82] It was again the moral aspect of the *Lives* which interested Goldsmith, and the following passage from one of his essays is of special importance for an understanding of what Plutarch meant to eighteenth-century England:

> . . . as the formation of the heart is of the first consequence, and should precede the cultivation of the understanding, such striking instances of superior virtue ought to be culled for the perusal of the young pupil, who will read them with eagerness and revolve them with pleasure. Thus the young mind becomes enamoured of moral beauty, and the passions are listed on the side of humanity . . . While the scholar's chief attention is employed in learning the Latin and Greek languages, and this is generally the task of childhood and early youth, it is even then the business of the preceptor to give his mind a turn for observation, to direct his powers of discernment, to point out the distinguishing marks of character, and dwell upon the charms of moral and intellectual beauty, as they may chance to occur in the classics that are used for his instruction. In reading Cornelius Nepos, and Plutarch's *Lives*, even with a view to grammatical improvement only, he will insensibly imbibe, and learn to compare ideas of great importance. He will become enamoured of virtue and patriotism, and acquire a detestation for vice, cruelty, and corruption.[83]

Although Nepos is mentioned with Plutarch here, it is especially Plutarch that we seem to hear speaking again, and when Goldsmith goes on to exemplify his remarks with reference to Aristides and Fabricius, it is surely Plutarch's account of them that he has in mind.

In 1762 a certain publisher named Newbery commissioned a series of biographies for young people, in the belief that 'great personages, both ancient and modern . . . are most worthy of their esteem and estimation, and most likely to inspire their minds with a love of virtue'. Goldsmith began the series with a translation of Plutarch's *Lives* 'abridged from the original Greek, and illustrated with notes and reflections for the use of young gentlemen and ladies',[84] and his introduction not only acknowledges Plutarch's influence on biographical writing but also is written quite in the spirit of Plutarch himself. Many young perople were set to read the *Lives*, and it was for this reason, as well as because the Dryden translation was regarded as defective and full of errors, that the Langhorne brothers published their translation in 1770. According to their *Preface*, 'If the merit of a work may be estimated from the universality of its reception, Plutarch's *Lives* have a claim to the first honours of literature.' The Langhornes again stress the educational value of the *Lives* in their dedication to Lord Folkestone, where they say, 'We put into your hands the best of political preceptors.'

An excellent example of the way in which Plutarch influenced the outlook of an eighteenth-century writer is to be found in the works of James Boswell. At the age of 23, Boswell began to read the *Lives* after finishing Xenophon. In a letter to his friend William Temple, dated 23 March 1764, he announces his intention to select 'some of them only'. In the *Journal of a Tour to Corsica* he says of General Pasquale de Paoli (of whom, incidentally, William Pitt is reported to have said, 'He is one of those men who are no longer to be found but in the *Lives* of Plutarch'), 'He just lives in the times of antiquity. He said to me "A young man who would form his mind to glory must not read modern memoirs, but Plutarch and Titus Livius." ' Writing afterwards about Corsica and General Paoli to Rousseau in 1766, he says:

> The voyage has done me a wonderful amount of good. It has affected me in the same way that Plutarch's *Lives* would if they were fused into my mind.

Speaking of Paoli's willingness to allow the Corsicans to believe that he could foresee future events from his dreams, he says:

> It may be said that the General has industriously propagated this opinion in order that he might have more authority in civilising a rude and ferocious people, as Lycurgus pretended to have the sanction of the oracle at Delphos, as Numa gave it out that he had frequent interviews with the nymph Egeria, or as Marius persuaded the Romans that he received divine communications from a hind.

The *Lives* were unfortunately not 'fused' so well into Boswell's mind that he was always able to attribute incidents of a hero's life to the right hero; nevertheless, his interpretation of the character and political position of General Paoli in Corsica is vividly represented in terms of what he had read in Plutarch, and he had formed his judgement here from the *Lives* of Lycurgus, Numa, and Sertorius. When he comes to write his *Life of Johnson*, he appeals to Plutarch, 'the prince of ancient biographers', as his authority for believing that 'the conversation of a celebrated man . . . will best display his character', and he quotes from the *Life* of Alexander[85] to support this view.

It was thus in the 1760s and 1770s in particular that Plutarch's value as a moral teacher was appreciated in England. At the end of the eighteenth century, however, as cultural standards changed, there was a reaction against him. Writers such as Macaulay and Mitford, the historian of Greece, were critical of his comparative lack of historical sensibility. Nevertheless, during the nineteenth century his influence was still felt from time to time, especially by writers who were able to sympathize with his moral outlook; and the *Lives* were still able to inspire a poet such as Wordsworth, whose *Dion* owes much to the *Life* of Dion in its conception and presentation of the hero.[86] In an introductory essay to a translation of the *Moralia*, Emerson commented as follows:

> Plutarch's popularity will return in rapid cycles. If over-read in this decade, so that his anecdotes and opinions become commonplace, and to-day's novelties are sought for variety, his sterling values will presently recall the eye and thought of the best minds, and his books will be reprinted and read anew by coming generations. And thus Plutarch will be perpetually rediscovered from time to time as long as books last.

NOTE ON THE LIVES OF GALBA AND OTHO

These two *Lives* are in many ways unlike the others. They were written singly and without parallels, like the *Aratus* and the *Artaxerxes*. Although Plutarch must have had at his disposal sufficient material of good authority concerning Galba and Otho to make longer works than some of the other *Lives* (e.g. the *Cimon* or the *Aristides*, which were probably restricted in length by a lack of material), the *Galba* and the *Otho* are both short. The *Otho* consists of only eighteen chapters and is, in fact, the shortest of the *Lives* in the number of its chapters. Their shortness can be accounted for by the absence of features that occur regularly in other *Lives*: there is little reference to the careers of the two men before A.D. 68 and none of the usual details of boyhood, education, and early political life; there are no long characterizations—in fact, the emphasis is not so much moral as political—and the treatment and style are not discursive. The narrative in each case is mainly chronological, beginning with the events that immediately preceded the death of Nero in A.D. 68 and continuing to that of Otho in A.D. 69.[87] The characters of both Galba and Otho emerge in their *Lives* from a few descriptions and from the events narrated; but Plutarch seems to be more closely concerned with historical narration and with the task of illustrating, from the events of A.D. 68–69, a principle derived ultimately from Plato, that there is nothing more dangerous to an empire than the undisciplined and unreasoning impulses of its soldiery.[88] From the fact that Plutarch wrote biographies, without Greek parallels, of all the Roman emperors from Augustus to Vitellius, it may be inferred that he treated them all in much the same way as the *Galba* and the *Otho*, the only ones which are now extant; that is to say, he wrote them more as a series of historical monographs, illustrating his view of the Roman empire, than as character studies, even though the characters of emperors like Gaius and Nero must have afforded him good material for moral reflection.

NOTES

[References to Plutarch's *Lives* are to the Loeb edition, for the convenience of the general reader.]

[1] For his dates, see K. Ziegler, in Pauly-Wissowa, *Realenzyklopädie der klassischen Altertumswissenschaft* (hereafter designated *RE*) xxi. 639–41. Cf. also C. P. Jones, 'Towards a chronology of Plutarch's Works', *JRS* lvi (1966), 61ff., and esp. 66.

[2] For Ammonius, see H. von Arnim, *RE* i (1862); R. M. Jones, *The Platonism of Plutarch*, Diss.Chicago (Menasha, Wisconsin, 1916), 7–8.

[3] His own admission: *Demosthenes* 2, 2–3. For misunderstandings of Livy, see especially the Budé edition of the *Lives*, vol. II, 143 ff.

On the other hand, it is equally clear from his general use of Roman sources and his discussions of various Latin technical terms that Plutarch must have had a fairly good working knowledge of the Latin language.

[4] *Praecepta gerundae reipublicae* 805 A–B; 813 D–E.

⁵ The practice did not, of course, begin with either Seneca or Plutarch. It is found in Valerius Maximus, the collector *par excellence* of *exempla*, and in the works of the elder Seneca, but it probably came to Rome originally with philosophers like Panaetius and was perpetuated by other philosophers and the schools of rhetoric in the first century B.C.

⁶ The twenty-two pairs, in their traditional order, are: *Theseus and Romulus, Lycurgus and Numa, Solon and Publicola, Themistocles and Camillus, Pericles and Fabius Maximus, Alcibiades and Coriolanus, Timoleon and Aemilius Paulus, Pelopidas and Marcellus, Aristides and Cato the Elder, Philopoemen and Flamininus, Pyrrhus and C. Marius, Lysander and Sulla, Cimon and Lucullus, Nicias and Crassus, Sertorius and Eumenes, Agesilaus and Pompey, Alexander and Julius Caesar, Phocion and Cato the Younger, Agis and Cleomenes and Tiberius and Gaius Gracchus, Demosthenes and Cicero, Demetrius and Antony, Dion and Brutus.*

⁷ *Pericles* 1, 3 ff. A briefer statement of a similar aim is expressed in *Aratus* 1, 2–4.

⁸ See above, p. 46.

⁹ In some editions (including the Loeb) this chapter is placed before the *Timoleon*, since it is introductory to the two *Lives* (*Timoleon* and *Aemilius Paulus*) which form the pair.

¹⁰ '. . . the arts and technical skills': Plutarch uses here the one Greek word τέχναι to include not only medicine and music but also the specific virtues. This rather loose application of what probably began with Socrates and Plato as an analogy between moral virtue and the arts is foreign to most modern ways of thought.

¹¹ Tacitus, *Agricola* 46, 2. The readings of Grotius (*similitudine*), Heinsius (*aemulatu*) and Pichena (*imitando*) all acknowledge this sense, which is corrupted by the MSS. *militum* or *multum*.

¹² D. R. Stuart, *Epochs of Greek and Roman Biography* (Berkeley, California, 1928), 120.

¹³ The Aristotelian influence is seen most clearly in the *de uirtute morali*. Cf. R. M. Jones, *The Platonism of Plutarch*, Diss. Chicago (Menasha, Wisconsin, 1916), 12–13. Jones rightly points out, however, that 'we have, of course, no reason for supposing that Plutarch in taking over the frame work [*sic*] of ethical theory from Aristotle rejects the Platonic ethics. We find throughout his writings numerous Platonic ethical ideas . . .' For direct references to moral observations, judgements or doctrines of Plato, cf. *Lycurgus* 5, 6; 7, 1; 15, 1; 29, 1; *Numa* 20, 6–7; *Aristides* 25, 6; *Pericles* 8, 1; 15, 4; *Coriolanus* 15, 4; *Comp. Alcibiades and Coriolanus* 3, 2; *Pelopidas* 18, 4; *Dion* 8, 3 (cf. 52, 4); *Cicero* 2, 3; *Comp. Demosthenes and Cicero* 3, 4; *Demetrius* 1, 7; 32, 5; *Antony* 36, 1; *Comp. Agis, Cleomenes and Gracchi* 2, 2; *Galba* 1, 3. In addition, Plato figures as a character in the *Dion*, and Plutarch quotes him frequently in other places without any reference to ethical matters. In general, see the list of parallel passages given by R. M. Jones, *op. cit.* 109 ff and 151, note 5. For Plato's influence on Plutarch in psychological analysis, see R. M. Jones, *op. cit.* 12, and *Plutarque, Vies III* (Budé, Paris, 1964), 172–3. For Plutarch's use of Peripatetic biographical concepts and terminology, see esp. A. Dihle, *Studien zur griech. Biographie* (Göttingen, 1956), 57–76.

¹⁴ Cf., for example, Seneca, *Epistles* xcv. 65 ff.

[15] *Pericles* 13, 11–12. For Plutarch's sources in general, see K. Ziegler, in *RE* xxi. 908–12 and the bibliography given in 911–12. To the bibliography should be added: C. Theander, *Plutarch und die Geschichte* (Lund, 1951), esp. 37–82. The sources for individual *Lives* are discussed with good sense and clarity in the new Budé edition, of which the first three volumes have so far appeared. For 'stories told in the schools', cf. *Pericles* 35, 2; *Philopoemen* 2, 3, etc.

[16] Cf. R. E. Smith, 'Plutarch's Biographical Sources in the Roman Lives', *CQ* 1940, 1–10; C. Theander, *op. cit.* 67–78.

[17] e.g. memories of local events in the civil war between Octavian and Antony, recalled by his great-grandfather (*Antony* 68, 4–5); details of life at the court of Cleopatra in the time of Antony, as told to his grandfather by a physician studying in Alexandria at the time (*ibid.* 28, 2–7); the story of Damon and the Roman officer on Lucullus' staff wintering in Chaeronea, as told, no doubt, by later members of Damon's family living in Plutarch's own day (*Cimon* 1–2). Oral traditions were used also in the composition of the *Demosthenes* (31, 4 *fin.*).

[18] e.g. *Publicola* 15, 3 ff; *Nicias* 1, 5; *Otho* 18, 1. For statues, see below, note 25. In most of these instances Plutarch reports what he himself had seen.

[19] For his visit to Bedriacum, see *Otho* 14. He must certainly have seen the sites of the two famous battles fought near his native Chaeronea, as is suggested by *Alexander* 9, 2 and *Sulla* 19, 5–6, and it is almost equally certain that he had visited the site of Sulla's battle at Orchomenus and seen the evidence he describes (*ibid.* 21, 4), even though he does not mention autopsy in these cases.

[20] *Demosthenes* 2.

[21] One wonders whether it was true of Plutarch, as it was of the elder Pliny, that 'nihil . . . legit quod non excerperet', and even whether perhaps he had the elder Pliny's attitude to the books that he read: 'dicere enim solebat nullum esse librum tam malum ut non aliqua parte prodesset' (Pliny, *Epistles* iii. 5, 10). For Plutarch's collections of notes, which were used for composing the *Moralia* as well as the *Lives*, cf. *Moralia* 475D and 464F; A. W. Gomme, *A Historical Commentary on Thucydides*, vol. I (Oxford, 1945), 78–79, and esp. note 1 on p. 78. For Plutarch's reliance on memory, cf. *Pericles* 24, 7, where he digresses briefly on the name and renown of Aspasia and then adds: 'As I remembered these details in the course of writing it was perhaps only natural that I should mention them.'

[22] φασί ('they say'), λέγεται (it is said'), and various expressions meaning 'some say . . . others say', without names of actual sources, are common in all the *Lives*.

[23] For this, see in particular A. W. Gomme, *op. cit.* 81 ff.

[24] See above, p. 53.

[25] e.g. *Pericles* 3, 2 ff; *Lysander* 1, 1; *Alexander* 4, 1–2; *Demetrius* 2, 2; *Philopoemen* 2, 1; *Flamininus* 1, 1; *Marius* 2, 1; *Sulla* 2, 1; *Antony* 4, 1.

[26] In the introductory chapter to the *Aemilius Paulus and Timoleon* Plutarch says that he selects 'the most important things and the fairest to know' from the careers of the men whose biographies he is writing. This, however, is not an analysis of his actual method of composition, which is more accurately described in the passage quoted above from *Cimon* 2, 3–5, nor does it mean that

he confines himself, in the *Lives*, to describing only what is noble, while deliberately suppressing base or ignoble deeds; it is rather an account of how noble deeds and characters affect his own outlook, and how, in his inner reflections, he selects the finest of them as examples for his own moral improvement.

[27] *Pericles* 5, 4; 13, 11–12. Plutarch's criticisms of Ion and Stesimbrotus as moralists are valid, but something more is needed in evaluating historical sources.

[28] This is the view of the Budé editors (*Vies*, vol. III, 202, note 1), who fail to notice the different treatment given to the same evidence in the *Comparison of Alcibiades and Coriolanus* 2, 2. Cf. also D. A. Russell, *JRS*. liii, 1963, 21.

[29] For the divine favour, see *Lycurgus* 5, 3; *Numa* 4, 7. The presentation of these two men is influenced by the traditional pattern of the good ruler, which occupied men's thoughts considerably in the Flavian period and the time of Nerva and Trajan.

[30] See F. Leo, *Die griechisch-römische Biographie nach ihre literarischen Form* (Leipzig, 1901), 178–92, and A. Weiszäcker, *Untersuchungen über Plutarchs biographisch Technik* (Berlin, 1931), esp. 3 ff, for a discussion of the terms employed. To discuss the implications of this analysis at any length would be beyond the scope of the present chapter and in any case it has been done with admirable thoroughness by Weiszäcker in the work mentioned.

[31] Weiszäcker (*op. cit.* 67 ff) has distinguished various specific types of *Eidologie* according to the point at which they occur in a *Life* ('Universaleidologie', 'Periodaleidologie'—e.g. 'Rand-Eidologie', 'Ersterfolgs-Eidologie', 'Akme-Eidologie', 'Alters-Eidologie'—and 'Gelegenheits-Eidologie').

[32] For a comparison of the *Lives* of Caesar by Plutarch and Suetonius, see Weiszäcker, *op. cit.* 71–72.

[33] *Alexander* 1, 3. The verb used by Plutarch here is εἰδοποιεῖν. For εἰδοποιία, see D. A. Russell, '*Longinus*' *On the Sublime* (Oxford, 1964) 133.

[34] *Alcibiades* 2, 2 ff; *Agesilaus* 25, 5. There is no need to quote more of the many examples; they can be found in nearly all the *Lives*.

[35] *Alexander* 1, 2. See above, p. 53. In this passage Plutarch includes witticisms with sayings. Similarly, in *Lycurgus* 20, 5 he says that one can judge the character of the Spartans even from their sayings.

[36] e.g. *Lycurgus* 19, 3–4; *Themistocles* 18; *Pericles* 8, 5–6; *Demosthenes* 11, 5–6; *Alexander* 58, 2 ff; *Flamininus* 17, 2–5; *Cicero* 7, 5–6; 24, 3–4; 25–7; 38, 2–6.

[37] *Demosthenes* 11, 6.

[38] e.g. *Aristides* 8, 3–4; *Pericles* 12, 3–4.

[39] e.g. *Lucullus* 40, 1 (combined with anecdotes and sayings); *Alexander* 23, 6; *Cato Major* 4, 3; *Cicero* 8, 2; *Tiberius Gracchus* 2, 3, etc.

[40] e.g. *Alexander* 39; *Antony* 4, 3–4 (mentioned in a chapter of *Eidologie* and in the wrong chronological sequence, as Plutarch admits in 5, 1).

[41] e.g. *Brutus* 2, 3–5.

[42] *Demetrius* 20, 1–3. Cf. *Dion* 9, 2.

[43] Catullus 65, 16.

[44] Virgil, *Georgics* ii. 176; cf. Propertius ii, 34, 77–78.

[45] Horace, *Epistles* i. 19, 23 ff.

[46] Propertius iii. 1, 1 ff; 3, 51–52; 9, 43–44; iv. 1, 64; 6, 3–4.

47 *Idem.* ii. 34, 66; i. 7, 3.

48 It appears from Nepos xxiii. (*Hannibal*) 13, 4 that the comparisons were of groups (e.g. Roman generals and foreign generals) rather than the detailed analyses of individual men instituted by Plutarch.

49 Quintilian, *Inst. Orat.* ii. 4, 21. Significantly, this passage is closely connected with what Quintilian considers a valuable mental exercise, namely 'laudare claros uiros et uituperare improbos' (*ibid.* 20). For comparisons in general, see F. Leo, *op. cit.* 149–51; H. Erbse, 'Die Bedeutung der Synkrisis in den Parallelbiographien Plutarchs', *Hermes* 84 (1956), 398–424.

50 e.g. *Theseus* 1, 2; *Cimon* 3, 1; *Phocion* 3, 4; *Sertorius* 1, 6; *Agis* 2, 4–6.

51 Quintilian, *loc. cit.* H. E. Butler translates this in the Loeb edition: 'This . . . involves a duplication of the subject matter and deals not merely with the nature of virtues and vices, but with their degree as well.' In view of Plutarch's practice one might almost translate *modus* as 'the defining limit'.

52 *Theseus* 2; *Cimon* 3. See also *Pericles* 2, 4; *Nicias* 1, 1 (very brief); *Pelopidas* 2, 5; *Dion* 1–2 (full statement); *Aemilius Paulus* 1, 4;* *Demosthenes* 3 (full statement); *Phocion* 3 (full statement); *Demetrius* 1, 7; *Agis* 2, 4–6; *Sertorius* 1, 6. [* In the Loeb edition this chapter is prefaced to the *Timoleon*.]

53 e.g. *Dion* 50, 3; *Phocion* 1, 3; 3, 3; *Timoleon* 3, 2; 30, 4–5; 36, 2–3; *Alexander* 20, 4; *Cleomenes* 39, 1; *Aemilius Paulus* 36 (of special interest); *C. Gracchus* 19, 3; *Marius* 40, 4; *Sulla* 6, 2 ff; 34, 2 ff; *Sertorius* 10, 4. Cf. also the chapters on the 'fortune' of Dionysius II of Syracuse, *Timoleon* 14–15.

54 e.g. *Comp.Theseus and Romulus* 3; *Demosthenes* 3, 4; *Comp.Agesilaus and Pompey* 2, 1; *Demetrius* 1, 7–8; *Comp.Demetrius and Antony* 1, 1; *Aemilius Paulus* 1, 4*; *Sertorius* 1, 6. [*In the Loeb edition this chapter is prefaced to the *Timoleon*.]

55 *Comp.Lysander and Sulla* 2, 1 and 4, 1 ff.

56 *Comp. Agis, Cleomenes and Gracchi* 5, 6. Cf. also *Comp. Lysander and Sulla* 5, 5; *Comp. Philopoemen and Flamininus* 3, 3. For specialized studies of the *Comparisons*, see A. Stiefenhofer, 'Zur Echtheitsfrage der biographischen Synkriseis Plutarchs', *Philologus* 73 (1916), 462 ff; H. Erbse, 'Die Bedeutung der Synkrisis in den Parallelbiographien Plutarchs'. *Hermes* 84 (1956), 398–424.

57 'Without use'—ἄχρηστα. Elsewhere (*Nicias* 1, 5) Plutarch says that it is not his purpose to collect useless material—οὐ τὴν ἄχρηστον ἀθροίζων ἱστορίαν. Most of his modern critics, especially historians, would interpret ἄχρηστος much more narrowly than Plutarch did.

58 *Romulus* 12, 6; *Lysander* 12, 7; *Timoleon* 15, 6; *Aemilius Paulus* 5, 5; *Brutus* 25, 4.

59 By far the best critical account of Plutarch as a historian is to be found in the masterly essay by A. W. Gomme, *A Historical Commentary on Thucydides,* vol. I (Oxford, 1945), 54–84, to which the brief account given here is greatly indebted.

60 See above, pp. 51–2.

61 See above, p. 56 and note 27. Similarly, in the *de malignitate Herodoti* many of Plutarch's objections to what Herodotus says are made on moral grounds or on grounds of 'probability'.

62 *Pericles* 13, 12. In this passage ἱστορία appears to be used in two distinct senses, recognized by lexicographers: (i) 'inquiry', and (ii) 'a written account

of an inquiry'. The second part of Plutarch's complaint, regarding the un-reliability of contemporary, oral or written, accounts is a commonplace of historians. It begins with Thucydides (i. 22, 2–3; cf. also ii. 35, 2) and is echoed through the ages by Polybius (xvi. 14, 6 ff; 17, 8 ff, Buettner-Wobst), Josephus (*de bello Iudaico* 1, 1–2), Tacitus (*Histories* 1, 1), Herodian (i. 1, 1–2), etc.

⁶³ *Theseus* 1, 3. This *Life* is a remarkable demonstration of Plutarch's inabi-lity or unwillingness to decide between conflicting sources, his arbitrary appro-val of some, his acceptance of majority opinions, and his general reliance on 'probability'—e.g. 2, 2; 10, 2–3; 14, 2; 17, 5–6; 19, 1–2; 20, 1–2; 22, 5; 26, 1; 27, 4–6 (admitting the difficulty of inquiry into matters of great antiquity); 28, 1–2; 29, 4–5; 30, 4–5; 31, 1 ('probability' supported by majority opinion); 32, 5; 34, 2. Despite the fact that in such remote antiquity 'inquiry wanders in uncertainty' (*Theseus* 27, 5; cf. *Lycurgus* 1, 3) it is quite legitimate to single out the *Theseus* in this way, since Plutarch's characteristic tendencies are thereby thrown into relief. The same tendencies are present in the other *Lives* to a greater or lesser extent, according to the number and nature of the sources available to him. He scarcely mentions sources in the *Galba* and *Otho*, no doubt because it was comparatively easy for him to learn the facts about these em-perors. For his acceptance of the 'authors who are least contradicted', cf. *Lycurgus* 1, 3. For his unwillingness to decide, *Demosthenes* 15, 3. For an example of criticism of a source based on good sense and 'probability', *Pericles* 28, 1–3.

⁶⁴ *Romulus* 8, 7. For εἰκός, see N. I. Barbu, *Les procédés de la peinture des caractères et la vérité historique dans les biographies de Plutarque* (Paris, 1934), 139 ff.

⁶⁵ See A. W. Gomme, *op. cit.* 54–61.

⁶⁶ *Themistocles* 2, 3; *Numa* 1, 4. For chronological discussions or observa-tions, cf. *Numa* 1, 1 ff; *Lycurgus* 1, 1–3; *Solon* 27, 1; *Themistocles* 27, 1.

⁶⁷ See above, p. 57.

⁶⁸ It should be added that it was also the fashion in the first century A.D. to collect 'first instances' of things; cf. Seneca, *de breuitate uitae* 13, 2 ff.

Gomme (*op. cit.* 72, note 1) rightly suggests that in the *Nicias* 'the descrip-tion of Nikias' φιλοτιμήματα in c. 3 is coloured more by Plutarch's experience of Roman magnificence than by his historical knowledge of the 5th century'. One might further observe that the very word φιλοτιμήματα belongs to the vocabu-lary of public benefaction in first century A.D. Greece, and the text of *Nicias* 3, 2, χορηγίαις ἀνελάμβανε καὶ γυμνασιαρχίαις ἑτέραις τε τοιαύταις φιλοτιμίαις τὸν δῆμον, ὑπερβαλλόμενος πολυτελείᾳ καὶ χάριτι τοὺς πρὸ ἑαυτοῦ καὶ καθ᾽ ἑαυτὸν ἅπαντας, with the possible substitution of another verb for the equivocal ἀνελάμβανε, might have been taken from the honorific decree on the statue base of a public bene-factor in any Greek town in Plutarch's day. The expressions can all be paralleled (e.g. *IG* v. 1, 531, 535, etc., for φιλοτιμία in this sense, in connexion with the tenure of the *gymnasiarchia*; *ibid.* iv¹. 606: ὡς ὑπερβαλεῖν τοὺς πρὸ αὐτοῦ πάντας, etc.).

⁶⁹ *Themistocles* 3; *Aristides* 2 ff.

⁷⁰ *Aristides* 8.

⁷¹ For Coriolanus, see the Budé edition of the *Lives*, vol. III, 172–3, where it is well suggested that 'sa biographie est-elle comme une illustration du traité *Sur la colère*'. Cf. also D. A. Russell, *JRS* liii, 1963, 27–8.

⁷² See above, p. 58.

[73] F. Leo regards Plutarch as primarily an artist (*op. cit.* 177: 'Plutarchs Biographien auf der Seite der Kunst gehören'), but he arrives at this conclusion on the basis of 'der Gegensatz von Kunst und Wissenschaft', which in itself is a hazardous methodology.

[74] e.g. 'He was thus when he was a boy, but when he was a man he changed his ways.'

[75] *Sertorius* 1, 1 ff. It is difficult to know how much of this chapter Plutarch wrote with his tongue in his cheek.

[76] For this aspect of Plutarch, see R. Hirzel, *Plutarch* (*Das Erbe der Alten*, Heft IV, Leipzig, 1912), esp. 74–180; 200–6.

[77] See esp. R. Hirzel, *op. cit.* 139 ff; T. J. B. Spencer (ed.), *Shakespeare's Plutarch* (London, 1964), and especially the useful bibliography on p. 20.

[78] The 'epitaph' read out by Alcibiades in Act v, sc. 4, is a curious combination of two separate epitaphs reported by Plutarch. Here Shakespeare reproduces North's translation word for word, except for the substitution of 'caitiffs' for 'wretches'.

[79] Compare, for example, Hamlet's speech, 'But to my mind, though I am native here . . .' (*Hamlet*, Act i, sc. 4) with Plutarch, *Antony* 24–25, 1; both passages deal with achievements and good qualities marred by a 'particular fault'.

[80] So J. and W. Langhorne in the *Preface* to their translation of the *Lives*.

[81] It has been well said by A. W. Gomme (*op. cit.* 54) that 'Plutarch himself belonged, as it were, to the eighteenth century of Greece'.

[82] This is no doubt a reference to Plutarch's interest in *philanthropia*. Dryden, in the dedication of his *Life of Plutarch* to the Duke of Ormond, had described Plutarch as one 'than whom antiquity has never produced a man more generally knowing, or more virtuous; and no succeeding age has equalled him'.

[83] Goldsmith, *Miscellaneous Essays* (1765), No. 13.

[84] For which, incidentally, he was paid $11\frac{1}{2}$ guineas.

[85] *Alexander* 1; see above, p. 53.

[86] Many of the details are taken directly from Plutarch's *Dion*, e.g. Plato's warning against 'self-sufficing solitude'; the five thousand warriors, 'each crowned with flowers', who accompanied Dion on his return to Syracuse, and their 'ruder weapons'; Dion's bright armour; the celebrations with wine at his return; his pelting with flowers; the vision of a woman 'vehemently sweeping', etc.

[87] Cf. F. Leo, *op. cit.* 156: 'Er führt also nicht einen βίος des Galba, sondern einen Abschnitt einer aus der römischen Geschichte excerpirten Kaisergeschichte ein.'

[88] *Galba* 1, 3.

IV
Suetonius and his Influence

G. B. TOWNEND

BY A.D. 120 Classical Latin literature was near its close. Of the major authors of the school and University syllabus, the historian Tacitus must have just about completed his *Annals* and was perhaps dead; Juvenal, the last of the satirists, was well advanced in his literary career, as the last representative of that elaborate and rhetorical style which we recognize as Silver Latin. The new emperor, Hadrian (117–138), was himself a keen poet and patron of poets; but during his reign literature was to lose almost all distinction until the dubious revival in the middle of the fourth century, falling for the most part into the hands of such scholars and pedants as Fronto and Aulus Gellius, whose interest harked back to the earliest age of Roman letters.

The transition from the Classical period to this age of scholarship is marked by the climax, such as it is, of Roman biography. Gaius Suetonius Tranquillus at once says the last word on the rulers of Rome during the first century after Christ and provides the pattern of the bookish writers of the Antonine age. He was born of an equestrian family about A.D. 70, perhaps at Hippo Regius in North Africa, perhaps in Italy—Ostia, Pisaurum, and Rome have all been tentatively suggested.[1] Educated partly in the capital, he became a *grammaticus*, or teacher of literature, before embarking on the public career open to men of his rank. He secured a posting to Britain as military tribune, as his father had been before him; but, although this was normally essential for the equestrian *cursus honorum*, he had it transferred to a relative and evidently confined his career to more sedentary offices.[2] From a fragmentary inscription found at Hippo (Bône) in 1952,[3] we know that he held a succession of posts at court: *a studiis* to the emperor (a scholarly appointment of uncertain scope),[4] *a bibliothecis*, in charge of imperial libraries in Rome; and *ab epistulis*, in charge of the emperor's correspondence. The last of these, which developed during the second century into a major civil service appointment in the increasingly centralized bureaucracy, he held under Hadrian; the two former seem, on grounds of both chronological probability and inscriptional evidence, to have fallen in the last years of Trajan's reign; and a lacuna in the inscription, which cannot now be filled, must have contained the titles of one or two earlier posts, perhaps of the same type, so that altogether Suetonius' employment in the palace will have occupied the better part of the second decade of the century. The next datable event in his career is the dedication of his main work of biography, the *Caesars*, to the praetorian prefect, Septicius Clarus,[5] who held office from 119 to 122; and finally a passage in the Augustan *Life of Hadrian*[6] states that Suetonius was dismissed, together with Septicius, for lack of respect towards the empress. After this we hear nothing of Suetonius' career: a reference towards the end of the imperial *Lives*[7] suggests that he was still writing after A.D. 130, and some such period as this seems essential to allow for the completion of his multifarious writings, of which little but the titles are now known. There is some plausibility in the suggestion that the lost work *On Public Offices* should be referred to this period,[8] when the majority of Hadrian's reforms in the imperial bureaucracy are probably to be placed; and this might indicate some return of Suetonius to favour. Other works[9] of a predominantly linguistic nature, such as the treatise on the correct names of articles of clothing or that on Greek terms of abuse, may well belong to his early career as a *grammaticus* or the years immediately following. But generally we must be content with the picture of the scholar extending his interests into all sorts of obscure branches of knowledge over a very long period, interrupted only to a limited extent by the loss of favour in 122. The particular ways in which he was able to take advantage of his position as head of the imperial archives will be considered below.

Suetonius' first work of biography, *On Illustrious Men*, has come down to us only in a mutilated form.[10] Of the various sections, we have that on *grammatici* more or less complete; and with it, in the same manuscript, the preface and the first five *Lives* from the *Rhetoricians*—all on a very small scale, and lacking any developed biographical plan. From the *Poets*, *Lives* of Terence, Virgil, Horace, and Lucan have come down to us, attached to MSS. of the authors' poems, though in variously abbreviated or expanded forms; and the brief extant *Lives* of Tibullus and Persius may be due to Suetonius in part or in whole. Fragmentary *Lives* of a single Orator and a single Historian survive from their respective sections. The work as a whole was used by St. Jerome to provide items for his chronological table of history; and from this a number of isolated sentences can be attributed to Suetonian *Lives*. We can hardly judge of the quality of the work as a whole from these odd fragments: only that the biographer was ready to quote literary works and other documents to establish controversial points or to illustrate such matters as the relationship of Horace and Maecenas. The literary biographies are almost certainly earlier and less developed than the *Caesars*, from which conclusions may more satisfactorily be drawn; but a remarkable proportion of our knowledge of Roman literary history today is derived from this ill-fated work.

The original model for a series of *Lives* of Roman emperors may have been some such Greek author as the obscure Phaenias of Eresus,[11] who wrote *Lives* not only of poets and philosophers but of the tyrants of Sicily. The latter appear not to have fallen under the category of panegyrics, to which so many of our extant biographies properly belong—the Greek *Lives* of Agesilaus by Xenophon and of Evagoras by Isocrates, as well as much of Nepos and the *Agricola* of Tacitus. Even Plutarch, writing during Suetonius' own time, partakes largely of the manner of panegyric. Whether or not Phaenias had shown the way, in writing *Lives* that were objective, or actually critical, Suetonius was presumably prompted to adopt this sort of attitude by the fashion of the time. Tacitus, in his preliminary remarks both to the *Histories* and to the *Annals*,[12] drew attention to the way in which earlier writers on the imperial period had tended to be either flatterers, writing to please the reigning monarch, or traducers, exploiting the reaction after a bad emperor's death; and had set out to combine elements from the two types into a coherent and objective whole. We may form our own opinions of Tacitus' success. But writers in the reign of Trajan or Hadrian were at last far enough removed in time from the Julio-Claudian emperors to make a critical assessment possible as well as necessary.

Suetonius could hardly contemplate rivalling Tacitus in writing history in the ordinary sense, a type of literature which required the stylistic artistry and grasp of major issues which the older man had recently demonstrated so notoriously. But even in Tacitus history continually threatened to become little more than the history of the emperor rather than the empire, for all that he still observed the rules of annalistic writing, with a year-by-year framework and occasional attention to provincial affairs. True biography, if it was to get away from Tacitean history, had to take an entirely different line of approach, and to abandon chronology almost entirely. It could be assumed that the main narrative of events would be known well enough from Tacitus or from earlier and fuller annalists. The pattern for the alternative analytic scheme was already provided to some extent by panegyric, which had dealt with the hero's virtues in succession, each with one or more anecdotes to illustrate it (this is clearly seen in Xenophon, or in Nepos' *Epaminondas*), and the inscriptions of Roman epitaphs had followed something of the same line.[13] None of these, however, appears to have developed the analytic method to the extent which we find in Suetonius.

The pattern may be seen clearly in the *Julius*, the first of the twelve *Caesars*. Family and birth, with accompanying omens, are now lost, apart from a stray fragment; then the career, up to the final victory and accession to supreme power—this section being far more protracted than in the following *Caesars*, for whom accession comes relatively soon and early life is less eventful. Next the celebrations of the victory, including public games (a subject which always interested Suetonius deeply, being dealt with in one of his lost works); then his reforms, and his plans for further projects. At this point (45.3) comes the first of those passages in which Suetonius explains his programme for the following sections—though it seems probable that in this, the first of the *Caesars*, the first half of the *Life* may originally have opened with a similar statement of headings. Here he says: 'As he acted and planned in this way, he was cut short by death. Before I describe this, it will not be irrelevant to set forth in outline details concerning his appearance and bearing, his personal habits and his character, and also his practices in civil and military life.' After these topics have in turn been dealt with in their respective ways, and with no regard for chronology, he proceeds to a discussion of Julius' dictatorial ways, and so on to the conspiracy against him, his death, will, and funeral, and the public reactions which followed. In this *Life* the analytic sections occupy a relatively small position, but the principle is the same. Although the pattern is reproduced more or less closely in all the following *Lives*, there is

no fixed list of headings. Even the sequence Family—Father—Birth
—Early life till accession—is varied in different ways. In *Augustus*
the fourth of these rubrics includes a long section on the civil wars,
in approximately chronological order; in *Tiberius* a long account of
the exile in Rhodes. In *Caligula*, there is nothing to be said of his
family, already dealt with at the beginning of Tiberius; but his
father, Germanicus, rates a short biography on his own, constructed
on something like the standard pattern. Again, the characteristics
discussed vary according to the individual: the really villainous
emperors have no virtues at all (except in so far as a display of piety
towards relatives regularly follows close on accession), but a large
catalogue of vices; others have a mixture of both. Then the sections
of personal appearance and habits come in different positions: sometimes at the beginning of the character as a whole, sometimes at the
end; after the death in others; early on in boyhood in the single case
of *Titus*. This degree of elasticity makes the scheme much more
tolerable, though it is difficult to assert that the variations are really
the result of careful calculation. There is certainly little evidence of
conscious effort to build up a coherent character, such as one finds
in Plutarch. This is largely because Suetonius avoids generalizations,
preferring a list of disconnected items which the reader must add up
for himself. As an example of this sort of passage, the following
chapter describes the stupidity of Claudius:

> When Messalina had been executed, shortly after sitting down to
> dinner he enquired, why the mistress did not appear? Many of
> those whom he had condemned on capital charges, on the very
> next day he ordered to be summoned to council or to play dice,
> and, as if they were slow in coming, sent a messenger to rebuke
> their laziness. When he was about to marry Agrippina, contrary to
> the laws of relationship, he did not refrain from referring to her in
> every speech he made as 'my daughter, my foster-child, born and
> brought up in the bosom of my family'. When he was about to
> adopt Nero, as if it were not enough that he was being criticized for
> adopting a stepson when he had a grown son of his own, he re-
> peatedly announced that this was the first time anyone had been
> adopted into the Claudian family. (*Cl.* 39)

In this paragraph the majority of the incidents described refer to
well-known persons, and can be dated precisely by anyone who
knows the main outlines of the reign. The second anecdote, of the
unnamed councillors, is typical of all too many pieces of information

which modern historians would like to be able to place in a satisfactory context; though there is some likelihood that it belongs shortly after Messalina's death. From this point of view Suetonius can be infuriating. Again and again he passes over some interesting topic with an oblique reference, as the expulsion of the Jews under 'Chrestus' in *Cl.* 25.4, or the Vinician conspiracy in *Nero* 36.1, of which we happen to have no other direct source of information. Again and again he quotes a story of dubious veracity, with no better authority than 'it is commonly said' or 'the tradition is'. In this latter respect he is no worse than other Roman writers, who realized that nothing so defaces the written page as the constant citation of earlier writers' names—and the footnote, of course, had not been invented; but the deficiency is the clearer in Suetonius simply because he so patently draws on a variety of inconsistent sources and makes no attempt to reconcile them. But if Suetonius irritates modern readers in this way, it is because they are hoping to use him as an historical source, to provide a factual account of the events of such-and-such an emperor's reign. This is not, of course, how Suetonius intended his *Lives* to be read. He could hardly have dreamed that an age would come when readers lacked even certain books of Tacitus' *Annals* and *Histories*, not to mention the less-brilliant historical works of Aufidius Bassus and the elder Pliny. His concern is deliberately withdrawn from topics other than the character and career of the central figure, and this meant that he was bound to follow what it is convenient to term the Law of Biographical Relevance.[14] Public affairs do not interest the biographer, except in so far as they reflect the emperor's position; provincial developments, wars, and disasters can be ignored almost completely; ministers and generals, even when as prominent as Aulus Plautius or Corbulo or Agricola, may not merit even a single reference. Modern prosopographers may believe that an emperor's choice of administrators throws much light on his character, but this is a very recent idea, and Suetonius can hardly be blamed for leaving these personages on one side.

Another feature of the *Caesars* (of which incidentally there seems to be no trace in the literary *Lives*) arises naturally from the method of arrangement *per species*: the announcement of a series of topics to be dealt with in order, followed by sections on the said topics. We have noted one such statement of programme in the *Life of Julius*; another appears in *Aug.* 61.1, summing up the previous material and introducing what follows: 'Since I have now described his behaviour in his commands and offices and in administering the state throughout the world in peace and in war, I shall go on to discuss his personal and private life, and the nature of his character and fortune at home and among his intimates from his youth until the end of his life.' This is in effect a device of rhetoric, called in Latin *partitio* or *divisio*, introduced to Roman oratory by Cicero's older contemporary Hortensius,[15] who earned ridicule by ticking off items on his fingers as he announced the plan of his speech. Cicero himself certainly employed such *divisiones* in the interests of clarity, and they are to be found in almost all Latin prose writers, and even some poets. In biography, they occur in the earliest extant Greek examples, as in Xenophon's *Cyropedia* (i. 1.6) and Isocrates' *Evagoras* (22); and there are a few examples in Cornelius Nepos, particularly in *Epaminondas* (1.4), the *Life* which most closely approximates to the Suetonian pattern. In Suetonius himself the precedent of these earlier *Lives*, all mainly panegyrical in tone, may have been reinforced by the grammarian's practice of classification. From his book *on Clothing* a simple example survives,[16] in which he first named the three types of priestly hat, and then dealt with them in the same order. At all events, having adopted *divisio* in order to make clear the scheme of his arrangement *per species*, he soon begins to use it more and more, until it becomes a positive mannerism and often tends to confuse the reader instead of assisting him. This is largely because once he has announced the topics to be dealt with he is likely to proceed from one to the next without repeating the key word or marking the transition in any way. For example, in *Aug.* 51.1 we have: 'There are many major proofs of his mercy and restraint.' The experienced reader can recognize at once that the following section, covering the rest of 51, consists of instances of mercy: the opening words of 52, 'He accepted no temples in any province . . .' contain no overt indication that they are the beginning of a long series of anecdotes on Augustus' restraint. Likewise in *Nero* 26.1 five major vices are listed; but when the first anecdote follows, it may not be clear that this illustrates Nero's violence, the first of the five, and the names of the other four are not set clearly at the opening of the sections in which they are in turn illustrated. There can be no doubt that much greater clarity would have been achieved if, instead of the introductory *divisio*, we had simply a reference to each quality at the beginning of its own section. Often, indeed, it is extremely difficult, even for the reader with his eye open for this particular feature of arrangement, to decide how the material is intended to be classified. This is especially true in *Nero* 33.1, where a long series of parricides is introduced by the *divisio* 'He began his parricides and murders with Claudius'. The list of deaths which follows continues down into 37, but it is far from clear whether Nero's aunt, wives, stepsister, and stepson are still under the heading of parricides or are ordinary murders, along with Seneca and others. And sometimes the actual meaning is lost altogether. In *Claud.* 21.1, Suetonius says: 'He also presented numerous magnificent games, not only the usual ones and in the normal places, but new inventions and ones revived from antiquity, and some where no one had previously held any'. This can only be a *divisio*, although the reader would hardly notice it unless he were deliberately watching out for this type of expression. Only then will he realize that the statement a little farther on 'He frequently held circus-games in the Vatican' picks up the item in the heading 'where no one had previously held any'; so that he eventually extracts the information (not known from any other source) that Claudius was the first to use Caligula's new circus in the Vatican gardens for shows of this sort.[17] This may be only one of a number of similar pieces of information which have escaped readers in the past. There can be no doubt that the abuse of *divisio* is a characteristic of Suetonius which must be borne in mind in reading and translating the *Caesars*. No other feature, perhaps, displays so clearly the method of the *grammaticus* turned biographer.[18]

Now, as I have remarked, Suetonius' exploitation of *divisio* begins only with the *Caesars*, not in the literary biographies. Likewise it is only in the first two *Lives* that we find the large-scale *divisiones* announcing the arrangement of major parts of the works. Comparable indications in *Cal.* 22.1 ('Thus far concerning him as emperor: the rest is to be related of him as a monster') and *Nero* 19.3 ('I have assembled this material partly as meriting no criticism, partly even as deserving considerable approval: this I have done in order to separate it from his weaknesses and crimes, to which I shall now turn') do not indicate subsequent topics in the same way—the simple *divisio* between *probra* and *scelera* in the latter passage, followed out in 20–25 and 26–37 or 38, is very minor and unobtrusive. The writer has evidently assumed that the reader will not need constant reminding of the regular scheme. At the same time it is in

the later lives that *divisio* begins to be pushed to the point of ob-
scurity. This links up with another very noticeable weakness of the
later *Lives*: the tendency to omit actual names of persons featuring
in anecdotes and to refer either to *quidam* (singular and plural
alike) or to vague descriptions, often arbitrarily multiplied into the
plural. Examples are the *immaturae puellae* in *Tib.* 61.5 (the daughter
of Sejanus, as Suetonius must have known), the aged matrons in
Nero 11.1 (simply Aelia Catella), *quidam tradunt* in *Otho* 7.1 (the
historian Cluvius Rufus); but all too often the real individuals can
no longer be identified, although their names were surely available
in Suetonius' sources. In *Julius* and *Augustus* there are hardly any
example of this deliberate anonymity and exaggeration. This seems
to be a further example of a decline in Suetonius' care and precision,
beginning apparently with the *Tiberius*.

In one further respect the biographer's method suffers a severe
setback at virtually the same point. In addition to his readiness to
quote verbatim from sources of all sorts, in prose or in verse, in
Latin or in Greek, as no reputable writer of formal prose appears to
have done before,[19] he makes particularly effective use of extracts
from letters of Augustus, sometimes of considerable length, to
illustrate questions which arouse his particular interest. There
seems no good reason to doubt[20] Suetonius' own assertion that he
studied the autograph version of most of these letters, evidently
while he was head of one of the imperial bureaux, as *a studiis, a
bibliothecis*, or *ab epistulis*—we do not know under which functionary
such a collection would come, but in any case any one of them
would presumably have been allowed access to his colleagues'
material. What is striking is the nature of the selection. Letters of
Augustus are quoted in the Donatus *Life of Virgil* (31), extensively
in the *Life of Horace* and in Augustus' own *Life*; after that, in *Tib.*
21.4 in *Cal.* 8.4, and in *Claud.* 4. All these quotations are apt and
revealing, adding immensely to the value of the passages in which
they appear. But they are all from letters by Augustus, and all cover
problems arising during Augustus' own reign, even when they
occur in the *Life* of an emperor who succeeded twenty-five years
after Augustus' death. It is extraordinary that Suetonius does not
quote a single letter, with the exception of *Nero* 23.1 (which is not
claimed to be, and probably was not, taken directly from the original) from any emperor after A.D. 14. It is conceivable that certain
of the emperors did not have their correspondence preserved in the

palace archives: it is not to be imagined that no letters at all were to be found, particularly ones to implement the rather thin material available on the last six Caesars dealt with. Two explanations present themselves: either that the use of the Augustan material displeased Hadrian, who put a ban on further exploitation of the archives; or that Suetonius was no longer able to consult the archives, because he was no longer employed in the palace. The fact that in the *Tiberius* the biographer was still able to use the Augustan letters in his published work, but was not able to draw on Tiberius' own letters, favours the latter explanation, which is supported by other indications.

In any case, there is evidence here as elsewhere of a distinct break between the *Augustus* and the *Tiberius*, for which Suetonius' dismissal in A.D. 122 is the best explanation. The main objection to this is that we know, on the authority of Johannes Lydus (*de Magist.* ii. 6), that the *Caesars* were dedicated to Septicius Clarus as praetorian prefect—an office which he ceased to hold when he and Suetonius both fell from favour. Thus 122 has normally been accepted as the date of publication of the *Caesars* as a whole. But *Julius* and *Augustus* together form a respectable book for publication on its own, even if as just the first instalment of a longer series; and the dedication may perfectly well have been attached to them alone. Among contemporary writers, both Tacitus and Juvenal are agreed to have published their works in successive parts,[21] and not many years earlier the books of Statius' *Silvae* and Martial's *Epigrams* had unquestionably appeared in this way, with the addition of dedications to a number of different patrons. Indeed, it is highly unlikely that the different parts of Suetonius' own *Lives* of literary men were published at one and the same time, so different is the scale and treatment of the *Grammatici* and *Rhetores* from that of the poets which have come down to us. There is a further consideration. Suetonius' first two *Lives* do not encourage comparison with the *Annals* of Tacitus, which had appeared at some time during the previous decade and begin with the accession of Tiberius. When the biographer came to the period dealt with so impressively by Tacitus, he may well have felt hesitant over publication, especially as he was notoriously dilatory in this respect (Plin. *Epp.* v. 10.2).

At the same time, there is reason to suspect that his reading of the *Annals* prompted some of the most interesting passages in the next group of *Lives*. It is most unlikely that Suetonius used Tacitus as an historical source,[22] for which purpose he was hardly suitable, especially when his own sources were still available; and where the two writers display close verbal similarities it is evident that both are echoing an earlier writer. But once in each of the next two *Lives* Suetonius exceptionally finds it necessary to refer to documentary evidence to settle a controversial point: in *Tib.* 21.2 he discusses Augustus' attitude to Tiberius, and quotes from Augustus' letters to disprove the view that he had deliberately selected Tiberius as his successor to show off his own good qualities; and in *Cal.* 8 he quotes another letter of Augustus to show the correctness of the public *Acta* in attributing Caligula's birth to the town of Antium. These are the only two problems tackled in this way in these two *Lives*, and there is no apparent reason within the *Lives* why these two should have been chosen. But in *Ann.* i. 10.6 Tacitus had suggested with some force the theory about the succession which Suetonius attacks; in i. 41.3 he casually mentions Caligula as 'born in the camp' (that is to say, on the Rhine). Without openly crossing swords with the older writer, Suetonius appears to have noted these errors, and searched for evidence to refute them: in both cases masking his criticism of Tacitus by going back to earlier writers who had put forward the same views and arguing from the original evidence. It is unfortunate that we have lost the book of the *Annals* in which Tacitus surveyed the early life of Claudius; but it may be inferred that Suetonius' references to Augustus' letters about the young prince's character (*Claud.* 4) were likewise stimulated by something in the historian's writings. However, the *Nero* provides certain confirmation concerning his use of the *Annals*. The only passage in which he quotes an actual document is where (52) he refutes the allegation that Nero's poems were not his own works by referring to an autograph copy of some of the best known poems, which could only have been written by a man actually in the process of composition. Here, in fact, he is not directly answering the view which Tacitus had propounded, which is rather that the poems were the results of a sort of combined operation over dinner (*Ann.* xiv. 16.2); but since it is the only use of documentary evidence in this life, or indeed in any of the later *Lives*, and is also the only passage in which Suetonius defends Nero against a current charge, it looks as if he was reminded generally of Tacitus' allegation when he came across the copy of the poems, but did not check the actual context in the *Annals*.

The conclusion that emerges is accordingly that, while still working on the records of Augustus' reign, Suetonius began noting details which would prove useful for the following *Lives*, where he could discreetly correct the misstatements of Tacitus. The next stage of research, in which he would have begun work on the archives for Tiberius' own reign, including that emperor's own correspondence, never took place. The only post-Augustan document, the text of Nero's poems, may have been noticed at any time: 'It came into my hands', is all Suetonius says. It would not be in the files of the *ab epistulis*, and did not need to be copied out, as the actual letters did.

Now although Suetonius seldom obtrudes himself into his works (only on the rare occasions when he can himself testify to the truth of some assertion, as in the *Lucan* or *Dom.* 12.2), there are certain indications[23] in the later *Lives* of a marked decline in the discretion and tactfulness *vis-à-vis* the emperor which had marked the original publication. In *Claud.* 44.2 he virtually invites comparison between the concealment of that emperor's death and of Trajan's, whereby Hadrian's accession had been facilitated; whereas he had been discretion itself in passing over similar accounts of the death of Augustus (*Aug.* 98.5, *Tib.* 21.1). In *Titus* 6.1 he refers gratuitiously to the unpopularity of Titus on his accession, as a result of arbitrary executions of distinguished citizens, in such a way as to suggest the notorious case which had disfigured the first year of Hadrian's reign. And in *Nero* 18 he criticizes that emperor for not extending the empire and nearly surrendering Britain, as if with deliberate reference to Hadrian's abandonment of Trajan's conquests across the Euphrates.

None of these passages can be taken as an overt attack on the reigning emperor, any more than the criticism of Tacitus had been obvious. But the discerning reader must have observed them with interest at the time.

Thus we have a fairly clear picture of the decline in Suetonius' biographical method as shown in the *Lives* from *Tiberius* onwards. Removed from the archives, of which he had just begun to make such significant use, generally embittered against the emperor, apparently deprived of much of his initial enthusiasm for the whole project, he may even have let the work lie for some years. Thus the later *Lives* are disappointingly short, even those of the three Flavian emperors, for whom oral material should still have been available in abundance (if Suetonius was still in Rome, and not perhaps at Hippo),[24] and on whom he might have written considerably more freely than Tacitus had done when he wrote the *Histories* some twenty years earlier. At the same time there is a deliberate affectation of vagueness and generalization, strongly contrasting with the detailed precision of the first two *Lives*; and there is no reference to documents later than Augustus, apart from the fortuitous mention of Nero's poems. It is tantalizing to conjecture how our knowledge of the Flavian period might have been improved if Suetonius had applied himself with the same thoroughness to the last of the *Lives* as he did to the first.

In assessing the value of the *Caesars* it is important to remember that many of the least favourable verdicts passed on them come from historians who are disappointed that Suetonius was not an historian, far less a source-book for later historians. But even judging the *Lives* as what they are, certain criticisms are hard to refute. The writer is far too quick to accept incredible or scandalous stories, even when we can tell that his sources included more plausible versions. Thus, while he knows two distinct and incompatible stories of the murder of Claudius (*Claud.* 44.2), he is prepared to quote anecdotes connected with each (*Nero* 33.1, based on the poisoned mushrooms, and 40.3, on the poisoned drink), both of which could not be true.[25] Again, he asserts flatly that Nero was responsible for the great fire of Rome (*Nero* 38.1); yet shows that he was aware of the alternative version, of an accidental outbreak (acknowledged in Tac. *Ann.* xv. 38.1), by a reference (43.1) to the account in which the worst charge that could be made was that four years later he *planned* to set fire to the city.[26] He blackens Tiberius' character by a tale of prolonged drinking (*Tib.* 42.1), which involves chronological confusions that he could easily have checked; and gives extraordinarily incomplete versions of prosecutions (e.g. *Tib.* 49.1, *Nero* 37.1) in a way calculated to throw the worst possible light on the emperor concerned. And the lack of authenticity of such unlikely scandals as those related of Galba (22) is demonstrated by the silence of other authorities. This tendency to believe, or at least to write down, the worst is apparent even in the earliest *Lives* (e.g. *Jul.* 49, *Aug.* 68); but at least it is clear that these were only a few of the large number of stories circulated at the time. In fact, there is little to the discredit of Tiberius or of Nero which is not similarly asserted by Tacitus, or at least quoted in such a way as to make the reader incline to believe it. In general it appears that, as both Tacitus and Josephus indicate,[27] every emperor attracted slander as soon as he was dead, and there is some indication that the most malicious of these writers were such impressive figures as the ex-consuls Servilius Nonianus and Cluvius Rufus, whose authority might override doubts of their credibility.[28] For the most part Suetonius seems to have decided that it was not his part to assess the validity of these stories, nor even to aim at a consistent character; but rather to report succinctly what the authorities alleged, and to leave it to the reader to draw his own conclusions. It remains true that he was seldom able to resist a scabrous anecdote, any more than the Greek Cassius Dio could. It is to be noted that when Tacitus (*Ann.* xiv. 2) rejects the story found in *Nero* 28.2, that Nero attempted to seduce his mother, he replaces it with an alternative considerably more salacious.

More serious, perhaps, is the charge that the *Caesars* lack the artistry and structure of Plutarch, as well as the Greek biographer's moral standpoint. Neither writer has much pretension to style as such, though the disjointed and staccato language of Suetonius is often displeasing and sometimes actually incomprehensible to the modern reader, when so much of an anecdote has been pared away that the point is lost. It is, of course, true that Plutarch has much greater appeal to those who admire noble sentiments and improving generalizations: that he has that combination of oratory and morality which is characteristic of so much inferior literature of the Classical period, especially of the Roman empire.[29] The modern age may have more sympathy with the attitude of that later biographer who applauded Suetonius, in contrast to the three great names of Latin historiography, Sallust, Livy, and Tacitus, for writing 'not so much eloquently as accurately' (*Script. Hist. Aug., Prob.* 2.7); for what Suetonius does is to edit and adapt far less than the major historians do, in their insistence on dignity of style and sentiment. He leaves it open to us to judge for ourselves, in a way that the eloquence of Tacitus seldom permits, as he constrains our agreement by the subtlety and force of his language. Indeed, one of the main criticisms of Tacitus' portraits of the Julio-Claudians is that he has prejudged the character, especially of Tiberius, and insists on his interpretation of it even when the facts that he relates fail to support it.[30] With Suetonius, the opposite failing is rather apparent: that he never makes up his mind about the true nature of his subject, nor seeks to give a consistent account, even by the simple expedient of recognizing that there could be a change for the worse as the result of circumstances. To some extent an initial judgement has determined the selection of anecdotes he makes, as when he virtu-ally ignores the possibility that Nero might have been innocent of setting fire to Rome; but even this tendency is probably to be put down to the specious nature of the more scandalous authorities, who could claim inside information about the wickedness of court life. Especially when documentary evidence was not to hand. Suetonius could hardly make a valid choice between discrepant sources. But where the modern reader is continually aware that the subtle complexities of Tacitus present a work of art rather than the truth, and that the gallery of noble Greeks and Romans presented by Plutarch's *Parallel Lives* could never quite have existed in that way, there is something solidly authentic about Suetonius' em-perors, even if individual stories remain suspect. He allows us to construct our own figures from his materials, and we feel that the results are real.

The final proof of Suetonius' success must be that he is intensely readable. Some readers may have treasured him for the obscenity of some of his anecdotes; but many more have read him again and again for the way in which he makes the Rome of the early em-perors come to life, full of vital characters and utterly convincing detail. The very dignity of Tacitus and Plutarch, as of Livy in his great history of the Roman republic, makes them avoid the trivial and commonplace, the cheap and sordid details of life which are to be found so abundantly in Suetonius. To illustrate this, I quote from a well-known passage, perhaps the most successful piece of continuous narrative in the *Caesars*, describing the last hours of Nero, after he had sacrificed the support of every class in Rome (*Nero* 47.3–49.1).

> Thus he put off his deliberation till the next day. He was roused about midnight, and when he learnt that the troops on guard-duty had vanished, he leapt out of bed and sent round to his friends; and because he received no reply from any of them, he visited their lodgings in turn, with a few attendants. But all their doors were closed and no one answered. He returned to his room, to find his bodyguards had also fled, having plundered his bedclothes and removed his box of poison as well. At once he asked for Spiculus the gladiator, or someone else who would kill him. When he could

find no one, he said, 'Have I neither a friend nor an enemy?' and rushed out, as if to throw himself into the Tiber.

So far, although the translation cannot reproduce the economy and speed of the Latin, the sheer amount of information contained in one short paragraph is manifest, as events follow one another in quick succession.

But recovering his spirit, he wanted some more secret hiding-place to collect his thoughts; and when his freedman Phaon offered him his suburban residence between the Salarian and Nomentan roads, about four miles out, just as he was, with one foot bare and wearing a tunic, he threw on a cloak of faded colour and mounted a horse, holding a handkerchief in front of his face, with only four companions, including Sporus. At once he was thrown into panic by an earthquake and a flash of lightning, and heard from the camp nearby the shouts of the soldiers, promising trouble to him and success to Galba. He also heard a traveller who met them saying, 'These fellows are after Nero', and another asking, 'Anything new about Nero in the city?' Moreover, his horse reared at the smell of a corpse lying by the road, so that his face was uncovered and he was recognised and saluted by a retired guardsman.

When they reached the side turning, he sent the horses away and made his way with difficulty among the bushes and brambles along a path in the reeds, having a coat thrown down for him to walk on, until he reached the rear of the house. There, when Phaon urged him to withdraw for the moment into a cave where sand had been dug, he said he was not going to be buried alive. He waited a little while, until a concealed entrance to the house should be made; and, wishing to drink some water from a pool close at hand he took some in the hollow of his hand and said 'So this is the water Nero drinks.' Then tearing his cloak on the brambles, he pushed himself through the twigs across his path and crawled through a narrow tunnel into a cellar which had been dug out and lay down in the adjoining store-room on a bed fitted with a moderate mattress and an old robe laid on it. And feeling hungry and thirsty again, he refused to touch some grimy bread that was offered him, but drank a little lukewarm water. Then as each of his attendants in turn pressed him to save himself as soon as possible from the impending disgrace, he ordered a grave to be made in his presence, measuring it by his own body, and some bits of marble to be arranged, if they were to be found, and water and firewood for dealing with his corpse forthwith, weeping at every juncture and repeating over and over again, 'What an artist perishes in me!'

Probably the most striking feature of this passage is the amount of vivid detail, including Nero's clothing, the exact position of the villa and the fact that the direct way (through the Colline Gate) would pass close to the praetorian camp; and then the exact description of the approach to the villa and the arrangements made for the emperor's reception. It is certain that a formal historian such as Tacitus would not have condescended to mention the presence of a dead body by the roadside, or have quoted the actual words of passers-by, or remarked on the brambles and reeds along the path to the house. Suetonius gains immensely from this lack of refinement. But at the same time his account leaves endless questions unanswered. Why did the party have to approach the villa surreptitiously? Why could he not have slipped into the house by a side-door, and, if the idea was to conceal his entry from Phaon's servants, how could they hope that no one would notice a tunnel being dug into the cellar? Why could Phaon not lay hands on some more palatable refreshments? Why did they so quickly decide that concealment was impossible, and urge Nero to commit suicide? Was Nero intending to be buried or cremated? Lastly, why, after all these precautions, were praetorian cavalry able to find their way directly to the villa and discover the dying emperor immediately, as the next paragraph shows? The whole course of events smells of treachery, which is never explicitly hinted at. In addition, there are phrases in the original which are almost incomprehensible: in particular, *traiectos surculos rasit* can only mean something like 'pushed his way through the twigs', but it is very difficult to see how the Latin words give this or any other precise sense. Most of these problems can be set aside, if not solved, by the recognition that Suetonius has organized his narrative entirely in accordance with his law of biographical relevance.[31] Every detail is given from Nero's own point of view, with sights, sounds, smells, taste, and feelings all contributing to reproducing the fugitive's feelings to a remarkable extent. In this way it is at least implied that the reasons for all the precautions barely entered Nero's consciousness; and if there was treachery he knew nothing of it.

At the same time Suetonius refuses, as always, to enter into his character's actual thoughts. One has only to contrast the later Greek historian, Cassius Dio, describing the same events (lxiii. 27–28); in particular, 'Everyone who passed he suspected had come for him; he started at every voice, thinking it to be that of someone searching for him; if a dog barked anywhere or a bird chirped, or a bush or branch was shaken by the breeze, he was greatly excited'— and so on. Dio's version, which proceeds to develop moral commonplaces and paradoxes, is little more than cheap rhetoric. Suetonius has avoided this pitfall altogether, with the possible exception of the earthquake, which is at least much less prominent than Dio's is.

By and large, Suetonius' narrative here is immensely telling. Admittedly it is his finest consecutive section of narrative, and also we have not got Tacitus' description of Nero's fall to provide a really challenging contrast. But we can contrast the two writers' versions of a similar episode, the panic and death of Vitellius, in *Vit.* 16 and Tac. *Hist.* iii. 84, where again Suetonius' richness in factual details makes him score several points against the historian's greater dramatic power. However, it is clear in those passages, as it is in the account of Nero's fall, that underlying all our extant versions is at least one earlier written source containing all Suetonius' details, and perhaps all Dio's rhetoric as well; and all that Suetonius has done is to select those parts which he thought relevant to Nero's predicament. We cannot judge his success properly without this earlier source or sources, now hopelessly lost. But, although we are bound to criticize Suetonius for sacrificing quite so much, we must admire the mastery of compression and concentration which makes the passage permanently readable and permanently vivid. It may, after all, be significant that posterity thought Suetonius worth preserving while it allowed his richer and more authentic sources to perish completely. Suetonius' main claim to importance is not as an original literary artist: he deserves our gratitude and our attention for the way in which he has selected and preserved what he regarded as most significant from the immense quantity of written material which the late empire and the Dark Ages were to discard.

THE THIRTEENTH CAESAR

For all his shortcomings, there is no doubt that Suetonius set the fashion for imperial biography during the following centuries. The series of *Caesars* was continued a century later by Marius Maximus; but his work is lost, and we cannot judge how closely he followed his model. His name is sometimes linked with that of Suetonius by the *Scriptores Historiae Augustae*, who profess to use him as a major source; but the contrast is made that, while Suetonius loved brevity, Marius Maximus was *homo omnium verbosissimus* (*Firmus* 1.1), and he seems to have quoted documents at excessive length (cf. *S.H.A. Comm.* 18.1, *Pert.* 15.8). The Augustan writers themselves are indebted to Suetonius in various respects; but the best among the *Lives* are arranged on a basically chronological plan, and the arrangement *per species* is seldom consistently or clearly carried out. An occasional *divisio* announces a seemingly Suetonian scheme, as in *Sev. Alex.* 29.1: 'Before I speak of his wars and expeditions and victories, I shall say a few words of his daily and domestic life.' But it is harder even than in Suetonius to follow up the sections promised. In *Max. et Balb.* 4. a direct appeal is made to Suetonius, as to other models apparently fictitious; and the following sketches resemble the *Caesars* fairly closely. Also considerable use is made of documents, especially letters and speeches, allegedly from the public records, though they are more likely pure forgeries. For the most part, the Augustan *Lives* lack all the tautness and richness of detail of Suetonius himself. Similarly the brief sections on the various emperors in the fourth-century compilers, Eutropius, Aurelius Victor, and the *Epitome* also attributed to the latter, owe something of their arrangement to Suetonius, as they apparently owe a good deal of their material; but the scale is so small that there can be no close similarity.

After this, signs of Suetonius' influence in biography are very slight. *Lives* of saints, which grow increasingly popular, could not well be fitted to the same sort of rubrics as the *Lives* of emperors, and mainly corrupt emperors at that. The *Life of St. Ambrose*, written early in the fifth century by his follower, Paulinus of Milan, has been claimed for the Suetonian school;[32] but, in fact, apart from a turgid section on the saint's character, it possesses not one of the characteristics of that manner. The arrangement is almost entirely chronological, there are no sections of illustrative anecdotes, no *divisiones*, no quotations from documents. But at least Paulinus is mainly factual, in contrast to the numerous hagiographers who do little but assemble a series of stock miracles, which appear in *Life* after *Life*, with the sole intention of edifying the faithful.

In Constantinople, where Suetonius was certainly known for a long time (for much of our information concerning his lost works is derived from the Byzantine encyclopedia known as Suidas, or the Suda), he might be expected to have influenced the *Lives* of emperors which were produced from time to time in Greek. Arrangement *per species* is noticeable in one of the best of these in particular,[33] the *Life of the Emperor Basil* written in the tenth century by his grandson Constantine VII Porphyrogenitus, which contains sections in order on Ancestry, Boyhood, Early Career, and then, after a digression on his predecessor, on Finance, Judicial Affairs, and so on, concluding with Basil's death and the succession. But nothing in this *Life* directly recalls Suetonius, and the work is rather to be attributed to the tradition of Greek panegyric, in which these sections had been usual as far back as Xenophon's time. The objective standpoint is lacking, and a section is devoted to attacking the memory of a previous emperor, exactly as in the *Panegyric of Trajan* written in Latin by Suetonius' friend, the younger Pliny. If Suetonius, or one of his imitators, suggested the idea of imperial *Lives* to the Byzantines, the old rhetorical patterns proved too attractive for a dispassionate school of biography to develop.

Meanwhile the library of the monastery of Fulda in Germany contained a copy of the *Caesars* (perhaps the only one surviving in western Europe) from which all our existing manuscripts are directly or indirectly derived.[34] More significant for the history of biography, it was read and studied by Einhard, a Frankish scholar attached to Alcuin, the English leader in the Carolingian revival of scholarship. Within twenty years of Charlemagne's death in A.D. 814, Einhard composed the *Vita Karoli*, the biography in which the model of Suetonius is most closely followed.[35] The reasons for his choice were undoubtedly complex.[36] In the first place, precedents for secular biography were not abundant, and the accepted framework used for the *Lives* of saints was totally inappropriate. Secondly, Einhard was evidently immensely impressed by his reading of Suetonius, whom he knew almost by heart by the time he began to write his own biography. And thirdly, Charlemagne had taken pains to ensure, especially by his coronation at Rome in the year 800, that he was to be accepted as the successor of the old Caesars of the Roman Empire, in at least as valid a sense as were the contemporary Greek emperors at Constantinople, whose succession from Augustus by way of Constantine I was vitiated mainly by their loss of contact with the heartlands of the original empire. Charlemagne's heirs, under whom Einhard was now living, were no less concerned to establish their position as genuine (and indeed holy) Roman emperors. From all these points of view, it is not surprising

that Einhard decided to represent Charlemagne as the second
Augustus, at once the subject of Suetonius' finest and most finished
biography, the most reputable of the twelve Caesars, and the founder of the original line of emperors as Charlemagne was of the
second, although the emperor himself looked rather to the model of
Constantine and Theodosius, as Christians. It was an additional
advantage that the Latin of Suetonius is simple and unpretentious,
much closer to the common learned Latin of the Middle Ages than
the splendours of Ciceronian oratory or the subtle complexities of
Tacitus. Einhard could never have attempted to reproduce the
effect of a Tacitean style: he makes a very convincing adaptation of
the Suetonian, without ever allowing his actual borrowing of
Suetonian words and phrases to stand out as intrusions into his
usual manner.

In general arrangement, Einhard does his best to follow Suetonius, especially in respect of abandoning chronological narrative,
such as was available especially in the various contemporary
Annals, which some have claimed also as a work of Einhard and on
which he certainly draws for a great deal of his material.[37] Thus he
begins with an account of the rise of the Carolingian family to
power (including a description of the Merovingian kingship, a
digression which Suetonius would not have admitted), the accession
of Charles and his brother, and the removal of the latter. At this
point he turns tardily to Charles's birth, boyhood, and youth, only
to report that he knows nothing whatever about them—a surprising
admission, when he emphasizes in his preface that he was himself a
witness of much that he recorded, and when much living tradition
on Charles's early life should have been still available. However, as
if to insist on his adherence to the Suetonian plan as far as possible,
he follows up with a good *divisio*: 'I have decided to pass on to
explain and illustrate his acts and character and the other parts of
his life, omitting what is unknown: in such a way that, in narrating
first his campaigns (*res gestas*) at home and abroad, then his character
and interests, then his government and death, I shall pass over
nothing worthy or necessary to be learnt' (4.2). The influence of the
Julius and *Augustus* is here especially evident, since in those two
Lives a long series of campaigns appears early on, because in both
cases they led directly to the seizure of supreme power and accordingly fall under the rubric of Early Life. In Einhard, the wars which
all come during Charles's reign become a separate section, and are

dealt with considerably more diffusely than in Suetonius, as if to give a survey of the wars in themselves, and not merely as items in the emperor's career.[38] In particular, there is a general description of the Saxons and the difficulties of overcoming them, which is hardly related to Charles at all, although their defeat naturally adds to his glory; and the disaster at Roncesvalles is described in some detail, although Charles was not personally involved. Despite occasional echoes of Suetonius, this whole section depends less on the biographical pattern, and contains rhetorical elements more proper to panegyric, such as 'Tota in hoc bello Hunorum nobilitas periit, tota gloria decidit' (13.2).

The list of wars leads on to a summary of the countries conquered, the treaties with foreign monarchs, and a list of major buildings, the latter a prominent feature in *Augustus* (28.3–30). There follows a further *divisio*, repeating in greater detail the second half of the earlier programme, and recalling in language the *divisio* in *Jul.* 44.4: 'It is agreed that this was his nature in protecting and increasing the kingdom, and at the same time adorning it. I shall now begin to describe his mental powers, his great constancy [consistency? fortitude?] in all circumstances, fortunate and unfortunate, and other things concerning his personal and domestic life' (18.1). In fact, these topics are not dealt with as promised. After a single reference to his patience in face of his brother's provocation, Einhard proceeds to a detailed account of Charles's wives and children, with details on their upbringing closely modelled on the similar section in *Aug.* 64.3, and his friendliness to strangers; then his personal appearance and way of life, the most Suetonian section of the whole work; a greatly extended section on religion (which certainly appears in many of the *Caesars*, but rather as a survey of superstitious observances, such as dreams); and the *Life* concludes much on the Suetonian pattern, with a description of Charles's tomb, including the epitaph (a detail never, in fact, found in Suetonius), suitable omens of his death (which are not listed before the actual death, but after, as in *Tib.* 74, *Claud.* 46, etc.), and the full text of his will, whereas Suetonius merely gives a paraphrase of the main points (*Jul.* 83, *Aug.* 101.). Einhard's reason for giving the entire document may be simply a reluctance to attempt the task of abbreviation; but there may well have been some factor in the contemporary political situation which encouraged him to quote it in full.

So far as the general layout is concerned, the *Vita Karoli* diverges from its main model, the *Augustus*, little more than do many of Suetonius' own *Lives*. But there is one important difference. Although reasonably objective, the work is still primarily panegyrical, lacking even the small element of scandal which appears in *Aug.* 68–70, not to mention the large sections on vices on most of the emperors. Indeed, one characteristic that Einhard has failed to borrow from Suetonius at all is the discussion of *mores* under separate headings. Despite the promise in the first *divisio* of an account of Charles's *mores*, and of his *constantia* in the second, no virtues are discussed as such, and he has no vices at all. Certain leading qualities, especially magnanimity, simply emerge from the tone of the work as a whole, which is warmer and more approving than in any of the Caesars.[39]

Moreover, Einhard is patently partial towards Charlemagne, in a way that Suetonius never is to his subjects; and his partiality is almost certainly his own, since he is close to the events described and does not so much copy already partial literary sources, as Suetonius did, as pervert the existing *Annals* to his own purposes.[40] Criticisms have been levelled at him for glossing over such features in Charles's life as his treatment of his brother Carloman and his family, or his frequent changes of wives and concubines. To some extent the explanation may be that Einhard simply did not regard these matters as meriting criticism; alternatively we must accept the fact that he was writing under Charlemagne's son, where hostile criticism might be unwelcome, while when Suetonius wrote the most recent of the Caesars had been dead for a score of years and was universally accepted as a tyrant. As for the alleged misrepresentation of Charlemagne's attitude to the papal crowning in Rome, it may be untrue that he was unaware of the Pope's intention when he entered the Church; but Einhard asserts only that this is what Charlemagne declared (28.2), and this may well have been the case.[41]

More alarming is the possibility that Einhard may have extended his borrowings from Suetonius from the use of words and phrases to the attribution to Charles of details which belong only to Augustus. Since the majority of close similarities belong to the account of personal appearance and private life, for which Einhard is our only authority, it is impossible to confirm or refute this suspicion. Halphen (p. 93) points out that the statement (19.4) that Charles never travelled without his children, his sons riding at his side and his daughters following behind, copied closely from *Aug.* 64.3, is demonstrably untrue, on the evidence we have of the occasions when the family were not in the same part of the kingdom as their father. Of course, it can hardly be true of Augustus either, on grounds of sheer probability; yet it certainly looks as if Einhard has asserted it simply because it was found in Suetonius. In the same way, the totally untrue assertion that the Byzantine emperors sent envoys on their own initiative (*ultro*) to request Charlemagne's friendship (16.4) owes at least its form of words to a similar claim in *Aug.* 21.3, where the word *ultro* appears justified. It is more hazardous to guess that Pepin (3.1) is stated to have died of a dropsy (*morbo aquae intercutis*) simply because Nero's father had done so (*Nero* 5.2)—at least this time there was no glory to be borrowed from either the person or the ailment. This last item may rather fall into the category of things in the *Vita Karoli* that are there because something in the *Caesars* suggested them; yet there was presumably something in the first place which warranted Einhard in selecting these rather than other possible details. One clear case of perversion of evidence is to be seen in 32, the list of portents before Charles's death. The eclipses given first in this list are real enough, but occurred not in the last three years of the reign, but in 807–810, according to the contemporary *Annals*, which from their nature are likely to be more reliable on chronology; and the portico at Aachen, whose collapse is stated to have foreshadowed his death, apparently fell in 817, three years later.[42] The other items in this list are harder to date or authenticate; but the general impression is that Charlemagne had to have as impressive a list of portents as Julius or Augustus, and that items have been amassed rather ruthlessly for the purpose.

The section which above all depends on Suetonius is that in which Einhard describes Charles's appearance, health, and ways of taking exercise (22). From the opening words—'Corpore fuit amplo atque robusto, statura eminenti, quae tamen iustam non excederet'—the reader's attention is called to the similar opening to *Tib.* 68: 'corpore fuit amplo atque robusto, statura quae iustam excederet;' while the 'statura eminenti' comes from *Cal.* 50.1. Almost every item has a Suetonian model in the same way. The eyes are a mixture of Julius' and Tiberius'; the beauty of his grey hair comes from Claudius; he has authority and dignity standing or sitting, like Claudius (who possessed these qualities also while lying down);

his fat neck is Nero's, his somewhat projecting belly is both Nero's and Titus'; his good health comes from Julius, Tiberius, and Nero, but his limp is from Augustus; and his avoidance of medical advice is fairly closely copied from Tiberius. The first impression from these and other minor verbal similarities is that Einhard was incapable of physical descriptions at all, and that his emperor is entirely composed of fragments from the twelve Caesars; but a closer examination reveals that whenever necessary he can produce entirely satisfactory descriptions for features which Charlemagne did did not share with his Roman predecessors. None of the Caesars possesses a rounded top to his head, nor enjoys a general 'corporis habitudine virili'. And Tiberius' avoidance of doctors does not share Charlemagne's particular reason for 'almost hating them because they urged him to give up roast meat, to which he was accustomed, and stick to boiled'. In particular, where Augustus' height is given exactly, on the authority of a confidential freedman (*Aug.* 79.2), Charlemagne's is calculated as equal to seven of his own feet—a sensible adjustment necessary in a society where a standard measurement was not in use. Again, in the second half of the chapter, his diversions include a taste for riding, like Julius and Titus, but hunting is peculiar to him, even if the phrase explaining that this was a characteristic of his race is taken almost exactly from one dealing with Tiberius' hair style (Tib. 68.2). But what Charles really enjoyed was bathing, which takes up the greater part of the paragraph and has no parallel among the Caesars.

Einhard's method over these details is thus not easy to define with precision. He has clearly welcomed the idea of a detailed physical description, and decided to employ Suetonian phrases where appropriate, while implementing with his own vocabulary in such a way that there are no glaring discrepancies of style. There is no reason to suggest that he has any intention of using Suetonian features in an attempt to make Charlemagne resemble any of the Caesars as a model; for it is noticeable that he has borrowed nothing from Augustus but his limp, and many more features come from the later Julio-Claudians, who were not particularly admirable either physically or morally. There would be no point in taking items from them if the idea was to glorify Charlemagne.[43]

It is perhaps not too fanciful to compare Einhard's borrowings for this biography to the methods employed by Charlemagne's architects in building the Palatine Chapel at Aachen, which now forms the core of the cathedral. Here the overall octagonal plan of the building closely recalls Justinian's S. Vitale at Ravenna, the seat of Roman imperial power most familiar to the Franks; and the porphyry pillars incorporated inside the building were actually brought from Ravenna, as Einhard expressly admits in 26.1. But one striking feature of the chapel, the external niche at first-floor level, is derived from the façade of the so-called Palace of Theoderic at Ravenna.[44] Ravenna perhaps more even than Rome was deliberately exploited as a source of imperial precedents, as it also provided Charlemagne with a type of imperial title which he found especially to his liking.[45] In a very similar way, Einhard has exploited the plan and materials of Suetonius' *Caesars* to construct a memorial to his former master.

But the Palatine Chapel is not S. Vitale, nor could it be mistaken for a building at Ravenna. So Einhard, for all his debt to Suetonius, never comes near to emulating him. Not merely has he no vivid narrative passages which might be compared to Suetonius' account of the crossing of the Rubicon (*Jul.* 31–33) or the flight of Nero (*Nero* 47–49); he never gives life to his subject by quoting Charlemagne's actual words or letters. At first sight this seems surprising, when many of the emperor's *ipsissima verba* should have been available from witnesses still alive, if Einhard could not recall them himself, and when he was himself secretary to Louis, as Suetonius had been to Hadrian.[46] But, as E. Auerbach points out,[47] the biographer had cut himself off from this resource by choosing Suetonian Latin as the vehicle for his expression. Charlemagne and his contemporaries did not use classical Latin, even as basic as that of Suetonius, for their normal conversation; and any notable *dicta* in which the mind of the emperor might have been revealed would be in Frankish. It is true that some of the more famous of the utterances of the Twelve Caesars were originally in Greek, but appear in Suetonius in Latin ('alea iacta est<o>' is the most famous example). But normally the original language is preserved, even in the original of 'Et tu, Brute ?' which was not Latinized until the sixteenth century; and even where translation has taken place, it is the work of writers to whom Greek and Latin were parallel and interchangeable—Suetonius himself wrote works in both. For all Einhard's facility, and despite the wide knowledge of Latin in learned Carolingian circles, Charlemagne was essentially a Germanic figure and could not fully reveal himself in the words of first-century Rome.

There could be no better example of the impossibility of trans-posing a style from one epoch to another. Einhard has enough ingenuity to find appropriate Latin words and phrases for whatever he wishes to express; but, apart from the fact that his choice of topic is initially limited by the vocabulary at his disposal, all too often the form of expression adopted is derivative, and makes true authenticity impossible. For example, when Charlemagne is stated (24.2) to have listened over dinner to 'aliquod acroama aut lectorem' the whole phrase is borrowed from *Aug.* 74, a context in which 'acroama' is perfectly natural, to signify an 'entertainment'. To Einhard, we cannot tell what the word may have meant: Garrod and Mowat opine that it may be 'a singer or court-jester', Halphen prefers not to guess. It clearly is not the word that Charlemagne would normally have used, nor Einhard himself. The whole picture immediately becomes second-hand and antiquarian in tone. Perhaps worse than anything, Einhard cannot rely on a body of readers with a large fund of common knowledge of the circumstances of the world he describes. He is writing rather for the literate class of posterity, who can indeed understand the *Vita Karoli* well enough, as far as it goes; but these are readers with whom the writer is not in direct touch, and the spark of communication is quenched. The succinct telling of a story in a few words has become impossible, and the language has become, as Auerbach says, 'lame and weak'.

There is one further respect in which Einhard may have drawn upon Suetonius to some purpose. This is in his preface, written in some of his most fluent Latin. Halphen in his edition (p. 3, n. 2) infers that some classical model underlies this passage, perhaps the original preface of Suetonius, which is now lost almost without trace. The indications are not very convincing. In the first place, Suetonius' preface included a dedication to his patron, Septicius Clarus; Einhard's mentions no recipient, even if at the same time it perhaps contains a trace of a model in which someone was so addressed, in the phrase 'en tibi librum . . .' Secondly, Einhard appeals to the value of the present age as worthy of record; Sueto-nius could not claim to be describing the present, or even the recent past, except in so far as even the Augustan age ranked as modern in the eyes of the archaizing school at the court of Hadrian. Thirdly, Einhard refers to himself as a witness of what he relates, as Sueto-nius could for only a very small part of the period. And fourthly, he mentions his debt of gratitude as a reason for undertaking the task—a consideration which could not conceivably have carried weight with Suetonius nor have produced such a work as the *Caesars*. It is true that we have no evidence when the opening pages of Suetonius were lost, so that Einhard may have read them in Fulda and derived thence a certain number of phrases. It would, on the other hand, be attractive to guess that the readiness with which he allows all Charlemagne's early life to go unrecorded was due to the model of *Julius*, which lost its opening at the same time as the preface perished. The discussion in section 4 will then be a subsequent addition based on a tardy realization that all the other *Caesars* contained this sort of information in full. On the whole, it is perilous to assume that Einhard had access to any more of Suetonius than we now possess.

In general, the *Vita Karoli*, thought historically not very reliable, is a biography of unusual interest and is almost the sole attempt during the Middle Ages to portray any individual, ecclesiastical or lay, as a whole, as opposed to the pious or panegyrical *Lives* of saints and kings which were produced in such abundance. Yet the idea of copying Suetonius seems never to have been repeated. Einhard himself was copied to a minor extent by the Frank Thegan, who within a few years composed a *Life of Louis the Pious*.[48] The degree of imitation of Suetonius, however, is far less than is claimed by. W. Schmidt:[49] the arrangement is almost entirely chronological, sections beginning regularly with 'eodem tempore', 'alio anno', 'sequenti anno', with no attempt at the Suetonian manner. Only in section 19, at the beginning of Louis's reign, has Thegan taken a hint from Einhard, with a full account of personal characteristics and customs, starting with 'erat enim statura mediocri, oculis magnis et claris, vultu lucido, naso longo et recto', and so on, with details of Louis's learning, piety, generosity, clothing, humour, and diversions. There are no illustrative anecdotes, and it is interesting to observe that Thegan has not thought of borrowing phrases or even words from his model. The converse is true of the notorious pillaging by the monk of Caen,[50] who described the last days of William the Conqueror and included a sketch of his appearance and character, which consists entirely of isolated sentences taken from *Vita Karoli* 22 to 26. Suetonius appears here at third hand, in the same combination of *Tiberius* and *Caligula* already quoted: 'corpore fuit amplo atque robusto . . .' The only divergencies from Einhard appear to be simple errors of copying or transmission.

On the other hand, a direct but sporadic use of Suetonius himself can hardly be denied for William of Malmesbury; who in his *Gesta Regum* IV, describing the life of William Rufus, has details which are not found in Einhard. A highly Suetonian section on physical appearance (321) contains items derived from the lives of Augustus, Claudius, Vespasian and Titus—including the *venter proiectior* of the last which is also ascribed to Charlemagne, but also additional features from the same sentence in *Tit.* 3.1—and a subsequent section on prophetic dreams combines *pridie quam excederet vita*, virtually as in *Jul.* 87, and *vidit per quietem*, as in *Nero* 46.1. Moreover, as M. Schütt points out,[51] Malmesbury has allowed his whole treatment of Rufus's reign to be affected by the Suetonian model, producing an uncomfortable blend of chronicle and biography; though the influence is felt only in odd passages, and Sallust is perhaps an equally important source for his treatment.[52]

With the coming of the Renaissance[53] and the great increase in the study of Suetonius and other classical writers, it might have been expected that he would again be imitated by biographers, especially when humanists were looking to the Classics for models of every type of literature. Despite the popularity of the *Caesars*, this seems never to have happened. For a writer like Petrarch, composing in the middle of the fourteenth century *Latin Lives of the Illustrious Romans*,[54] and of Julius Caesar in particular, Suetonius is a major source, but rather in the way that he is to a modern scholar: he never becomes a model, except in so far as Petrarch imitates him very relevantly in quoting extant letters of Caesar to illustrate his real intentions in the Civil War, and borrows from him a section on Caesar's appearance and habits, which he incorporates somewhat awkwardly into what is fundamentally a straightforward narrative. Indeed, Petrarch, who claims in his preface 'It is my purpose to write history', shows little sign of a true biographical pattern. As the Renaissance advanced, and more and more elaborate lives were composed, both in Latin and in the vernaculars, the influence of Suetonius becomes increasingly indirect.

In the sixteenth century, at Milan, we find what appears to be the last direct appeal to the Suetonian mode. Gerolamo Cardano, the doctor and scientist, wrote in 1576 an account of his own life in Latin,[55] which has often been compared with the more exciting and imaginative Italian autobiography of his contemporary, Benvenuto Cellini. But, perhaps because the analytic nature of his own studies so inclined him, Cardano chose to write almost entirely *per species*, rather than in the continuous narrative which was normal and which the popularity of Plutarch had tended to encourage. He begins with his place of origin and his ancestors; then his birth, with the addition of details of his horoscope, which his age regarded as very significant; then his parents. At this point (4) he departs from the Suetonian model in a way which emphasizes his general acceptance of it; by giving a brief chronological summary of the main phases of his life, with precise dates (this last an amenity which the wide acceptance of the Christian era had made far easier than it was in antiquity); and he remarks: 'Perhaps if Suetonius had observed this, he might have increased the convenience of his readers; for, as philosophers say, there is nothing which is not a unity.' This is an extraordinarily sensible modification of the pattern. What he has failed to note is that Suetonius could safely assume in his readers a general knowledge of the history of the period, which would include the main events in the imperial biographies. For Cardano himself, in no sense a public figure, the chronological framework was essential. With this established, he reverts to Suetonian rubrics: appearance (dealt with much as in Suetonius, though with no actual borrowings), illnesses, clothing, diet, and so forth, with long sections on various mental characteristics. A typical section, recalling *Vesp* 22–23, is that on *dicta familiaria* (50), a collection of his own sayings, often with the occasion on which they were made. The work as a whole naturally differs from Suetonius in fundamental respects: it is written in the first person and is essentially subjective, though to nothing like the extent of Cellini's or Rousseau's; there is a good deal of polemic, as Cardano takes issue with enemies and rivals, of whom he seems to have an inordinate number; and he is uncontrollably diffuse, with no desire or ability to restrict the scope of anecdotes to the demands of the context, and is always prepared to insert a fresh rubric for the sake of discoursing on some topic which interests his curious mind. The conciseness and the avoidance of moralizing and conjecture which Suetonius might have bequeathed to modern biography were already too remote for Cardano to revive them; and only in the more objective of newspaper obituaries is anything like them to be found today.

NOTES

[1] R. Syme, *Tacitus* (Oxford, 1958), pp. 778–81; A. Macé, *Essai sur Suétone* (Paris, 1900), pp. 31–84.

[2] Plin. *Epp.* iii. 8. There is no need to assume, with F. Della Corte, *Suetonio, eques Romanus* (Milan, 1958), p. 12, that he must have held a tribuneship subsequently.

[3] *Ann. Ep.* (1953), no. 73: fully discussed in *Historia* x (1961), pp. 99–109.

[4] A handy discussion in Della Corte, pp. 19–20.

[5] Johannes Lydus, *de Mag.* ii. 6.

[6] *S.H.A.Hadr.* 11.3.

[7] *Titus* 10.2; Syme, *op. cit.*, p. 780.

[8] Macé, *op. cit.*, pp. 106–7.

[9] For a list of titles and fragments, see Roth's edition, pp. 275–306, and Reifferscheid, *Suetonii Reliquiae* (Leipzig, 1860).

[10] Roth, *op. cit.*, pp. 287–301; Reifferscheid, *op. cit.*, pp. 3–104.

[11] D. R. Stuart, *Epochs of Greek and Roman Biography* (Berkeley, 1928), pp. 132–4, etc.; fragments in Müller, *Frag. Hist. Graec.* ii. 293–301.

[12] *Hist.* I, 1; *Ann.* I. 1.

[13] Cf. W. Steidle, *Sueton und die antike Biographie* (Munich, 1951), pp. 114 ff, and *passim* on the origins of Suetonian biography.

[14] Stuart, *op. cit.*, p. 78, on the same principle in Greek biography.

[15] *Brutus* 302; *Div. in Caec.* 45; *Inv.* I. 31.

[16] Reifferscheid, *op. cit.*, p. 268; Roth, *op. cit.*, p. 282.

[17] *A.J.A.* lxii (1958), p. 216.

[18] Unless it be the closing words of the life of Vitellius, with a philological explanation of a Gallic nickname (*Vit.* 18).

[19] Cf. *Hermes* lxxxviii (1960), pp. 98–99.

[20] So M. A. Levi, *Divus Augustus* (Florence, 1951), pp. xliv ff; Della Corte, *op. cit.*, pp. 168–9, for an uneasy compromise. Cf. *C.Q.*, N.S. ix (1959), pp. 286 ff.

[21] e.g. Syme, *Tacitus*, pp. 471, 776–7; Highet, *Juvenal the Satirist* (Oxford, 1954), pp. 10–16; Macé, *op. cit.*, p. 209, not accepting the same possibility for Suetonius.

[22] Syme, *op. cit.*, pp. 502, 781–2; Macé, *opl cit.*, pp. 206–7.

[23] Fully discussed in *C.Q.*, N.S. ix (1959), pp. 290–3.

[24] The opening of *Vespasian* suggests personal investigations in central Italy for the specific purposes of this Life: especially 1.4: 'I did not find a trace of this, although I enquired with considerable care.' If *Titus* 4, on the evidence of statues and busts in Germany and Britain (*sicut apparet*), indicates personal observation, as suggested by Syme, *op. cit.*, p. 779, it may be from a tour with Hadrian in 121–122, immediately before his dismissal. But the observation need not be Suetonius' own, and is singularly lacking in archaeological confirmation.

[25] For the full implications, see *Hermes* lxxxviii (1960), pp. 109–11.

[26] *Ibid.*, pp. 111–12. The alternative version, not connecting Nero with the fire at all, is echoed in Aurelius Victor, *Caes.* 5.13.

[27] *Ann.* I. 1.5; *Hist.* I. 1.1–2; *Ant.* XX. 154.

[28] *A.J.P.* lxxxv (1964), pp. 337 ff; Syme in *Hermes* xcii (1964), pp. 419–20.

29 Cf. the comparison in J. A. Garraty, *The Nature of Biography* (1958), pp. 55–57, largely missing the point.

30 e.g. B. Walker, *Annals of Tacitus* (Manchester, 1951), pp. 82 ff.

31 *N.B.* how the four freedmen are introduced: Phaon is named twice, as owner of the villa; Epaphroditus at the end, where he assists his master's suicide; Neophytus is not named at all by Suetonius, although the common source certainly mentioned him. Sporus alone is specified initially (48.1: quattuor solis comitantibus, inter quos et Sporus erat), being a regular symbol throughout the *Life* of Nero's degeneracy, named more often than even Agrippina or Seneca.

32 Originally by W. Schmidt, *de Romanorum . . . arte biographica* (Marburg, 1891), p. 66, repeated uncritically by numerous subsequent scholars. For the text, see Migne, *Patrol. Lat.* xiv, pp. 28–50.

33 P. J. Alexander, in *Speculum* xv (1940), pp. 194–209.

34 Cf. E. K. Rand, in *Harv. Stud. in Class. Phil.* xxxvii (1926), pp. 1–48.

35 Most easily accessible in editions by H. W. Garrod and R. B. Mowat (Oxford, 1915); L. Halphen (Paris, 1938, with French translation); S. Painter (paperback, Ann Arbor, 1960, English translation alone).

36 Cf. S. Hellman, *Ausgewählte Abhandlungen* (Darmstadt, 1961), pp. 168 ff.

37 L. Halphen, *Etudes Critiques* (Paris, 1921), pp. 78 ff.

38 He claims, however: 'I should describe at this point the difficulties he had to face . . . were not my purpose in the present work to record the manner of his life rather than the event of the wars which he fought' (6.3)—a straightforward statement of the divorce of biography from history, which he does not altogether succeed in establishing.

39 Cf. H. Löwe, in Wattenbach-Levison, *Deutschlands Geschichtsquellen im Mittelalter* (Weimar, 1952), p. 276.

40 Halphen, *op. cit.,* pp. 82–98.

41 *Ibid.,* pp. 95, 223.

42 *Ibid.,* pp. 95–96.

43 E. K. Rand, *op. cit.,* pp. 43–48, suggests that many of the closer similarities to Augustus, especially in Charlemagne's way of life, may be the result of a genuine imitation of that emperor, as a result of hearing a reading of Suetonius at table. It is difficult to find a single example which carries conviction.

44 These parallels were brought to my notice by Dr. R. A. Markus, of Liverpool University. Cf. J. Beckwith, *Early Medieval Art* (1964), for a simple exposition, with illustrations; though he prefers to regard Justin II's Chrysotriclinion at Constantinople as the main influence.

45 Cf. H. Löwe, in *Deutsches Archiv für Erforschung des Mittelalters* ix (1952), pp. 393–4.

46 Halphen, *op. cit.,* p. 77.

47 *Literatursprache und Publikum in der lateinischen Spätantike* (Bern, 1958), pp. 86–87.

48 Published in *Mon. Germ. Hist., Scriptores in Folio* ii, pp. 589–604.

49 *Op. cit.,* pp. 67–68.

50 Published in T. D. Hardy, *Catalogue of Materials* ii (1865), p. 15; and in an English translation in Douglas-Greenaway, *English Historical Documents* ii (1961), pp. 279–80.

[51] In *Eng. Hist. Rev.* xlvi (1931), 255–260; quoted by R. W. Southern, 'Saint Anselm and his Biographer' (1963), 325–326.

[52] e.g. the clear echo in 305 of Sall.*Cat.*54.4–6.

[53] For the influence of Suetonius in the eleventh and twelfth centuries, cf. ch. VI and VII.

[54] Published as vol. ii of *Edizione Nazionale delle Opere di F. Petrarca,* ed. G. Martellotti (Florence, 1964). Part ii, containing *de Gestis Cesaris,* is apparently to appear shortly.

[55] Published in Cardano's Complete Works (Lyon, 1663), and in an English translation by J. Stoner (1931).

V

The Augustan History

A. R. BIRLEY

THE second and third centuries A.D. are among the worst documented in the history of Rome, as far as literary authorities are concerned. To emphasize the importance of this period would be to enunciate a truism. The second century, or the years A.D. 96–180, from the death of Domitian to the accession of Commodus, is in Gibbon's famous judgement 'the period in the history of the world during which the condition of the human race was most happy and prosperous'.[1] Half of the third century—the years A.D. 235–84— was a period of continuous anarchy: civil war, repeated invasion from without and military catastrophe when external assaults were countered. But after Diocletian's successful seizure of power, there began a new era of stability, if not of happiness and prosperity; and the nature of the empire was transformed. There are profound differences between the fourth-century empire, as revealed in the pages of Ammianus Marcellinus and the Theodosian Code, and the age of Antonines. They cannot be ascribed to Diocletian or to Constantine alone—or for that matter to the triumph of the Christian Church alone. Christianity was a symptom long before it became a cause of the change. The origins of the transformation of the empire must be sought in the second and third centuries A.D., especially in the period A.D. 168 onwards—that is, from the outbreak of the Marcomannic Wars.

It is precisely here that the difficulty arises. For the second century and the first quarter of the third century the work of Cassius Dio is the major source. Unfortunately his account of the reign of Antoninus Pius, A.D. 138–61, the longest reign of any emperor between Augustus and Constantine, is entirely missing, as it has been since the time of his Byzantine epitomator.[2] For much of the remaining portion of the period what has been preserved is in any case merely a feeble and truncated abridgement.[3] For the years A.D. 180–238 there is the *Roman History* of Herodian, a Greek of supposedly Syrian origin, who had lived in Rome and had some official position, probably of a very lowly kind.[4] Herodian's stock as an historian has risen and fallen with the years. Where comparison with other accounts is possible, Herodian does not always shine.[5] But he is useful, in spite of his irritating vagueness and his trite rhetoric; and occasionally he supplies facts not found elsewhere, which can, in some cases, be accepted.[6] For the rest of the third century up till A.D. 284, and indeed for all parts of the second century not covered by Herodian or what survives of Dio, there remain brief chroniclers of a later era, such as Aurelius Victor; contemporary litterateurs such as Aulus Gellius, Fronto, Lucian, and Philostratus the biographer of the sophists; the legal sources; and the histories, martyrologies, and theological treatises of the Christian Church. To all of these coins, inscriptions, papyri, and the results of archaeological investigation provide some framework and some control. There remains another literary source, a work preserved in a codex of the ninth century written in a Frankish minuscule hand, the *Codex Palatinus Latinus* 899, from which seventeen other copies complete or partial, of varying accuracy, are derived. The work is called in the *Palatinus* 'vitae diversorum principum et tyrannorum a divo Hadriano usque ad Numerianum diversis conpositi' [*sic*]. But it has been known since the early seventeenth century as the *Historia Augusta*, the name given to it by its great editor Isaac Casaubon, who found the phrase in the work itself, applied, however, to Tacitus, who is described as 'scriptorem historiae Augustae'—much more appropriately, as Ernst Hohl the most recent editor dryly comments in his preface:

> Nomen Casaubonus a vita Taciti Augusti 10, 3, in qua Cornelius Tacitus appellatur scriptor historiae Augustae, haud scio an parum apte mutuatus esse videatur, dum respicias, quantum discrepet harum vitarum genus ab illius annalibus.[7]

For his first twelve chapters in particular, and thereafter to a lesser extent, Edward Gibbon relied heavily on the *Augustan History* as a source. For that reason it is of some interest that he drew attention in his very brief preface to the octavo edition of the *Decline and Fall* to a difficulty—admittedly a minor one in comparison with those raised just over a century later and thenceforward—which he himself found when using the *Augustan History*.

After stating that 'diligence and accuracy are the only merits which an historical writer may ascribe to himself', he adds:

> At present I shall content myself with a single observation. The biographers who, under the reigns of Diocletian and Constantine, composed, or rather compiled, the lives of the emperors, from Hadrian to the sons of Carus, are usually mentioned under the names of Aelius Spartianus, Julius Capitolinus, Aelius Lampridius, Vulcatius Gallicanus, Trebellius Pollio, and Flavius Vobiscus [*sic*]. But there is so much perplexity in the titles of the MSS., and so many disputes have arisen among the critics (see Fabricius, Biblioth. Latin, lib. iii cap. 6) concerning their number, their names, and their respective property, that for the most part I have quoted them without distinction, under the general and well-known title of the *Augustan History*.

Hence the *Augustan History* had raised problems at an early stage. Gibbon's annotation, with its references to learned works long since forgotten, makes it plain that others had grappled seriously with some of the more obvious defects of the work. Gibbon's comments in text and notes show that he had his own complaints. Thus in chapter 4, in a note to his description of the character of the Emperor Pertinax, and in particular his style of entertaining:

> Dion speaks of these entertainments, as a senator who has supped with the emperor. Capitolinus like a slave, who had received his intelligence from one of the scullions.

In chapter 7 he is obliged to add to his account of the murder of Severus Alexander a note that 'I have softened some of the most improbable circumstances of this wretched biographer'. Describing the same emperor's Persian war, he prefers the account of Herodian, commenting that 'the old abbreviators and modern compilers have blindly followed the *Augustan History*'. Unfortunately all too often Gibbon himself did likewise, and some of the more celebrated passages in the first part of his work, although incomparably more elegant than the wretched biographer, are based solely on him, and are, as history, worthless.[8]

So much by way of preface. The title assigned to the work in the Palatinus has already been quoted. The work contains lives of different emperors and usurpers from Hadrian to Numerian, composed by different authors. That is, it covers the period A.D. 117–284. There is an important gap in the second half. The lives of the emperors who reigned between Gordian III and Valerian are missing, as is most of the life of Valerian himself, which begins in its present form with the aftermath of Valerian's capture by the Persians. Thus the period A.D. 244–*c*.260 is not dealt with, years which saw the first millenary of Rome's foundation, the two major persecutions of the Christian Church before the great persecution by Diocletian, those of Decius and Valerian, the first major Gothic invasion and the death in battle of Decius, and the capture of Valerian by Sapor.[9]

A work of biography of this nature falls into a recognizable category of classical biography, that inaugurated by Suetonius' *Twelve Caesars*. The *Augustan History* was not the first work to imitate Suetonius' plan, but these two are the major surviving examples. The method is well known: the *Life* begins with the subject's date and place of birth, his family and ancestry, early life and career up till his accession, and goes on to describe the reign largely by category, with little regard for chronological narrative. The biography ends with the subject's death, frequently with omens, and some personal details.[10] Suetonius, as *ab epistulis* of Hadrian, had access to imperial archives, and made use of these and other documentary sources in his work, frequently citing his authorities, as an historian should, or at least quoting them verbatim. The *Augustan History* also quotes documents and cites authorities.

But at this point the differences between the two must be emphasized. The *Augustan History* is assigned in the manuscript adscriptions to a plurality of authorship, as its title proclaims. The authors are six in number, Aelius Spartianus, Julius Capitolinus, Vulcacius Gallicanus V.C. (i.e. *vir clarissimus*, the title of senatorial rank), Aelius Lampridius, Trebellius Pollio, and Flavius Vopiscus Syracusius, 'the Syracusan'. These writers are nowhere else recorded in any ancient source—although they know about one another, in some cases.[11] The second major difference is that the *Augustan History* includes *Lives* not only of emperors but also of heirs to the throne and usurpers—all who rightly or wrongly held the title or name of *Caesar*. This was an innovation in which some pride is taken, although reference is made to predecessors who had specialized in biographies of usurpers.[12] There are some thirty *Lives* in the work, but several *Lives* cover more than one man: thus the *Maximini duo* and *Gordiani tres*, and of course the *quadrigae tyrannorum* and *tyranni triginta*.

The contributions of the six authors fall into two main categories. The last two, Pollio and Vopiscus, are responsible for the *Lives* from Valerian to Numerian. The earlier *Lives*, from Hadrian to Gordian III, are divided among the other four, to one of whom, Gallicanus, is assigned only the *Life* of the usurper Avidius Cassius. Hence Spartianus, Capitolinus, and Lampridius virtually cover the period A.D. 117–244 between them. But their contributions are not evenly divided. Spartianus wrote the *Lives* of Hadrian, of Aelius Caesar, Hadrian's first heir, and then, after a long interval, come his *Lives* of Didius Julianus, Severus, Severus' unsuccessful rival Niger, and his two sons Caracalla and Geta. Capitolinus evidently wrote the *Lives* of Pius, Marcus, and L. Verus, then those of Pertinax, Clodius Albinus (Severus' other rival), and Macrinus, and finally the group of *Lives* covering the years A.D. 235–44: Maximinus Thrax and his son, Gordian I and Gordian II, Balbinus and Pupienus, and Gordian III, all those, in fact, who were emperor at some stage in the year A.D. 238. Lampridius is credited with the *Lives* of Commodus, Diadumenianus the son of Macrinus, Elagabalus, and Severus Alexander. A number of *Lives* by the first four authors are prefaced by dedications in which the authors address themselves to Diocletian or to Constantine. Pollio and Vopiscus do not dedicate their work to an emperor, but from references to persons and events it appears that they, too, are, broadly speaking, contemporaries of the other *scriptores*.

Vopiscus speaks directly to his readers more than the other five, but they, too, speak of their intentions and views from time to time. Particularly interesting is the fact that Spartianus, for example, in the preface to his *Aelius*, tells Diocletian that he intends to compose *Lives* of all those 'qui principum locum in hac statione quam temperas retentarunt', and this, he says, he has already done, as far as Hadrian (whose *Life* is, in fact, the only one before that of Aelius in the *Augustan History*); and in addition, *Lives* of all who

vel Caesarum nomine appellati sunt nec principes aut Augusti fuerunt vel quolibet alio genere aut in famam aut in spem principatus venerunt. (*Ael.* 1.1)

Yet Spartianus' ambitious project is sparsely represented in the *Augustan History*.

Capitolinus' first contributions are unprefaced. In the address to Constantine which opens his *Maximini duo* he implies that he, too, will be writing other *Lives*, an intention reiterated in the preface to the *Gordiani tres*. In neither case, however, does this necessarily imply anything more than what has survived under the name of Capitolinus. Vulcacius Gallicanus, in the only *Life* to his credit, announces that he has set himself the task of writing the *Lives* of all 'qui imperatorium nomen sive iusta causa sive iniusta habuerunt . . . ut omnes purpuratos, Auguste (sc. Diocletiane), cognosceres' (*Av. Cass.* 3.3). Lampridius is a little more guarded. In his *Life of Elagabalus* he claims that he has written other *Lives* already (those of Commodus and Diadumenianus alone survive, in that case): 'cum iam aliorum ante tulerimus'—but that it was only when Constantine forced him, 'invitum et retractantem', that he wrote the life of *Elagabalus* (*Ant. Heliog.* 35.1). But he says that he is going on to write *Lives* of subsequent rulers, among which he mentions the Gordians, Claudius II, and Aurelian, in addition to Alexander (the only other one in the *Augustan History* which is, in fact, ascribed to Lampridius). Then, most remarkably, he goes on to promise *Lives* of Diocletian and Maximian, and of four other figures:

> his addendi sunt Licinius, Severus, Alexander atque Maxentius, quorum omnium ius in dicionem tuam venit, sed ita ut nihil eorum virtuti derogetur. non enim ego id faciam, quod plerique scriptores solent, ut de his detraham, qui victi sunt, cum intellegam gloriae tuae accedere, si omnia de illis, quae bona in se habuerint, vera praedicaro (*Ibid.* 35.6–7)

This is indeed a bold project, to propose to treat in favourable fashion Constantine's rivals Flavius Severus and Maxentius, the rebel L. Domitius Alexander, and the final enemy Licinius.

This rapid survey of the nature of the authorship makes one thing plain. To quote A. Momigliano:

> If we take this evidence *prima facie*, it follows that somebody must have chosen from among biographies of the first four authors those which seemed worthy to be included in the present *Historia Augusta*.[13]

Momigliano goes on to add that 'one can of course dispute the attribution of individual *Lives* with the help of various arguments'— as people were doing in Gibbon's time—'but the general picture of disorder will not be modified'. He further points out that the internal chronological evidence for the date of composition does not help to clarify the picture. This evidence must now be considered.

Spartianus addresses four of his *Lives* to Diocletian and one to Constantine. The first of those dedicated to Diocletian, the *Aelius*, refers to the appointment of Galerius and Constantius as Caesars:

> eo prope genere, quo nostris temporibus a vestra clementia Maximianus atque Constantius Caesares dicti sunt, quasi quidam principum filii, virtute designati augustae maiestatis heredes. (*Ael.* 2.2)

This seemingly dates the composition of the *Aelius* to the period A.D. 293–305. In the preface to the *Geta*, Constantine is addressed as Augustus. No further precision is given, and the life might thus belong to any moment between the years A.D. 306 and 337. Capitolinus dedicates three *Lives* to Diocletian and three to Constantine. The dedications to Diocletian give no further clue to precise dating, and these three *Lives* might thus belong to any part of the period A.D. 284–305, or even, theoretically, to the years of Diocletian's retirement. The *Gordiani tres*, of the *Lives* which he dedicates to Constantine, appears to belong to a period late in the reign, after the defeat of Licinius, to judge from a slighting reference to the latter:

> quem titulum evertisse Licinius dicitur eo tempore quo est nanctus imperium, cum se vellet videri a Philippis originem trahere. (*Gord.* 34.5)

Lampridius also, as already indicated, seems to be writing after the fall of Licinius.

The *Lives* by Pollio and Vopiscus lack these grandiloquent addresses to emperors. Pollio seems to be writing his work to a friend, who is related to one Herennius Celsus:

> quare scire oportet Herennium Celsum, vestrum parentem, cum consulatum cupit, hoc quod desiderat non licere. (*tyr. trig.* 22.12)

The ambitions of Celsus suggest that the friend of Pollio must be, likewise, of high rank. One might assume that had earlier lives by Pollio been available the recipient of his work might have been more directly addressed. Various items give some precision, however. Constantius is Caesar at the time of writing; and Claudius Gothicus is described as 'principe generis Constanti Caesaris nostri' and as the man from whom 'Constantius, vigilissimus Caesar, originem duxit'. Mention of this relationship is frequent in the

Claudius itself.[14] Hence the work of Pollio began after A.D. 293; and a reference to the Baths of Diocletian in *tyranni triginta* 21.7 suggests that part at least was composed not earlier than A.D. 298. The fact that Vopiscus, early in his first life, the *Aurelian* (2.1), discusses the biographical writings of Pollio would make A.D. 304 the *terminus ante quem*.

Vopiscus, of all the *scriptores*, reveals his personality the most. The preface to his *Aurelian* is an engaging piece of writing. It records a conversation between the writer and the Urban Prefect Junius Tiberianus, at the festival of the Hilaria, in the prefect's carriage:

> Hilaribus, quibus omnia festa et fieri debere scimus et dici, impletis solemnibus vehiculo suo me et iudiciali carpento praef. urbis, vir inlustris ac praefata reverentia nominandus, Iunius Tiberianus accepit. (1.1)

Author and prefect then dicusssed the Emperor Aurelian—for their drive took them past the Temple of the Sun consecrated by that emperor, from whom the prefect claimed descent. Tiberianus lamented the lack of biographies in Latin of the great man—'clarissimum principem, severissimum imperatorem, per quem totus Romano nomini orbis est restitutus' (1.5). He invites Vopiscus to undertake the task and gives him the freedom of the Ulpian Library, making available in particular 'linen books' (*libri lintei*), in which Aurelian's *ephemeridae* were set down 1.6–7). Vopiscus tells his friend (whose name is not correctly recorded in the MSS., but may be Pinianus, as proposed by Hohl), that he has carried out his task of research (1.9). Before commending his account of Aurelian's life he records further details of his memorable discussion with Junius Tiberianus. He himself criticized the work of Trebellius Pollio, for its carelessness and brevity. The prefect reassured him that no historian had failed to tell some lies, citing the examples of Livy, Sallust, Tacitus, and Pompeius Trogus. Finally he stretched out his hand and jokingly gave Vopiscus *carte blanche* to say whatever he liked:

> 'scribe', inquit, 'ut libet. securus, quod velis, dices, habiturus mendaciorum comites, quos historicae eloquentiae miramur auctores'. 2.1–2)

A Junius Tiberianus is recorded as Urban Prefect on two occasions, from 18 February A.D. 291 to 3 August A.D. 292, and from 12

September A.D. 303 to 4 January A.D. 304. It is now apparent that there were two men of the same name, presumably father and son.[15] The latter's prefecture is unsuitable, as the festival of the Hilaria took place on 25 March, and the second Tiberianus was not prefect during the month of March. Hence, at first sight, the conversation between Vopiscus and the prefect can be assigned firmly to 25 March A.D. 291. But, as must have been made plain already, this creates a major difficulty, for Vopiscus and Tiberianus discussed the work of Pollio—who was writing most of his work, if not all, not earlier than A.D. 293, and some of it, at least, not before A.D. 298. The only real solution is to suppose either that the Hilaria took place at an unusual time of year in A.D. 303 (or that some other festival is meant), or that the second Tiberianus' prefecture lasted longer than the dates which the chronographer of A.D. 354 assigns to it, to 4 June A.D. 304, for example, as proposed by Mommsen, who emended 'prid. non Ian.' to 'prid. non Iun.'[16] This conclusion is given support by the reference later in the *Aurelian* to Constantius as Augustus—'et est quidem iam Constantius imperator' (44.5)— and to Diocletian as a private citizen—'Diocletianum principem iam privatum' (43.2). This would date the work closely to A.D. 305–6.

At this stage another noteworthy feature of the work must be considered: the documents. Relevant in this context is an important distinction established by Mommsen, among the first sixteen *Lives* (those from Hadrian to Diadumenianus), between 'major' and 'minor' *Lives*.[17] The major *Lives* are those of regnant emperors; the minor *Lives* are those of Caesars, junior emperors, and usurpers or pretenders—namely L. Aelius Caesar, L. Verus, Avidius Cassius, Pescennius Niger, Clodius Albinus, Geta, and Diadumenianus. The writing of biographies of these lesser figures was something of an innovation. It is precisely here that the documents abound, precisely where the authorship was in most need of extra material to pad out the scanty evidence, as is admitted in the preface to *Pescennius Niger*:

> Rarum atque difficile est, ut, quos tyrannos aliorum victoria fecerit, bene mittantur in litteras, atque ideo vix omnia de his plene in monumentis atque annalibus habentur. (1.1)

But the authenticity of these documents was questioned at an early date: a study published in 1870 showed that the documents in the *Avidius Cassius*, ostensibly letters by L. Verus, M. Aurelius, a praetorian prefect, the Empress Faustina and Cassius himself, were unquestionably all composed by one and the same hand.[18] Indeed, even *prima facie* something was wrong: in an oration of Marcus reported in *oratio obliqua* (8.5), the emperor is made to express opinions on violent deaths of emperors, and to refer to Nero, Caligula, Otho, Vitellius, Galba—and Pertinax, who was made emperor nearly thirteen years after his own death. Similar investigation has produced the same results with the other documents. Of some 150 letters, speeches, decrees, and acclamations, only the two acclamations in the *Commodus* (18–19) are now accepted as genuine. In fairness it should be observed that as far as the speeches are concerned—and they account for about a third of the total—ancient authors were generally allowed this licence. This was pointed out by L. Homo.[19] On the other hand, few ancient authors attempted to give speeches of their own composition such an air of verisimilitude as did the *scriptores*. One may cite, for example, the way in which a speech of Valerian is introduced in Aurelian (12.3–13.1), in a passage too lengthy to cite here *in extenso*: Vopiscus says that he is going to include the speech 'fidei causa,' and says where he found it: 'ex libris Acholii, qui magister admissionum Valeriani principis fuit, libro actorum eius nono'. It is, in fact, only too plain that the minor *Lives* of second-century figures, and all the third-century *Lives* (after that of Severus, at any rate) contain only a very thin framework of fact. The minor *Lives* have clearly been composed by the simple process of extracting from the appropriate major *Life* a basic minimum of facts, which was then elaborated by fiction. In some cases the facts were simply repeated, in both major and minor *Life*; in other cases some facts were reserved for the minor *Life*. The procedure with third-century *Lives* was analogous, except that here, for a large part of the period, the *scriptores* had little source-material to rely on at all.

Now that the credentials of the *scriptores* have been called in question thus far, the delineation of the 'problem' of the *Augustan History*, which has dominated work on the subject since 1889, can no longer be postponed. In that year Hermann Dessau, in a remarkable article in *Hermes*,[20] produced the startling but closely and impressively argued hypothesis that the work was a fraud: that it was not written by six authors in the time of Diocletian and Constantine; but by one man, whom Dessau designated the *Fälscher*, 'forger', nearly a century later, in the reign of Theodosius the Great.

Dessau's main arguments, after surveying the awkwardnesses

which have already been surveyed, were twofold. First, he pointed out a series of names of personages mentioned in the *Augustan History* which seemed to indicate knowledge of or allusion to persons living after the apparent time of composition. Second, he showed a close dependence, particularly in two lengthy passages, on Aurelius Victor and Eutropius, whose work was published in A.D. 360 and 369 respectively—a generation after the death of Constantine.[21] It is not the purpose of the present account to attempt to summarize the enormous literature which Dessau's article has engendered. But certain features in the continuing debate may be singled out for scrutiny or mention, before one can return to examine the *Augustan History* itself in more detail.

Dessau's case can be refuted by a determined conservative by the use of certain *a priori* arguments. It is not difficult to claim that apparent anachronisms only appear to be so because of the lack of evidence. Thus, allusions to certain families and persons—Ceionii and Petronii Probi, Ragonius Celsus and Toxotius—might not appear quite so anachronistic, it is argued, if more were known of prosopography of the early fourth century.[22] Institutional anachronisms, such as the much-debated instance of Junius Tiberianus' *iudiciale carpentum* (and his title *vir inlustris*) in a passage just quoted can also be defended.[23] Because the earliest date otherwise known for these two things is many years later than the apparent date of writing of the *Augustan History*, it does not follow that they did not exist earlier. Even the blatant case, greatly emphasized by Dessau, of the Claudian descent of Constantius Chlorus and Constantine, need not involve forgery. Although this alleged descent of the second Flavian dynasty from Claudius Gothicus is otherwise first recorded in A.D. 310,[24] whereas the *scriptores* are apparently writing when Constantius is still Caesar, this need not occasion such great suspicion as it did to Dessau.[25] After all, in any case, the *scriptores* could easily have touched up their work within a few years of publication. The borrowing from Aurelius Victor and Eutropius can, similarly, be countered in simple fashion: all three writers can have drawn from a common source.[26]

Nevertheless, when this has been said, it must be admitted that the seed of doubt sown by Dessau is difficult to ignore. Nor is there much comfort for a traditionalist in the alternative line of defence, to suppose that the text of the *Augustan History* in its present form has been radically tampered with, and that anachronisms, illusions most easily explicable as being aimed at fourth-century personages, and the borrowings from Victor and Eutropius, are all the product of such interference.[27]

It was necessary for Dessau to explain why the forger that he had postulated should have attempted such a deception: he had to find a motive once he had discovered the crime. His answer was simple and unambitious. The thing was done to give the work the appearance of greater antiquity, and hence greater authority. One might add, as did A. Rosenberg, the suggestion that the man was an unprincipled member of the bookselling profession, and imagine that he turned out a set of *Augustan Histories* to make himself a profit.[28] Evidence is certainly to hand of the wide popularity of such reading-matter among the better-off in the sacred city in the late fourth century, a matter of some disgust and puzzlement to Ammianus Marcellinus:

> quidam destestantes ut venena doctrinas Iuvenalem et Marium Maximum curatiore studio legunt, nulla volumina praeter haec in profundo otio contrectantes; quam ob causam non iudicioli est nostri.[29]

Marius Maximus was the continuator of Suetonius; and his work is known, apart from this reference, solely by a mention in a Scholiast on Juvenal (appropriately enough in view of Ammianus' categorization), and by citations in the *Augustan History*.[30]

Dessau's explanation was deemed insufficient by Mommsen, who posed the question 'cui bono?'[31] A number of vigorous attempts have been made to answer this question, which must be discussed briefly. For a number of years Dessau's views won wide acceptance, although some went beyond them, and at the same time the conservative position found its champions.[32] In 1926, N. H. Baynes in a brief monograph contended that the *Augustan History* was produced in the reign of Julian the Apostate, and that it was intended as propaganda on his behalf.[33] Baynes thus found a striking answer to the question of motive. At the same time his theory provided a satisfying explanation of the glorification of the second Flavian dynasty. There was no difficulty over the use of Aurelius Victor. Apparent use of Eutropius had to be explained as use of a common source. Baynes's theory attracted a number of supporters; but it now seems to number few adherents. The favoured view at present is much closer to Dessau's original hypothesis, but with an important variation in that serious political intentions are ascribed to the authorship. W. Hartke put forward in 1940 the theory that the work was composed in the year A.D. 394 by a member of Symmachus' circle—he actually named the author, Nicomachus Flavianus junior. Hartke himself modified his views a little subsequently,[34] but there is now a strong body of opinion which favours the hypothesis that the *Augustan History* was composed at the end of the fourth century as a piece of pro-pagan and pro-senatorial propaganda.[35]

Mommsen's 'cui bono?' has been repeatedly answered from 1926 onwards. But it must here be affirmed that the question of 'Tendenz' is one on which there is serious room for doubt. It may, indeed, be accepted, that the work is pro-pagan and pro-senatorial in outlook. But it is another matter to insist that the authorship seriously intended to influence the course of events through the work. Somehow, to take the *Augustan History* too seriously seems faintly absurd.

In any case, as far as the *Augustan History*'s attitude to Christianity is concerned, one important aspect of the question seems to have been overlooked. Stress has been laid on the fact that references to Christianity are sparse and ambiguous.[36] Yet there is no doubt that it would have been impossible for any writer covering the reigns of Decius and Valerian to have avoided discussing the persecution of the Christian Church by those two emperors. Is it conceivable that the lacuna in the text of the *Augustan History* is not a genuine lacuna; in other words, that the authorship of the work never, in fact, covered that vital period from A.D. 244 to *c*. A.D. 260? It must certainly be admitted that plenty of texts have been handed down damaged in this way, but nothing would have been easier for an unscrupulous person who claimed to have 'discovered' a collection of biographies written several generations earlier than to give such a discovery a still greater semblance of genuine age by demonstrating regretfully that the manuscript was damaged.[37] There is no doubt that where references to Valerian and Decius do occur in the *Augustan History* they are highly laudatory. By contrast, comments on Philip, the supposedly philochristian emperor, are unflattering, to say the least. There is a curious passage in the *Aurelian* where Philip and his son are classed with Vitellius, Caligula, Nero, and Maximinus Thrax, whereas Decius and his son are highly praised. Vopiscus has given his short list of good emperors. Then he goes on:

Valerianum enim, cum optimus fuerit, ab omnibus infelicitas
separavit. vide, quaeso, quam pauci sint principes boni, ut bene
dictum sit a quodam mimico scurra Claudii huius temporibus in
uno anulo bonos principes posse perscribi atque depingi. at contra
quae series malorum! ut enim omittamus Vitellios, Caligulas et
Nerones, quis ferat Maximinos et Philippos atque illam inconditae
multitudinis faecem? tametsi Decios excerpere debeam, quorum
et vita et mors veteribus comparanda est. (42.5–6)

One may perhaps speculate whether there is some hidden meaning
in the last sentence (although the *Augustan History* has been to an
excessive degree a happy hunting-ground for hidden meanings):
'although I must leave out the Decii, whose life and death must be
compared to men of old'. It is surely conceivable that the author was
thinking, as he composed that sentence, that he had had to leave out
the Decii, not only from this list of emperors, but from the whole
series of biographies. However this may be, it would have removed
a considerable embarrassment to have omitted biographies of
Decius and Valerian; and at the least it should be remembered that
a genuine assessment of the attitude of the authorship of the
Augustan History towards Christianity can scarcely be formed without taking this question into consideration.

Many passages could be quoted to illustrate the direct interest of
the authorship in boosting the claims of the senate—direct interest
because the attitude of the authorship is conveyed directly in the
bogus documents for which it alone is responsible. This alleged
private letter quoted at the end of the *Tacitus* may perhaps suffice:

Autronio Iusto patri Autronius Tiberianus salutem. nunc te, pater
sancte, interesse decuit senatui amplissimo, nunc sententiam dicere
cum tantum auctoritas amplissimi ordinis creverit ut reversa in
antiquum statum re publica nos principes demus, nos faciamus
imperatores, nos denique nuncupemus Augustos . . . etc.
(19.1–2)

The attitude here expressed seems to have borne fruit, in a modest
way. The earliest use made of the *Augustan History*, indeed the only
use made of it in antiquity (and by the same token this is the true
terminus ante quem for its composition) was by a later member of
the family of the Symmachi, Q. Aurelius Memmius Symmachus,
consul in A.D. 485, father-in-law of Boëthius, and the author of a
Roman History in seven books.[38]

It cannot be denied that the question of the identity, date and purpose of the *Augustan History* is one of vital interest and importance. If it could be solved unequivocally, the work would stand revealed as a social document of high value. But it must be admitted that general agreement on this question has not been and perhaps never will be reached. However, it is perhaps possible to concede, at least, that the *Augustan History* was conceived at a single moment, and that it is the work, if not of a single hand, at least of a team working in unison. This conclusion reached long ago by Dessau has been given support by the detailed study of clausulae, alliteration and assonance.[39]

This makes it legitimate to study the *Augustan History* as a unity. One of the most striking statements in the work is the admission at the end of the preposterous *tyranni triginta*:

> neque ego eloquentiae mihi videor pollicitus esse, sed rem, qui hos libellos, quos de vita principum edidi, non scribo sed dicto, et dicto cum ea festinatione, quam, si quid vel ipse promisero vel tu petieris, sic perurges ut respirandi non habeam facultatem. (33.8)

This statement may be a literary artifice—and indeed it could be accepted as such and no more in many contexts. In the *Augustan History* it has the ring of an all too self-evident truth: the whole work bears every sign of hasty and careless composition, of being a 'rush job'. It may be mentioned in passing that Hartke's original hypothesis about the time of writing involved the supposition that the job was done in the space of three months.[40] Some have found this impossible to accept.[41] Yet anyone familiar with the methods and products of modern journalism—and the term 'political journalist' was applied to Trebellius Pollio by E. Klebs[42] before Dessau opened the controversy—would not find this so difficult to credit. Indeed, there seems little reason why a determined man with a team of stenographers, a sheaf of sources to plagiarize, and a ready tongue, could not have taken considerably less than three months.

This view of the way in which the work was produced conflicts, of course, with the smokescreen which the authorship elsewhere diligently puts out, to convey the impression that the various biographies are the product of intensive research, which is indeed alluded to, sometimes even described at length, in a manner unparalleled in antiquity. Vopiscus brings the collection to a close with a smug observation on this topic:

Habe, mi amice, meum munus, quod ego, ut saepe dixi, non elo-
quentiae causa sed curiositatis in lumen edidi, id praecipue agens
ut, si quis eloquens vellet facta principum reserare, materiam non
requireret, habiturus meos libellos ministros eloquii. te quaeso, sis
contentus nosque sic voluisse scribere melius quam potuisse con-
tendas. (*Carus* 21.2–3)

The invitation to Vopiscus by the Prefect Tiberianus, to make use
of the Ulpian Library, has already been mentioned. Reference to
this library is made several times, to disarm criticism:

ac ne quis me temere Graecorum alicui Latinorumve aestimet
credidisse, habet in Bibliotheca Ulpia in armario sexto librum
elephantinum, in quo hoc senatus consultum perscriptum est, cui
Tacitus manu sua subscripsit. nam diu haec senatus consulta quae
ad principes pertinent in libris elephantinis scribebantur. (*Tac.*
8.1–2)

This is indeed a rare and helpful author, who supplies his readers
not only with references but indicates the right place to find them
in a particular library. In the *Probus* this standard of scholarship is
surpassed. The author tells his friend that he has used chiefly books
from the Ulpian Library (adding that in his time it is housed in the
Baths of Diocletian), but that other sources have also been laid
under contribution:

et item ex domo Tiberiana, usus etiam regestis scribarum porticus
Porphyreticae, actis etiam senatus et populi, et quoniam me ad
colligenda talis viri gesta ephemeris Turduli Gallicani plurimum
iuvit, viri honestissimi ac sincerissimi, beneficium amici senis
tacere non debui. (2.1–2)

All that is lacking here is the courteous proviso that his friend
Turdulius Gallicanus must not be held responsible for the use that
Vopiscus has made of his material, to make this preface identical in
tone with the kind customarily composed by modern scholars.

Another procedure employed by the authorship is lavish citation
of sources, frequently with a recommendation added that any
readers who want to study some particular matter further should
consult the works of So-and-so. One of the writers most frequently
cited is Aelius Junius Cordus, who is rated as somewhat inferior:
'quae qui volet nosse, Aelium Cordum legat, qui frivola super huius
modi ominibus cuncta persequitur' (*Clod. Alb.* 5.10). But care is
taken, none the less, to include a large number of trivial details, 'ne,

quis Cordum legeret, me praetermisisse crederet aliquid quod ad rem pertineret' (*Maximini* 28.10). In a later *Life* excuses of this sort are no longer thought necessary: 'Frivola haec fortassis cuipiam et nimis levia esse videantur, sed curiositas nil recusat' (*Aurel.* 10.1). However, Cordus' approach is roundly criticized:

> non enim nobis talia dicenda sunt, quae Iunius Cordus ridicule ac stulte composuit, de voluptatibus domesticis ceterisque infimis rebus. quae qui velit scire, ipsum legat Cordum, qui dicit, et quos servos habuerit unusquisque principum et quos amicos et quot paenulas quotve chlamydes, quorum etiam scientia nulli rei prodest . . . (*Gord.* 21.4)

Other sources are mentioned from time to time, such as Aemilius Parthenianus, 'qui adfectatores tyrannidis iam inde a veteribus historiae tradidit' (*Av. Cass.* 5.1), and a host of others—Annius Cornicula, Julius Atherianus, Julius Titianus, Suetonius Optatianus, Vulcatius Terentianus, and so on. Neither Cordus nor any of these writers are otherwise recorded, and there is little doubt that they are creations of the *Augustan History* itself.

From time to time, however, genuine sources are cited, and can be detected even where they are not cited. The two chief examples are Marius Maximus and Herodian; there is also Dexippus. Marius Maximus is clearly the same as L. Marius Maximus Perpetuus Aurelianus (cos. II ord. 223), son of an Italian procurator and grandson of a *scriba quaestorius*. His senatorial career began under Commodus, at the time of whose murder he was commanding the legion I Italica in Lower Moesia. An adherent of Severus presumably from the first—no doubt he was one of those northern army commanders referred to in *Severus* 5.3, who had prepared the way for Severus' proclamation on 9 April A.D. 193: 'cum iam Illyriciani exercitus et Gallicani cogentibus ducibus in eius verba iurassent'—he conducted the lengthy siege of Byzantium, commanded an army corps at the battle of Lugdunum, and went on to govern Belgica, Lower Germany, and Syria Coele under Severus. Under Caracalla he had the unusual experience of being proconsul of both Africa and Asia, in the latter province for two years, and Macrinus had to use him as a substitute for the semi-literate Oclatinius Adventus, when the latter found that the public speaking which the Urban Prefecture involved was too much for him. Finally, Severus Alexander made him *consul ordinarius* for A.D. 223, the first full year of the new reign.[43] This was when the opportunity first arose of writing a second *Twelve Caesars*, in continuation of Suetonius: Nerva, Trajan, Hadrian, Pius, Marcus, Commodus, Pertinax, Didius, Severus, Caracalla, Macrinus, Elagabalus. This is what Maximus seems to have done, and although the *Augustan History* in one place criticizes him as 'homo omnium verbosissimus, qui et mythistoricis voluminibus se implicavit' (*quad. tyr.* 1.2), there is good reason to believe that Maximus may have been the only continuous source of the *Augustan History* for at least the second-century major lives.[44]

For a long time much was made of an alleged duality of sources in the first part of the *Augustan History*—a narrative, chronological, factual source, sometimes identified with the anonymous, so-called 'last great historian of Rome'; and a biographical source of low value, full of scandalous matter, sometimes identified with Maximus himself.[45] But it is now recognized that this distinction is artificial and that it may be misleading. For one thing, there is not such a clear distinction in method, among historians of the imperial period, between the biographers and the annalistic historians. Cassius Dio, for example, includes potted biographies of emperors as a kind of preface or postscript to his account of their reigns year by year. Suetonius' approach is narrative in the portion of his *Lives* which deals with the subject's career before his accession.[46] At the same time, in the case of emperors such as Hadrian, whose reign was easily covered in annalistic fashion by giving an account of his journeys, one after the other, any biographer would naturally adopt an annalistic procedure; whereas in the case of Pius, who spent his entire long reign in Italy, and kept the empire at peace for almost all of it, even an annalistic historian would find it a problem to recount events year by year.

Herodian is used extensively by the *Augustan History*, sometimes being cited as Herodianus, sometimes as Arrianus, for no obvious reason. It seems reasonable to suppose that the authors turned to Herodian when Marius Maximus failed them.[47] This took them up to the accession of Gordian III, and no further; and this is precisely where the lacuna in the work begins.

The latter part of the *Augustan History*, for which Trebellius Pollio and Flavius Vopiscus are supposed to be responsible, teems with bogus material to an even greater extent than anything that goes before. The *tyranni triginta* of Pollio, for example, is a farrago largely compounded of nonsense. To make up the magic number of thirty it is clear that some of the personalities have been freely invented. Particularly suspect is Piso, who took power in Thessaly, 'Thessalicusque appellatus . . . vir summae sanctitatis et temporibus suis Frugi dictus et qui ex illa Pisonum familia ducere originem diceretur, cui se Cicero nobilitandi causa sociaverat' (21.1). All the later lives bristle with forged documents; especially suspicious are the lists of *dona* awarded to the virtuous hero by grateful emperors:

> pateras gemmatas trilibres duas, scyphos aureos gemmatos duos, discum corymbiatum argenteum librarum viginti, patenam argenteam pampinatam librarum triginta . . . etc. etc. (*Claud.* 17.5)

In spite of this, there runs through the *Lives* a thin substratum of fact. In the *Claudius* for example, there can be no gainsaying the statement that 'breve . . . in imperio fuit tempus' (2.1), but that is almost the only acceptable fact in the first three pages of the *Life* (apart from a passing mention of the victory over the Goths). There follows an account of his disposal of Aureolus, and of his Gothic war, where once more a thin sprinkling of fact is overlaid with a flood of jejune and uninformative rubbish—letters, a series of rhetorical questions, oracles. Then comes an account of his death, which is followed by a further massive selection of documents— these amount to a third of the total *Life*. The much longer *Aurelian* is little better in this respect. Indeed, in the first fifteen chapters it would be hard to find a single acceptable fact. The brief *Tacitus* contains virtually nothing of historical value—but much that has proved misleading. The first chapter is concerned entirely with the origin of the *interregnum*. Ten of the remaining eighteen chapters (3–9, 12, 18, 19) are largely composed of documents. Chapter 10 gives some personal details, including the statement that the emperor claimed Cornelius Tacitus as a relative. Chapter 11 gives further, even more trivial personal details—his taste in food, in particular, with a recommendation to those who want full details to read the *Life* by Suetonius Optatianus. Chapter 13 has a few facts: the invasion of the Eruli and his death. Chapter 14 describes the accession, reign, and death of Florian. In chapter 15 the most remarkable and absurd prophecy of all occurs: a descendant of Tacitus and Florian will extend Roman rule as far as *Taprobane* (Ceylon) and *Iuverna insula* (Ireland). But the *haruspices* who made the prophecy had covered themselves, Vopiscus sagely remarks: the prophecy was to be fulfilled a thousand years after the giant statues of Tacitus and Florian at Interamna had been struck by lightning. Chapter 16 contains merely conversational titbits about the prophecy, and an introduction to Probus, the subject of the next *Life*. Chapter 17 contains the omens predicting the rule and the death of Tacitus, and 18 and 19, as already mentioned, consist of documents.

The 'problem' of the *Augustan History* will undoubtedly remain a problem. But what is needed—and can be achieved—is careful historical analysis of the material which it contains, which will bear considerable fruit. This is what was urged long ago by Mommsen,[48] and it is still worth doing. To begin such a task a new and unbiased approach to the better early *Lives* would be valuable. Every name and every statement must be tested, not with *a priori* assumptions about the category of source from which it comes, but with a view to establishing what evidence there is to support it. Great caution is necessary, even by those practised in the methods of prosopography. To cite an instance, the treatment given by A. von Domaszewski to the praetorian prefect Veturius Macrinus is instructive. Domaszewski dismissed this person, stated in the *Didius Julianus* (7.5) to have been made praetorian prefect by Didius and to have been confirmed in office by Severus, as a fiction, compounded of a *nomen* in Cicero and the *cognomen* of the Emperor Macrinus.[49] But the man has since been revealed by epigraphic evidence, with the *praenomen* Decimus, both as praetorian prefect and as prefect of Egypt and procurator of Mauretania Tingitana at earlier stages in his career.[50] This instance suggests that material in the better *Lives* of second-century emperors should not be too easily discredited. A recent example may be examined: in the *Marcus* (2.3) one Eutychius Proculus is stated to have been among the instructors of M. Aurelius. This man comes in a list of teachers, together with Trosius Aper and Pollio. J. Schwartz casts doubt on all three, pointing out in the case of the two latter that the *Augustan History* knew the consular pair 'Pollione et Apro' (*Comm.* 2.4—the consuls of A.D. 176), and suggesting further that the *nomen* of Aper might be a corruption of the *nomen* of the consul Pollio, namely Vitrasius, distorted into Trosius.[51] As for Eutychius Proculus, a 'Siccensian', as he is described—from Sicca Veneria in proconsular Africa—Schwartz suspects that this person has been created on the basis of a character in the *tyranni triginta*.[52] It might be so. But it should be borne in mind that the curious nomenclature of Proculus might be explicable on reasonable grounds. Eutychius could be a *signum*, not an implausible attempt at a *nomen*.[53] Besides this, Greek names are found at Sicca Veneria.[54] Alternatively, one may draw attention to the Severan governor of Thrace *Equitius Proculus*.[55] As in so many other instances in the *Augustan History*, *Eutychius* could be a simple error, at what stage perpetrated one cannot easily determine.[56] As it happens, a simple and satisfying explanation is to hand: an inscription from Sicca records a procurator named M. Tuticius Proculus, surely the same man as the teacher of M. Aurelius, or a relative.[57] As for Aper and Pollio, emendation will again supply an answer. The text reads: 'Trosio Apro et polono'. The emendation 'et Polano' eliminates Pollio and gives an *origo* for Aper—Pola, in a part of Italy where most of the other members of the *gens Trosia* are recorded. Clearly caution is indicated. The same caution must apply even in lives where far greater freedom of invention is observable, for example the *Alexander Severus*, notoriously more of an historical novel than factual history. Thus, Aelius Serenianus, 'omnium vir sanctissimus', alleged to have been a counsellor of Alexander (68.1), may have existed—and he might be the same as the Serenianus, *praeses* of Cappadocia, described by Firmilian as 'acerbus et dirus persecutor'.[58] Should the identification be correct, one might almost suggest that the description of Serenianus in the *Augustan History* was intended as a deliberate, if muted, anti-Christian insinuation. At the time of writing Serenianus might have been remembered with some bitterness.

This brief investigation underlines an important fact about the *Augustan History*: its fondness for personal names. It is a sad fact that a high proportion of them are bogus, but in the earlier lives genuine names recur again and again, and can be authenticated, frequently only by epigraphic evidence. In this respect, the *Augustan History* is a welcome contrast to, for example, Xiphilinus:

> Dio, because those who were killed were very well known in those days, gives a list of their names; but for me it is enough to say that he disposed of all that he wanted to, alike, 'whosoever was guilty and whosoever was not', and that he mutilated Rome by depriving it of good men.[59]

Even Dio himself may on occasion have tired of such details:

> I should make my history wearisome if I were to describe exactly in every case those who were killed by him (sc. Commodus) . . .[60]

In this case one cannot be sure whether it is Dio or Xiphilinus who is speaking directly—one suspects the latter. By contrast the *Augustan History*, however crudely and ineptly its material is put together, does in these early *Lives* fulfil the claim made by Vopiscus at the end of the work, that 'si quis eloquens vellet facta principum reserare, materiam non requireret' (*Car.* 30.2).

From what has been said already, and from the extracts that have been quoted, it should be clear that the literary qualities of the *Augustan History* are minimal. None the less, it will doubtless continue to exert a fascination, as something *sui generis*. Whatever view is taken of the authorship, no one can seriously now believe that individuals existed in the reigns of Diocletian and Constantine, with the names of Vulcacius Gallicanus, for example, and the rank of *vir clarissimus*, or with the name Flavius Vopiscus and an origin in Syracuse. The work is certainly some kind of forgery. Here one may question whether 'forgery' is the best description.[61] It might be better to describe the work as a hoax, or even as a 'spoof'. But to do so would be implicitly to deny any serious political intention on the part of the authorship, and that is something that few students of the work would be prepared to do, at present, even though Dessau, who opened the controversy, thought otherwise. Parallels are hard to find. There were plenty of forgeries in antiquity, but the predominant category is that in which a work is falsely credited with the name of an already known author. To compose a pseudonymous work to which the names of non-existent persons are assigned is something different. Macpherson's *Ossian* and Chatterton spring to mind—but they had some genuine literary merit. The authorship of the *Augustan History* defies analysis. Perhaps it should supply its own verdict on itself:

> sum enim unus ex curiosis, quod infitias ire non possum incendentibus vobis, qui, cum multa sciatis, scire multo plura cupiatis. (*Probus* 2.8)

NOTES

The literature on this topic is vast. For accounts, one may refer to A. Momigliano, 'An unsolved problem of historical forgery: the *scriptores historiae Augustae*', *Journal of the Warburg and Courtauld Institutes* 17 (1954), 22 ff; and more recently to A. Chastagnol, 'Le probleme de l'historie Auguste: État de la question', *Historia-Augusta-Colloquium, Bonn 1963*, ed. J. Straub (Bonn, 1964), 43 ff. The standard text of the work is that by E. Hohl (Leipzig, 1927), revised 1955, most recent reprint 1965, with *addenda et corrigenda*, in the Teubner series. It is not the intention of the present article to supply a full bibliography, but various important studies will be referred to. The Latin passages cited are translated in the Appendix, pp. 199–201.

[1] *Decline and Fall of the Roman Empire*, 3.

[2] Xiphilinus 256, 6: Ἰστέον ὅτι τὰ περὶ τοῦ Ἀντωνίνου τοῦ Εὐσεβοῦς ἐν τοῖς ἀντιγράφοις τοῦ Δίωνος οὐχ εὑρίσκεται.

[3] On Dio, see now F. Millar, *A Study of Cassius Dio* (Oxford, 1964).

[4] On Herodian's status, see H.-G. Pflaum, reviewing the first work referred to in n. 5, *Revue des Études Latines* 32 (1954), 450.

[5] Cf. especially E. Hohl, *Kaiser Commodus und Herodian, Sitzungsberichte d. deutsch. Akad. Wissensch.* (Berlin, 1954), 1.3; *idem., Kaiser Pertinax und die Thronbesteigung seines Nachfolgers im Lichte der Herodiankritik, ibid.* (1956), 2.3. The defence of Herodian by F. Grosso, *La lotta politica al tempo di Commodo* (Turin, 1964), 30 ff, has not led me to revise my opinion.

[6] e.g. in 3.10.6 he states that Plautianus was related to Severus. This is confirmed by the papyrus *SB* VI, 9526, 11.47–48, in which Plautianus is described as οἰκεῖος ἡμῶν (sc. Severus and Caracalla) in A.D. 200, several years before the marriage of Plautilla and Caracalla.

[7] p. VII, n. 1.

[8] Thus the famous description of the emperors Gordian I and II in chapter 7—'Twenty-two acknowledged concubines, and a library of sixty-two thousand volumes, attested the variety of his inclinations; and from the productions which he left behind him, it appears that the former as well as the latter were designed for use rather than ostentation', with the note: 'By each of his concubines, the younger Gordian left three or four children. His literary productions, though less numerous, were by no means contemptible'—is as worthless as its source, the *Gordiani tres Iulii Capitolini*. For a critique of the biographer's account of Gordian I, see my paper 'The origins of Gordian I', *Britain and Rome*, ed. M. G. Jarrett and B. Dobson (Kendal, 1966), 56 ff.

[9] The statement by A. Chastagnol, *op. cit.* (in preliminary note), p. 43, 'avec une lacune (pour Philippe, Decius, Trebonianus Gallus et Volusianus) s'étendant sur les annees 244–253' is misleading: the *reign* of Valerian is not covered either.

[10] On Suetonius' method, cf. for example *RE* IV. A (1931), art. Suetonius Tranquillus, 613 ff (G. Funaioli); H. Peter, *Die Geschichtliche Litteratur über die römischen Kaiserzeit* (Leipzig, 1897) II. 328 ff.; F. Leo, *Die griechisch-römische Biographie* (Leipzig, 1901), 1 ff; and G. B. Townend, in ch. IV of this volume.

[11] The obvious example is Vopiscus' familiarity with Pollio (*Aurel.* 2.1). Vopiscus also refers to Capitolinus and Lampridius (*Probus* 2.7).

[12] *Av. Cass.* 5.1: 'Aemilium Parthenianum, qui adfectatores tyrannidis iam inde a veteribus historiae tradidit.'

[13] *Op. cit.* (in preliminary note), p. 24. He also suggests that elucidation on the nature of the work might have been provided in a now lost preface. As it stands, the work plunges *in medias res*: originally, biographies of Nerva and Trajan might have belonged to the collection.

[14] *Gall.* 7.1; 14.3; *Claud.* 1.1; 3.1; 9.9; 10.7.

[15] Cf. A. Chastagnol, *Les fastes de la préfecture de Rome au bas-empire* (Paris, 1962) 17 ff, 40–41.

16 T. Mommsen, 'Die *Scriptores Historiae Augustae*', *Hermes* XXV. (1890) 228 ff (= *Gesammelte Schriften* (Berlin, 1909) VII. 302 ff), p. 257 (= 329).

17 *Ibid.*, esp. 246 ff.

18 C. Czwalina, *De epistolarum actorumque quae a scriptoribus historiae Augustae proferuntur fide atque auctoritate* I (Bonn, 1870).

19 See, for example, L. Homo, 'Les documents de l'histoire Auguste et leur valeur historique', *Revue historique* CLI. (1926) 161 ff, CLII. (1926) 1 ff. In other respects a traditionalist, Homo too allows authenticity only to *Comm.* 18–19. Cf. also J. Hasebroek, *Die Fälschung der vita Nigri und vita Albini in den S.H.A.* (Heidelberg, 1916).

20 H. Dessau, '*Über Zeit und Persönlichkeit der Scriptores historiae Augustae*', *Hermes* XXIV. (1889) 337 ff.

21 Namely: Eutropius VIII. 11–14 = *Marcus* 16.3–18.2; Aur. Victor, *Caesares* XX. 1–30 = *Sev.* 17.5–19.4.

22 A. Momigliano, *op. cit.* (in preliminary note), 34–35.

23 A. Chastagnol in *Historia-Augusta-Colloquium* (*op. cit.*, in preliminary note), 60 ff, pursuing an idea of A. Alföldi; his views are criticized by A. Momigliano, 'Per la interpretazione di Simmaco *Relatio* 4', *Rendiconti dell' Accademia nazionale dei Lincei* VIII. 19 (1964), 225 ff.

24 In the *paneg. Lat.* 6 (7), 2, it is presented as something 'quod plerique adhuc fortasse nesciunt'.

25 Cf. Momigliano, *op. cit.* (in preliminary note), 33.

26 This was the view adopted by H. Peter, *Die Scriptores Historiae Augustae* (Leipzig, 1892), 80 ff.

27 This was the view of Mommsen (*op. cit.*, n. 16), 277 ff. On this question the keen arguments of E. Hohl, 'Die *Historia Augusta* und die *Caesares* des Aurelius Victor', *Historia* IV. (1955) 220 ff, in favour of the *Augustan History* having used Victor, should be consulted.

28 A. Rosenberg, *Einleitung und Quellenkunde zur römischen Geschichte* (Berlin, 1921) 231 ff.

29 Amm. Marc. XXVIII. 4.14.

30 *Schol. ad Iuvenalem* IV. 53.

31 *Op. cit.* (in n. 16), p. 229.

32 See the surveys by Momigliano and Chastagnol quoted in the preliminary note. The introductions to vols. I and II of D. Magie's Loeb text and translation (1921–32) are also very useful; and Magie's notes to the translation, in the absence of any modern historical commentary, are also valuable.

33 N. H. Baynes, *The Historia Augusta. Its Date and Purpose* (Oxford, 1926).

34 W. Hartke, 'Geschichte und Politik im spätantiken Rom', *Klio*, Beiheft XLV (Neue Folge XXXII) (1940). His views are amplified, and varied, in *Römische Kinderkaiser, eine Strukturanalyse römischen Denkens und Daseins* (Berlin, 1951).

35 Cf., for example, A. Alföldi, *A conflict of Ideas in the Late Roman Empire* (Oxford, 1952) 125–6; J. Straub, *Heidnische Geschichtsapologetik in der christlichen Spätantike* (Bonn, 1963).

36 A. Momigliano, *op. cit.* (in preliminary note) 39–41.

37 It is worth quoting this comment by Isaac Casaubon: 'Quid caussae sit cur hodie in isto Caesareae historiae corpore pars haec desideretur, difficile

dictu est. Scimus tamen, non hodie atque heri, sed ante aliquot secula, factam esse hanc iacturam: *imo fortasse nihil est amissum*, neque eorum quicquam periisse, quae in hoc corpus sunt ab iis conjecta, qui illud olim ex diversis scriptoribus concinnarunt' (my italics), *Historiae Augustae Scriptores VI cum integris notis Isaaci Casauboni Cl. Salmasii et Jani Gruteri* (Lugduni Batavorum, 1671) II. 166. Casaubon suggests that Christian antipathy to Decius may have been the cause for omitting the account of this emperor. The reason suggested in the text is equally valid.

[38] W. Ensslin, 'Des Symmachus Historia Romana als Quelle für Jordanes', *Sitzungsberichte der Bayerischen Akademie der Wissenschaften, phil.-hist.Klasse* (1948), Heft 3, 5 ff.

[39] H. L. Zernial, *Über den Satzschluss in der Historia Augusta, Deutsche Akademie der Wissenschaften zu Berlin, Schriften der für Altertumswissenschaft* II (Berlin, 1956); H. Szelest, '*Observationes nonnullae ad scriptores Historiae Augustae*', *Meander* XV. (1960) 141 ff (in Polish).

[40] W. Hartke, *op. cit.* (1940) (in n. 34) 82, 85 ff, 106 ff, 112 ff, 149 ff.

[41] J. A. MacGeachy, *Quintus Aurelius Symmachus and the senatorial aristocracy of the west* (Chicago, 1942) 181-4, followed by A. Chastagnol, *op. cit.* (in preliminary note), p. 67, n. 1. The speed of composition is only one of the grounds on which MacGeachy rejects Hartke's views. He is attacking here particularly Hartke's ascription of the authorship of the *Augustan History* to Nicomachus Flavianus junior; and his conclusion is worth quoting: 'Yet as a contribution to historiography, the *Historia Augusta* seems a dubious honor for any intellectual circle and a criterion which permits only a sorry judgment of the historical interests of the Roman senatorial nobility' (*op. cit., p.* 184).

[42] E. Klebs, 'Das dynastische Element in der Geschichtschreibung der römischen Kaiserzeit', *Historische Zeitschrift* LXI. (Neue Folge XXV) (1889) 213 ff, p. 227.

[43] Cf. G. Barbieri, *L' albo senatorio da Settimio Severo a Carino* (Rome, 1952), nos. 35, 1100. On the family, see now H.-G. Pflaum, *Les carrières procuratoriennes équestres sous le haut-empire romain* (Paris-Beirut, 1960-1), no. 168.

[44] This view is criticized by G. Barbieri, 'Mario Massimo', *Rivista di filologia e istruzione classica* XXXII. (1954) 36 ff, 262 ff. I prefer to follow E. Hohl, *Kaiser Commodus*, etc. (*op. cit.* in n. 5), p. 3, and H. Nesselhauf, 'Patrimonium und res privata des römischen Kaisers', *Historia-Augusta-Colloquium, Bonn* 1963, ed. J. Straub (Bonn, 1964), 73 ff, p. 92, with further references in n. 24. It should be noted that the account given of the career of Marius Maximus makes implausible the suggestion by F. Millar, *op. cit.* (in n. 3), p. 134 with n. 10, that he was present when the senate uttered the *adclamationes* reported in *Comm.* 18-19.

[45] This approach was initiated by J. M. Heer, 'Der historische Wert der *Vita Commodi* in der Sammlung der *Scriptores historiae* Augustae', *Philologus*, Supp. IX. (1904) 1 ff. The approach of J. Schwendemann, *Der historische Wert der vita Marci bei den SHA* (Heidelberg, 1923), and others, is similar.

[46] On Dio, cf. F. Millar, *op. cit.* (in n. 3), p. 40. On Suetonius, see the works cited in n. 10, above. In general, for a critique of the approach of Heer and others, cf. G. Barbieri, 'Il problema del cosidetto ultimo grande storico di Roma', *Annali della Reale Scuola normale superiore di Pisa, lettere, storia e filosofia*, ser. II. 3 (1934), 525 ff, esp. 535-8.

[47] On the use made of Herodian, cf. T. Mommsen, *op. cit.* (in n. 16), 261 ff; H. Peter, *op. cit.* (in n. 26) 49 ff.

[48] *Op. cit.* (in n. 16), p. 281.

[49] A. von Domaszewski, *Die Personennamen bei den S.H.A., Sitzungsberichte der Heidelberger Akademie, phil-hist. Klasse* (1918), p. 117.

[50] Cf. H.-G. Pflaum, *op. cit.* (in n. 43), no. 179 *bis*.

[51] J. Schwartz, 'L' Histoire Auguste et la fable de l'usurpateur Celsus', *L' Antiquité Classique* XXXIII. (1964) 419 ff, pp. 429–30.

[52] *Tyr. trig.* 22.14.

[53] Cf. Triarius Maternus Lascivius (*Pert.* 6.4); and earlier in the second century Ti. Claudius Iulianus, *signo* Naucellius (cos. suff. A.D. 159) *PIR* 2 C 902).

[54] Cf. *C.I.L.* VIII. 1640, 1666, 1689.

[55] *AE* 1959, 57.

[56] Cf. the examples of erroneously transmitted names in my paper 'Two Names in the Historia Augusta', *Historia* XV. (1966) 168 ff.

[57] *CIL* VIII 1625. I deal with this passage in my contribution to the 1966 Bonn *H.A. Colloquium* (forthcoming).

[58] Firmilian, *ap.* Cyprian, *Epist.* 75.10: 'Serenianus tunc fuit in nostra provincia praeses, acerbus et dirus persecutor.' See W. H. C. Frend, *Martyrdom and Persecution in the Early Church* (Oxford, 1965) 333, 391, who identifies the two without discussion.

[59] Dio, 77.6.1.

[60] *Idem.* 72.7.3.

[61] A. Momigliano, *op. cit.* (in preliminary note) 26.

VI

William of Poitiers: 'Gesta Guillelmi Ducis'

T. A. DOREY

IN his account of Curtius Rufus (ch. II), E. I. McQueen discusses the differences between biography and history, and concludes that Curtius's *Alexander* represents a fusion of the two genres.[1] The *Gesta Guillelmi* of William of Poitiers falls into the same category. It is not pure biography, concentrating on the character and personality of the subject, like Eadmer's *Vita Anselmi*;[2] nor, on the other hand, is it the history of the events of the reign, as is the case with the *Gesta Stephani*.[3] Although the work contains very few anecdotes, conversations, or personal glimpses, the narrative of events is entirely dominated by the heroic figure of the central character, William the Conqueror. It is, in effect, a panegyric,[4] with a very strong content of propaganda. In the arrangement of the material there is no attempt to follow the influence of Suetonius, a writer with whom the author was acquainted. The events are narrated in chronological order (with the exception of William's marriage and his religious reforms), there is little anecdotal material, no mention of any vices (the one quality which the author admits did incur some criticism—William's youthful recklessness—is considered justified by its successful results), there are no *divisiones*,[5] and the examples of William's various qualities are mentioned as they occur in the narrative. As opposed to Suetonius, William of Poitiers directs the reader's attention to his hero's deeds rather than his life.

William of Poitiers was a contemporary of William the Conqueror, and may have been distantly related to him. He was for a long time his chaplain, and was an eyewitness of many of the events that he described—though not, it seems, the Battle of Hastings.[6] Of his *Gesta Guillelmi*, the beginning and the end are lost. The surviving portions of the work begin with the death of Canute in 1035, though the earliest event mentioned in Normandy is William's arrival at the

full age of knighthood, in about 1042. It is probable that little was
said about his early years. The work breaks off in 1067, with the
murder of Coxo, Earl of Northumbria, though we know from the
Historia Ecclesiastica of Orderic Vitalis that it went on to 1071, and
that the author outlived William the Conqueror, but was prevented
by adverse circumstances from continuing his work up to the end of
the reign. Further information given by Orderic is that William of
Poitiers was of Norman stock, from Préaux, but was given his
surname *Pictavinus* because he had studied at Poitiers (then an
important centre of Classical learning). On his return to Normandy
he became Archdeacon of Lisieux. Before becoming a priest he had
been a knight, and had been in many dangerous battles, but in his
more advanced years devoted himself to silent contemplation and
prayer, and had greater skill in writing than in preaching. He also
composed a number of verses for the instruction of the young. The
picture presented by Orderic is that of a man gradually forsaking a
life of action for a life of study.

The two most important passages in the *Historia Ecclesiastica* of
Orderic Vitalis are:

> De cuius (Guillelmi ducis) probitate et eximiis moribus ac prosperis
> eventibus, et strenuis admirandisque actibus Guillelmus Pictavinus
> Lexoviensis archidiaconus affluenter tractavit, et librum polito
> sermone et magni sensus profunditate praeclarum edidit. Ipse si
> quidem praedicti regis capellanus longo tempore extitit, et ea quae
> oculis suis viderit et quibus interfuerit, longo relatu vel copioso
> indubitanter enucleare studuit; quamvis librum usque ad finem
> regis adversis casibus impeditus perducere nequiverit. (Book III,
> ch. 15)

and,

> Huc usque (1071) Guillelmus Pictavinus historiam suam texuit, in
> qua Guillelmi gesta (Crispi Salustii stilum imitatus) subtiliter et
> eloquenter enucleavit. Hic genere Normanus, de vico Pratellensi
> fuit, ibique sororem, quae in monasterio Sancti Leodegarii sancti-
> monialibus praeerat, habuit, Pictavinus autem dictus est, quia
> Pictavis fonte philosophico ubertim imbutus est. Reversus ad suos
> omnibus vicinis et consodalibus doctior enituit, et Lexovienses
> episcopos Hugonem et Gislebertum archidiaconatus officio in
> ecclesiasticis rebus adiuvit. In rebus bellicis ante clericatum asper
> extitit, et militaribus armis protectus terreno principi militavit,
> et tanto certius referre visa discrimina potuit, quanto periculosius

inter arma diris conflictibus interfuit. In senectute taciturnitati et orationi studuit, et plus in dictando seu versificando quam sermocinando valuit. Subtiles et concinnos versus atque ad recitandum habiles frequenter edidit, studioque iuniorum, quibus ipsi emendarentur, sine invidia erogavit. Contextionem eius de Guillelmo et eius pedisequis breviter in quibusdam secutus sum; non tamen omnia quae dixit, nec tam argute prosequi conatus sum. (Book IV, ch. 7)

Most of the information contained in these two passages has already been mentioned; further points will be discussed later in this chapter.

The *Gesta Guillelmi* was probably published some time between 1071 and 1077, the date of the death of Hugo, Bishop of Lisieux, of whom the author always speaks as if he were alive, and certainly before the arrest of Odo of Bayeux in 1082.[7] It was used as an important source by Orderic Vitalis (1075–*c*.1142), but it is not known what further influence it had. The earliest printed edition was that of Du Chesne, in 1619. Most recently it has been edited, with a French translation, by Professor Raymonde Foreville (Societe d'Edition 'Les Belles Lettres': Paris, 1952). This is a scholarly work of inestimable value, with a very full bibliography.

For part of his narrative William of Poitiers would have been an eyewitness of what he described; for other parts he would have been able to obtain first-hand information from eyewitnesses. But Professor Foreville has shown that there are numerous passages indicating that he also made use of two slightly earlier works, the Latin poem on the Battle of Hastings by Guy, Bishop of Amiens, *De Hastingae Proelio*, and the *Gesta Normannorum Ducum* of William of Jumieges.[8] The *De Hastingae Proelio* was a poem in elegiac couplets, of which 855 lines survive, and was written, according to Orderic, in imitation of the epics of Virgil and Statius:

Maronem et Papinium gesta heroum pangentes imitatus Senlacium bellum descripsit, Heraldum vituperans et condemnans, Guillelmum vero collaudans et magnificans. (III. 15)

It is mainly in verbal echoes and reminiscences that William's debt consists. The fact that he and Guy of Amiens took the same attitude towards the events they narrated is best explained by the common link of their Norman patriotism. The relationship between William of Poitiers and the *Gesta Normannorum Ducum* is slightly different.

The earlier work is far more compressed and less detailed, and generally the resemblances between the two works consist in the echoing of certain phrases or words. For example, in the account of the Battle of Hastings, the landing and the occupation of Pevensey and Hastings is described in very similar terms:

> Trans mare Penevesellum apulit, ubi statim firmissimo vallo castrum condidit. Quod militibus committens, festinus Hastingas venit, ibique cito opere alium firmavit. (William of Jumièges, *GND* vii. 14)
> Gaudentes arrepto littore Normanni primi munitione Penevesellum, altera Hastingas occupavere. (William of Poitiers, *Gesta Guillelmi* ii. 9)

William of Jumièges then proceeds:

> Quem Heroldus incautum accelerans praeoccupare, contracta Anglorum innumera multitudine, tota nocte equitans, in campo belli mane apparuit. Dux vero, nocturnos praecavens excursus hostis, ad gratissimam usque lucem exercitum iussit esse in armis. (vii. 14–15)

William of Poitiers describes this incident as follows:

> Accelerabat enim eo magis rex furibundus, quod propinqua castris Normannorum vastari audierat. Nocturno etiam incursu aut repentino minus cautos opprimere cogitabat. . . . Dux propere quotquot in castris inventi sunt . . . omnes iubet armari. (*Gesta Guillelmi* ii. 14)

The resemblances between these two passages are close enough to suggest that William of Poitiers had read and remembered what his predecessor had written. However, in the *Gesta Guillelmi* the account of the landing and the description of Harold's approach, which follow directly on each other in the *Gesta Normannorum Ducum*, are separated by several chapters in which the author describes the embassies and counter-embassies; the battle is condensed by William of Jumièges into less than fifty words, while it is narrated by William of Poitiers in very great detail, and there is considerable divergence between the two accounts on points of material fact. It is clear, therefore, that the *Gesta Normannorum Ducum* provided William of Poitiers with very little of the information that he used for his account of the Battle of Hastings.

There are, however, one or two other passages where William of

Poitiers seems to have used William of Jumièges as his source. The most notable example is the account of Harold's visit to Normandy. The incident is described by the two authors as follows:

> Edwardus quoque, Anglorum rex, disponente Deo, successione prolis carens, olim miserat duci Rodbertum, Cantuariorum archi-praesulem, ex regno sibi a Deo attributo illum statuens heredem. sed at Heroldum postmodum illi destinavit, cunctorum suae domi-nationis comitum divitiis, honore et potentia maximum, ut ei de sua corona fidelitatem faceret, ac Christiano more sacramentis firmaret. Qui, dum ob hoc negotium venire contenderet, velificato freto ponti, Pontivum appulit, ubi in manus Widonis, Abbatis-villae comitis, incidit. Quem idem comes cum suis confestim in custodiam trusit. (William of Jumièges *GND* vii. 13)
>
> Per idem fere tempus Edwardus rex Anglorum suo iam statuto haeredi Guillelmo, quem loco germani aut prolis adamabat, gra-viore quam fuerat cautum pignore cavit. Placuit obitus necessita-tem praevenire, cuius horam homo sancta vita ad caelestia tendens proximam affore meditabatur. Fidem sacramento confirmaturum Heraldum ei destinavit, cunctorum sub dominatione sua divitiis, honore atque potentia eminentissimum, cuius antea frater et fratrue-lis obsides fuerant accepti de successione eadem. Et eum quidem prudentissime, ut ipsius opes et auctoritas totius Anglicae gentis dissensum coercerent, si rem novare mallent perfida mobilitate, quanta se agunt. Heraldus, dum ob id negotium venire conten-deret, itineris marini periculo evaso littus arripuit Pontivi, ubi in manus comitis Guidonis incidit. Capti in custodiam traduntur ipse et comitatus eius. (William of Poitiers, *Gesta Guillelmi* i. 41)

From this point, however, the two narratives diverge, and William of Poitiers seems deliberately at one point to correct a fact stated by his predecessor:

> violenter illum extorsit *GND* vii. 13.
> nec violentia compulsus *Gesta Guillelmi* i. 41.

This indicates that although he knew the work of William of Jumièges he did not make great use of it.

According to Orderic, William of Poitiers wrote in imitation of Sallust (IV. 7). There are throughout the *Gesta Guillelmi* a number of borrowings from Sallust. The two most notable are in I. 44, where the polygamous habits of the Bretons are compared to those of the ancient Moors (*Jugurtha* LXXX. 6), and in II. 9, where the author mentions how Marius earned a triumph after bringing Jugurtha to Rome in chains (*Jugurtha* CXIV. 3). But there are similar borrowings from Caesar, Cicero, St. Augustine, Suetonius, and Virgil, as well as references to Juvenal and Statius.[9] From a stylistic point of view, there is little deliberate imitation of Sallust; there are echoes of Sallust from time to time, as there are of other Classical Latin authors. It seems that the correct interpretation of Orderic's statement was that, in an age when Tacitus was unknown and Livy not widely read, the name of Sallust was taken to represent the whole genre of Classical Roman historians, as Statius and Virgil were mentioned by Orderic to represent writers of Epic, and was used here to indicate that William had written a secular history, and not biography, ecclesiastical history or memoirs.

In this chapter it is my intention to examine and discuss the author's presentation of the exploits and character of William the Conqueror rather than the veracity of the picture or the truth of the events recorded. The latter task has already been undertaken in recent years by historians who have specialized in this period,[10] and the scope of the present study is purely literary.

The *Gesta Guillelmi* consists of a mainly chronological account of the achievements of Duke William's adult life, with the author concentrating his attention on certain clearly defined qualities and aspects of his hero's character. The characteristic to which he gives the greatest prominence—and it was a characteristic of the most vital importance for a king or prince in those days—was William's military skill and valour. This is stressed on numerous occasions. At the start of the book, when he has just 'taken up the arms of knighthood', he is described as a warrior without equal:

> Alium non habebat Gallia qui talis praedicaretur eques et armatus. Spectaculum erat delectabile simul ac terribile, eum cernere frena moderantem, ense decorum, clipeo fulgentem, et galea teloque minitantem. (i. 6)

His fearlessness as a young knight is described in the story of how, with four companions, he charged a group of fifteen, unhorsed one, captured seven, and pursued the others for four miles (I. 12). Another example is at the siege of Domfront, when William, with only fifty knights, beat off a surprise attack of three hundred knights and seven hundred foot:

> Pectus vero intrepide ille obvertens, deiecit humo quem audacia maxima primum sibi impegerat. Ceteri statim amisso impetu ad munitionem refugiunt. (i. 16)

His skill as a general is constantly illustrated, at the capture of Brionne (I. 9), at the siege of Arques (I. 25), at Varaville, where he attacked the army of the King of France when it was half across the River Dives (I. 34), during the campaign in Maine (I. 38), and at the capture of Mayenne by the use of fire (I. 40).

It is, however, in the account of the Battle of Hastings that these qualities are most clearly shown. There is William's calmness at a moment of crisis during the voyage (II. 7), his personal reconnaissance with a small party of knights (II. 9) and his courage in stopping the flight of the Normans and leading them back into battle, his sword flashing, cutting down anyone who opposed him:

> Fugientibus occurrit et obstitit, verberans aut minans hasta . . .
> Primus ipse procurrit, fulminans ense, stravit adversam gentem.
> (ii. 18)

His behaviour in the battle is summarized in the following passage:

> Guillelmus vero, dux eorum, adeo praestabat eis fortitudine, quemadmodum prudentia, ut antiquis ducibus Graecorum sive Romanorum qui maxime scriptis laudantur, aliis merito sit praeferendus, aliis comparandus. Nobiliter duxit ille cohibens fugam, dans animos, periculi socius; saepius clamans ut venirent, quam iubens ire . . . Cor amisit absque vulnere pars hostium non modica, prospiciens hunc admirabilem ac terribilem equitem. Equi tres ceciderunt sub eo confossi. Ter ille desiluit intrepidus, nec diu mors vectoris inulta remansit. Hic velocitas eius, hic robur eius videri potuit corporis et animi. Scuta, galeas, loricas, irato mucrone et moram dedignante penetravit; clipeo suo nonnullos collisit. (ii. 22)

> But William, their leader, so far outshone them both in valour and in wisdom that he deserves to be compared with, or even set above, the most famous commanders of ancient Greece or Rome. Splendidly did he lead his men, checking their flight, giving them courage, sharing in their danger; more often calling them on from in front than ordering them forward from behind . . . At the mere sight of this amazing and terrifying warrior many of the enemy lost heart without receiving a blow. Three horses were killed beneath him. Three times he leaped down undaunted, and soon had avenged the death of his steed. It was here that the strength and speed of his body and spirit could best be seen. Shields, helmets, breast-plates, he cut through with his angry and impatient sword, and many a man fell beneath the blow of his shield.

Another quality that is often stressed is the justice, wisdom, and firmness of his rule. This, too, is made clear at the start of the book:

> Hinc namque summo studio coepit ecclesiis Dei patrocinari, causas impotentium tutari, iura imponere quae non gravarent, iudicia facere quae nequaquam ab aequitate vel temperantia deviarent, imprimis prohibere caedes, incendia, rapinas . . . Denique coepit omnino a familiaritate sua removere quos imperitos aut pravos dinoscebat, sapientissimorum vero optimorumque consiliis uti. (i. 6)

> He now began jealously to protect the churches of God, to uphold the weak, to impose laws that were not burdensome, to dispense judgements that were always in accordance with equity and moderation, and above all to prevent murder, arson, and robbery . . . Finally, he began to remove from his personal following men whom he knew to be ignorant or evil, and to employ the counsels of the wise and virtuous.

His success in enforcing law and order throughout Normandy is often mentioned. After the establishment of William's undisputed sway, early on in his reign, all classes, churchmen, merchants, and farmers, rejoiced that they could go about their work without fear:

> Gaudebant dehinc ecclesiae, quia divinum in tranquillitate celebrare mysterium licebat, exultabat negotiator, tuto, quo vellet, iturus; gratulabatur agricola quod securum erat novalia scindere, spem frugum spargere, nec latitare milite viso. (i. 10)

These peaceful and orderly conditions even attracted the envy of foreigners:

> Homines advenae cernentes apud nos equites hac, illac pergere inermes et quodque iter cuique vianti tutum patere, huiuscemodi beatitudinem quotiens exoptavere suis regionibus! (i. 59)

Even when a large army was assembled for the crossing of the Channel, adequate means were provided for feeding the soldiers, and all pillaging or foraging was forbidden. Flocks, herds, and standing crops were left undamaged; the unarmed traveller would ride singing on his way, and at the sight of a band of knights would feel no fear:

> Provincialium tuto armenta vel greges pascebantur seu per campestria seu per tesqua. Segetes falcem cultoris intactae expectabant, quas neque attrivit superba equitum effusio, nec demessuit pabulator. Homo imbecillis aut inermis, equo cantans, qua libuit

vectabatur; turmas militum cernens non exhorrescebat. (ii, 2; repeated in ii. 45)

Conditions in Normandy under the Duke's firm rule are contrasted with the lawlessness that prevailed in territories under the control of his enemies, such as Geoffrey Martel:

sub quo licenter quaestum latrociniis contraherent (i. 17),

the Bretons:

rapinis, latrociniis, caedibus domesticis aluntur, sive exercentur (i. 44),

and William of Arques:

Ecclesiarum bona, agrestium labores, negotiatorum lucra militum praedam iniuste fieri (i. 25).

There is here a deliberate verbal parallel to the language used in I. 10. A similar comparison is drawn in the long discussion at the end of Book I on William's piety and justice:

Eius animadversione et legibus e Normannia sunt exterminati latrones, homicidae, malefici. Sanctissime in Normannia observabatur sacramentum pacis, quod effrenis regionum aliarum iniquitas frequenter temerat. (i. 48)

Thanks to his enforcement of law, Normandy was freed of brigands, murderers and criminals. In Normandy the oath of peace, so often disregarded by the undisciplined wickedness of other lands, was scrupulously observed.

Moreover, William himself would hear the cause of the widow, the orphan, and the poor, and would give his decisions with humility and compassion. No man was so powerful, or stood so high in the Duke's favour, that he could rob or oppress his weaker neighbour.

Not only did William of Poitiers portray the Duke as a man who governed Normandy with complete justice, but he also represented him as a man who always had justice on his side in his dealings with other kings and princes. He was in the right when he crushed his rebellious vassals at Val-des-Dunes, and when he gave loyal support to his overlord, King Henry, in the latter's quarrel with Geoffrey Martel that led to the capture of Mouliherne. The hostility that later arose between the King and the Duke was caused by the unjust behaviour of King Henry (I. 13), and by the jealousy of the king and his advisers (I. 29). His campaigns against Maine and Britanny are shown to be a proper exercise of his lawful overlordship (I. 36–37, 43). The whole account is, of course, highly tendentious. Finally, every effort is made to demonstrate that William had an irrefutable claim to the English throne, in virtue of his blood-relationship with Edward, by reason of Edward's formal nomination of him as his heir, and on the strength of Harold's oath to acknowledge his claim (II. 31; I. 14, 41; II. 11–12; I. 42).

The rightfulness of all William's actions is given further justification by the emphasis that is continually placed on the evil nature and viciousness of the opponents against whom he acts. At the very start of the book the reader learns of the murderous treachery of Godwin, Harold's father, towards the Anglo-Norman prince Alfred, and then is told how the abominable crime of the cruel murderer will be requited on Godwin's son, a man similar to him in cruelty and treachery, by the avenging sword of William (I. 3–4). William is frequently portrayed as an avenger, bringing requital upon wrongdoers. Apart from the above reference to the *vindice gladio*, he is described as *partis vindicantis ductor* in the campaign against the rebellious Normans (I. 8), and as *fortissimus vindex* at the Battle of Varaville (I. 34), while at Hastings the English are said to submit to punishment as if admitting their guilt by their lack of strength:

quasi reatum ipso defectu confitentes, vindictam patiuntur. (ii. 21)

Reference is also made to the madness—*vesania*—of the rebellious Normans (I. 7), the viciousness—*nequitia*—of Guy of Burgundy (I. 9); the boundless and destructive greed—*immanis cupiditas* (I. 15), *perniciosa cupiditas* (I. 36)—of Geoffrey Martel, whose evil conduct is continually stressed; the cowardly treachery and unbridled wickedness of William of Arques (I. 23), and the insolent effrontery and villainy—*impudens audacia, impudens iniquitas*—of Geoffrey of Mayenne (I. 44). But it is the unfortunate Harold who is most persistently stigmatized. He is referred to as *vesanus* and *periurus* (II. 1), as a man corrupted with luxury, a violent murderer, made arrogant by his rich plunder, the enemy of right and justice—*luxuria foedum, truculentum homicidam, divite rapina superbum, adversarium aequi et boni* (II. 8), as *vesanus* and *furiosus*—terms which refer to criminal lunacy, but had passed into the language of political propaganda (II. 25), and on several occasions as a tyrant—though in Classical terminology this often meant nothing more than a usurper (II. 25, 31, 32).

Another quality that is highlighted is William's clemency. Guy of Burgundy and his fellow rebels, blockaded in Brionne, make a plea for mercy—*pro clementia*. William deals with them without harshness —*non acerbius vendicavit*. He restores Guy to favour, and refrains from executing his supporters, as he would have been fully justified in doing (I. 9). In his attempt to capture the castle of Arques, he preferred to reduce it by blockade; the real reason clearly was that the place was so strong that it was difficult to take by storm, as the author himself admits. But William of Poitiers then goes on to make a virtue out of necessity, and says:

> Sane more suo illo optimo, rem optans absque cruore confectum iri.
> Hoping, of course, in accordance with his noble custom, that the matter would be brought to a conclusion without bloodshed. (i. 25)

William of Poitiers then proceeds to enlarge on the Duke's habitual clemency:

> quam pia continentia caedem semper vitaverit,

and tells how, in contrast to other rulers, he always avoided, where possible, inflicting the death penalty, remembering how God watches over the exercise of earthly power, and rewards each man as he has deserved, whether for acts of mercy or for acts of savagery:

> moderatae clementiae ut immoderatae saevitiae . . . sua cuique decernens.

When the castle of Arques is starved into surrender, the Duke's *celebranda clementia* manifests itself by allowing William of Arques to remain in Normandy and even to retain much of his possessions (I. 28). In his attack on Le Mans, though he could have destroyed the city and put the garrison to the sword, his habitual moderation —*solita illa temperantia*—made him prefer to spare the blood of his fellow men, however guilty, and to resort to a policy of attrition (I. 38). After the Battle of Hastings it was in his power to massacre or banish the surviving English nobles, but he resolved to proceed with moderation and rule with clemency. From his earliest youth it had been his custom to crown his victories with mercy.

> Posset ilico victor . . . quosque potentes alios iugulare, alios in exilium eiicere. Sed moderatius ire placuit atque clementius dominari. Consuevit namque pridem adolescens temperantia decorare triumphos. (ii. 26)

His clemency and compassion after his coronation are also recorded:

> Omnes ille clementibus oculis respexit, clementissimis plebem.
> Saepe vultu miserantem animum prodidit, iussit multotiens miseri-
> cordiam. (ii. 35)

Towards Edgar the Atheling, whom a section of the English had chosen king after the death of Harold, he showed not only mercy, but great liberality.

Finally, the author gives great prominence to William's piety. This was a particularly important quality, as it gained him what was one of his most important assets, the support of the Pope. The first example given is the desire attributed to him to destroy the tyrant, Geoffrey Martel:

> Tyrannum fortasse absumi desiderabat adolescens piissimus. (i. 18)

But in general there are three aspects of his piety that are portrayed —his humility towards God and his devotion to his faith, his religious orthodoxy, and his generosity to the Church. As regards his humility, all that he achieved, he is said to ascribe, with the wisdom of humility—*humili prudentia*—to the gift of God (I. 21). He and his ancestors fully realized the transitory nature of all temporal power, with the spiritual world alone having any permanence and providing any true rewards (I. 47). Immediately before Hastings he strengthened his spirit by taking the Sacrament, and then suspended from his neck the relics over which Harold had falsely sworn (II. 13). In the battle he was supported by the prayers of priests and monks, and after his coronation he continued to serve God with renewed zeal (II. 30). It is said more than once that William received special divine favours as a result of his devoutness. When he fell ill, God granted him recovery as a reward for his piety:

> Creditur, et dignissime quidem, piae devotionis arbitrum supernum
> strenuo maiestatis suae clienti sospitatem praestitisse. (i. 59)

His wisdom, too, was granted him as a reward for the piety he had practised ever since infancy:

> 'Pie agentibus Deus dedit sapientiam', ait quidam peritus divino-
> rum. Ille autem ab infantia pie operabatur. (ii. 1)

William's orthodoxy is shown in his fierce opposition to the Berengerian heresy, that denied the doctrine that the bread and wine, when consecrated, became the true body and blood of Christ

(I. 49). It is interesting to note that Lanfranc, who became William's chief religious adviser, published an important attack on this heresy. Another example of his orthodoxy is his strictness in punishing serious offences on the part of the clergy (I. 51) and his deposition of unworthy or irregularly appointed prelates such as Mauger, Archbishop of Rouen (I. 53), and Stigand, Archbishop of Canterbury (II. 1, 33). A counterpart to his refusal to condone clerical indiscipline was his appointment to bishoprics and archbishoprics of men of the highest character, such as Maurilius, Lanfranc, Gerbert, and Hugh of Lisieux.

William's generosity in founding new religious houses and in enriching established ones is mentioned on three occasions. First, in the account of his religious activities, we are told of his generous patronage in encouraging the building of churches and himself providing for their enrichment:

> In pluribus vero ecclesiis dominum collaudat patria nostra, sui principis Guillelmi benigno favore extructis, prompta largitate adauctis (i. 50);

and also of his munificent gifts of land, gold, silver, and other treasures to his newly founded monastery of St. Stephen at Caen, of which he made Lanfranc the first abbot (I. 52). Then, after his coronation, he sent rich gifts to the Pope (including Harold's banner —the Fighting Man), and to the churches in France, Aquitaine, Burgundy, Auvergne, and, above all, Normandy, making use of the great wealth that had been accumulated in England (II. 31). Finally, after his return to Rouen, there is a further account of gifts made to the churches of Normandy, on a scale so lavish that it had never been surpassed by any king or emperor:

> Nullius umquam regis aut imperatoris largitatem in oblationibus maiorem comperimus. (ii. 42)

In making these gifts, William was acting in a spirit of true piety, with his mind fixed not on the glory that perishes, but on the hope of eternal reward:

> mente ad spem interminae mercedis, non ad gloriam quae deperibit, intentus. (ii. 42)

William of Poitiers frequently introduces Classical parallels. The Duke's opposition to Geoffrey Martel is compared to the act of tyrannicide that was held so praiseworthy in ancient Greece and Rome:

> Quod ex omnibus praeclaris factis pulcherrimum iudicavit senatus Latinus et Atheniensis (i. 18),

and a similar comment is made about his killing of the tyrant Harold (II. 32).

His leading counsellors are compared with the Senate at Rome: Rome would not have needed as many as two hundred senators if she had had men as wise as these (II. 1). Rome itself, that Pyrrhus, King of Epirus, regarded as a city of kings, would have been glad to have been ruled by him (II. 32). He is also continually being compared to individual heroes of ancient history or epic, the comparison nearly always being favourable to William. Agamemnon had a fleet of a thousand ships; William had even more (II. 7). Agamemnon, with many other kings to help him, took ten years to capture Troy: William, with little foreign help, conquered England in a single day (II. 26). Xerxes joined Sestus and Abydus with a bridge of boats, and went on to meet defeat; William joined Normandy and England with the bond of his authority, and was never defeated (II. 7). It was the custom of great generals like Pompey and Marius to send out reconnaissance parties rather than to lead them in person; William took a scouting party of twenty-five knights to explore the unknown country, and returned carrying a comrade's chain-mail as well as his own (II. 9). William is also compared to Theodosius the Great for his piety (I. 52), to Titus, the 'darling of the world', to Augustus and Pompey for the affection that they inspired in their fellow countrymen (II. 32, 41), and to Tydeus and Achilles for warlike valour (II. 22).

Yet there are two characters in particular with whom William of Poitiers seems to be trying to identify his hero. In the account of the Duke's calmness at the breakfast taken in mid-Channel, when none of the other ships had come into sight, there is a deliberate identification with Aeneas:

> Non indignum duceret Mantuanus poetarum princeps laudibus Aeneae Troiani, qui priscae Romae ut parens gloria fuit, securitatem atque intentionem huius mensae inserere.
>
> Virgil, prince of poets, would not think it unworthy to include the lack of anxiety and the self-control shown at this meal among the praises of Trojan Aeneas, the father and glory of ancient Rome. (ii. 7)

There is a further comparison with Aeneas in William's attempt to meet Harold in single combat (II. 22). Apart from these specific examples, there seems to be a latent identification of William with Aeneas throughout the book. *Pietas* was the most notable quality of Aeneas; it is also one of William's characteristics to which very great prominence is given. Both William and Aeneas are portrayed as men endeavouring to fulfil a destiny marked out for them by the will of Heaven. In the struggle with their principal adversary, both William and Aeneas attempted to settle the issue by single combat. In both cases, too, the hero was seeking what had been rightfully promised to him; in both cases he was being frustrated by a treaty-breaker. The emphasis continually placed on Harold's perjury calls to mind the bad faith of Turnus. Finally, there is an implied comparison between Aeneas, the founder of the Roman race, and William, who with his Normans would found a new nation in England.

The other identification is with Julius Caesar. Of the borrowings from Suetonius, more are taken from the *Divus Julius* than from any other *Life*. Caesar's famous words, '*Veni, vidi, vici*' are applied to William's speed in capturing Alencon (I. 19). Caesar is cited as an example of how even the most experienced military commander would be alarmed by an army the size of the French host that was threatening Normandy (I. 30). There is the long and detailed comparison between Caesar's achievements in Britain and William's conquest of England, in which Caesar's setbacks, difficulties, and losses are contrasted with William's speedy, complete, and permanent success (II. 39–40). Finally, just as the stress that is placed on William's piety brings Aeneas to mind, so the reader is led to think of Caesar by the repeated references to William's clemency. The Duke's desire to avoid bloodshed, the humane nature of his punishments, and his readiness to forgive and reinstate the leaders of the opposing party form an interesting parallel with Caesar's much-vaunted habitual policy. It is interesting to note, too, that the underlying ruthlessness of them both is deliberately glossed over in the *Commentarii* and in the *Gesta Guillelmi*. There is, then, a definite indication that, just as Caesar saw himself as a second and greater Marius, William of Poitiers saw William the Conqueror as a second and greater Caesar.

Such, then, is the *Gesta Guillelmi*, a panegyric with a strong content of Norman propaganda, a work in which the author seems to present his subject mainly in terms of the well-known heroes of Classical history or epic. Such a treatment results in an overidealized presentation, which is, perhaps, inevitable in the circumstances in which the work was written. But there are other things that the reader will miss apart from impartiality. There is nothing like the clear picture that we get in Eadmer of William's relations with men like Lanfranc and Anselm,[11] or the vivid portrait furnished by William of Malmesbury of his personal appearance and habits:

> Iustae fuit staturae, immensae corpulentiae, facie fera, fronte capillis nuda, roboris ingentis in lacertis . . . magnae dignitatis sedens et stans, quanquam obesitas ventris nimis protensa corpus regium deformaret; . . . convivia in praecipuis festivitatibus sumptuosa et magnifica inibat; nec ullo tempore comior aut indulgendi facilior erat.

> He was of moderate height, but enormous physique, with fierce features and receding hair, and had immense strength in his arms; he possessed great dignity both sitting and standing, though the royal appearance was marred by an excessively protuberant belly; on the important feast days he held lavish and splendid banquets . . . and on no other occasion was he more affable and ready to grant favours. (*Gesta Regum* iii. 279)[12]

This, however, is the work of a succeeding generation. The biography of one's king, written in his own lifetime, will inevitably have a somewhat stilted air.

NOTES

[1] See pp. 17–19.

[2] For this work, and for a most useful discussion on medieval biography, see R. W. Southern, *St. Anselm and his Biographer* (Cambridge, 1963), pp. 320–8, and also ch. VIII of this volume.

[3] Now shown by R. H. C. Davis to be the work of Robert, Bishop of Bath (English Historical Review 1962, p. 209).

[4] See E. Jenkinson, ch I of this volume, pp. 2–3, for the Panegyric as a form of biography.

[5] For a discussion of the use of *divisiones*, see G. B. Townend, ch. IV, pp. 84–5.

[6] This is indicated by II. 19: 'a man who had seen that battle with his own eyes would have difficulty in describing all the details'. For the relationship with the Conqueror, see Foreville, p. vii.

[7] For a full discussion of the problem, see Foreville's edition, pp. xvii–xx, and the notes to relevant passages. The reference to Aquitania in n. 4 on p. 71 should be *de Bello Gallico* III. 20.

8 For William of Jumièges, see the edition of J. Marx (Rouen and Paris, 1914), especially pp. xvii–xix.

9 See Foreville, pp. xxxviii–xliii for the author's debt to the Classics.

10 See, in particular, D. C. Douglas, *William the Conqueror* (London, 1964); H. Korner, *The Battle of Hastings, England and Europe* (Lund, 1964); F. Barlow, *William and the Norman Conquest* (London, 1965).

11 e.g. *Historia Novorum*, pp. 15–16, 28–29.

12 This is one of the sections of William of Malmesbury's *Gesta Regum* where there is a strong Suetonian influence. Cf. also ch. IV p. 107, and ch. VII, p. 167, and n. 27.

VII

Two Biographies by William of Malmesbury

D. H. FARMER

WILLIAM OF MALMESBURY, the Benedictine monk, librarian and precentor of his Wiltshire abbey (c. 1093–1143), is generally considered as the most notable historian and Latin scholar of his generation in England. His reputation has long stood high. Even Milton, whose poor opinion of monastic chroniclers is well known, said that William 'must be acknowledged both for stile and judgment to be by far the best writer of them all'. M. R. James thought that 'whatever the sources of it, the mass and variety of William's learning are phenomenal: and no less notable are the pains he took in making it available for others'. Professor V. H. Galbraith, writing in 1951, said that 'among experts the historical reputation of William of Malmesbury stands higher than ever before'. Most recently his importance in the transmission of both halves of the collection of Seneca's Letters has been rightly emphasized.[1]

This does not mean that William cannot be criticized. Like most historical writers of his time, he had something of the historical novelist about him. His longer works, the *Gesta Regum* and the *Gesta Pontificum*, are ill proportioned; they also abound with anecdotes and sometimes bitter personal judgements which reflect both his strength and his weakness as a writer. It is fair to record that he altered many of these judgements when he revised his works in middle age; but his reputation as the most entertaining as well as the most comprehensive historian since Bede is based in part on his less praiseworthy qualities.[2] Close scrutiny, however, of the magnitude and versatility of his achievement compels admiration when we consider the difficulties under which he worked. Many of his weaknesses can be traced to the events, influences, and limited opportunities of his life.[3]

A West Country man of mixed Norman and Anglo-Saxon

parentage, William was educated and professed at the Abbey of Malmesbury. This had been founded in the seventh century by the Irish monk Meildub and been made famous by the learned and capable St. Aldhelm, who was abbot there from *c.* 675 and Bishop of Sherborne from 705 until his death in 709. The first notable Anglo-Saxon writer (his works were still read on the Continent and in England in the eleventh century), Aldhelm, though long dead, continued to influence the community which William joined. Very probably some manuscripts which belonged to him or were copied from books in his possession survived in the library and may have inspired some of William's interests.[4] And the cult of Aldhelm as a saint took a new lease of life when St. Osmund of Salisbury translated his relics to a new shrine in the abbey church in 1078 after a temporary opposition to the cult on Lanfranc's part. Miracles continued to occur at the tomb, one of which was witnessed by William himself when a boy.[5]

As a student William was extraordinarily precocious and industrious. By the age of 30 he had written the most important history of England since Bede and had done so on a foundation of the Latin classics and, as he himself records, logic, medicine, and ethics.[6] He seems to have been almost entirely self-taught: in vain does one search in his works for any acknowledgement to a living master. Godfrey of Jumièges, Abbot of Malmesbury from 1091 till 1109, was praised by William only for building up a good library, not for teaching him what he did not know. William himself, as precentor, later imitated and surpassed his former abbot.

At this time only a Benedictine monastery could have produced a William of Malmesbury; William had at once the advantages and the disadvantages of his upbringing. Only in a monastery would he have had access to the books he needed and the education to make good use of them. At the time when he became a monk the Norman abbots of English monasteries had brought from the Continent fresh intellectual interests and a higher standard of Latin: at Canterbury, St. Albans, and elsewhere they had accomplished a revolution in scriptorium and library. But with the intellectual opportunities of the twelfth-century Benedictine monk went almost inevitably a lack of knowledge of the world and a lack of experience of the characters of the great. Unlike Eadmer, William had never known at close quarters any of the most notable people of his day. He managed to travel a good deal to other English monasteries and cathedrals, but, again unlike Eadmer, he had never been abroad. His account of Rome, for instance, while containing much that is valuable, was entirely second-hand. When he came to write history, his judgements could be bookish and one-sided. The surprising thing is not his failure to achieve impartiality, but his succeeding in general as well as he did.

While realizing what he owed to the Norman abbots of Malmesbury, William had the deepest sympathy for his country's past. This came in part from his Anglo-Saxon mother, in part from his monastery. Malmesbury was connected not only with St. Aldhelm, but also with Kings Ina and Athelstan, with Lul and St. Dunstan. It was Dunstan who revived monastic life at Malmesbury, Dunstan, the artist and goldsmith, who had left tangible proof of his interest in the shape of an organ and a holy-water vat, reputedly made with his own hands.[7] Such relics, like Aldhelm's long red chasuble woven with black roundels enclosing peacocks, may well have fired the imagination of a young and impressionable monk. In his study of the English saints, whether in historical or biographical form, William could satisfy his deepest interests: admiration for the Christian heroes of the Anglo-Saxon past and opportunity to express himself in the fluent Latin that was peculiarly his. In this chapter his *Lives* of St. Dunstan and St. Wulfstan will be studied.

The difficulties were enormous. There was hardly any English secular biography. Asser's unsatisfactory *Life of Alfred* was known to him only through extracts in John of Worcester, while works like the curious *Encomium Emmae* also enjoyed only a very limited circulation. The most notable biographies produced were *Lives* of saints, but these, if of the heroic type, were often so filled with miraculous stories, Biblical parallels and lists of virtues that they were of little value as an authentic portrait of their subject. Some readers of the early Middle Ages wanted their saints to be presented almost without human traits, so that the divine power, as seen in miracles and prophecy, could shine through all the more clearly. They seemed to want almost the exact opposite to the modern reader. Physical descriptions of the saint's appearance, for instance, are extremely rare. Even more rare are real portraits.

William of Malmesbury had a poor opinion of his community's literacy in the period immediately preceding the Conquest. Although they had produced an amateur aeronaut Eilmer, who in his flight from the church tower broke a leg, and at least one practitioner of medicine, in general they 'only stammered at vernacular letters' and achieved nothing in Latin literature.[8] In this Malmesbury was only slightly below the standard of the other houses of the Dunstan revival. The low standard of Latin and the sparse hagiography are disappointing features of the tenth-century monastic revival, whose artistic achievements were so high. The contemporary biographies of Dunstan are poor; that of St. Oswald of Worcester is an excellent example of overcharged rhetoric and pomposity. Its verbiage, rightly criticized by William, serves only to draw attention to the paucity of information and invention. Of the three saints of the monastic revival St. Ethelwold was perhaps the least unfortunate in his biographers. The *Lives* of these three saints of the tenth-century monastic revival are notably inferior to those of Wilfrid, Cuthbert, and the Abbots of Wearmouth and Jarrow, written in the age of Bede.[9]

The *Lives* of Dunstan written in the early eleventh century by 'B' and by Adelard are unworthy of the importance of their subject.[10] It has been well said that 'the tenth century gave shape to English history and St. Dunstan gave shape to the tenth century'.[11] His early work of restoring Glastonbury and other monasteries to the normal life of the Rule of St. Benedict was followed by the more general and important work he accomplished for Church and State as Archbishop of Canterbury. These two achievements of his life were closely connected, for it was, in fact, mainly through the monastic order that the religious and cultural life of the country was built up, and it was largely from the ranks of the monasteries that the most important and influential bishops were drawn until the Conquest. From Dunstan's monastic revival also came the peculiarly English arrangement of having Black Monks as the chapters of several important dioceses. Yet the near-contemporary *Lives* of Dunstan give us a colourless and inadequate sketch of his character. Here was a splendid opportunity for a commemorative biography like those written of the Cluniac abbots; instead, we are given, in prose alternating with verse, 'a strange and inconsequential mixture of visions and miracles'.[12] We learn little of Dunstan's thoughts, talents, or plans, or his reminiscences which he shared with a circle of friends.

Notwithstanding the inadequacy of the *Lives*, Dunstan was venerated as early as 999 as 'the chief of all the saints who rest at Christ Church', Canterbury.[13] His cult diminished under Lanfranc, but revived to fresh intensity soon afterwards. The *Lives* of Dunstan written by the Canterbury monks Osbern and Eadmer were both signs of this revival. Its cause was both religious and patriotic. It represented the aspirations and the pride of the defeated Anglo-Saxon majority. Their saints had been derided by the Norman conquerors and their richness in relics of these saints was matched only by their poverty in literary records of them. Osbern, Eadmer, and William aimed at making good this deficiency.

One thing on which all these three agreed was the inadequacy of the early *Lives*. Osbern derided them for writing 'in a style which the prince of Roman eloquence (i.e. Cicero) calls puffed up'; William for being inelegant in style.[14] But criticism did not end there. Eadmer and William both criticized Osbern, but not each other. Their attack seems petty to modern historians, and aimed at the wrong target. Both William and Eadmer shared the prejudices of the monastic order; both oversimplified the issues involved in conflicts between the civil and ecclesiastical authorities and between monks and clerics; both wrote anachronistically, seeing in the tenth century some of the problems and outlook of the twelfth. Both fell into the common error of projecting the ideals of the present into the past, of raising the time of Dunstan to the status of a Golden Age, all the more vividly imagined through the contrast with the sombre realities of the present, and difficult to refute because of the scant documentation of the previous age. William nowhere acknowledged the existence of Eadmer's *Life*, although he praised his other writings elsewhere.

Some of William's detailed criticism of Osbern was justified; some was not. He was on sure ground rebuking him for verbosity and pomposity, notably in his description of Dunstan's studies as a boy, and for inventing imaginary conversations between Dunstan and the Devil, without making it clear to the unwary reader that they were imaginary.[15] He was much less well inspired to accuse Osbern of heretical teaching on original sin when he described Dunstan's birth as *sacrum puerperium*. William's list of Osbern's historical errors is not impressive; like Eadmer's list, it seems composed either of trivialities or of opinions which Osbern was not entirely wrong to hold. It is difficult to resist the impression that William resented Osbern's success. The errors include Osbern's saying that Edgar founded the nunnery of Shaftesbury when, in fact, he refounded a much older establishment there, which had begun in the reign of Alfred; that he made Dunstan first Abbot of Glastonbury, whereas William had established a list of abbots there extending over 454 years before Dunstan was born; that Osbern said Edgar had married a nun, which was neither historically accurate nor decently loyal. With regard to Dunstan's work at Glastonbury, at least, modern historians are far nearer Osbern's view than William's.[16]

William's *Life of Dunstan* was competent but unremarkable. If it had been entirely lost instead of surviving in a single manuscript completed shortly before the Dissolution of the monasteries, we would have lost little or nothing about Dunstan, but we would have known less about William.[17] It is not dull—nothing that William wrote could be that—but he really had nothing new to say. He could only tread once again the well-worn path of the episodes of Dunstan's life as told by 'B' and repeated by the later biographers, adding occasionally dramatic details or personal judgements. He wrote at the request of his near neighbours, the monks of Glastonbury, who furnished him, he says, with ancient materials written in Latin and English from their ancient archives to help him in his task. If this statement is anything more than a scholar's smokescreen, it is certainly surprising that the *Life* shows no trace of the use of any new documents: there are, it is true, citations from the contemporary *Lives* of Oswald and Ethelwold, from Goscelin's *Life of Edith* and Eadmer's *Life of Oda*, but William knew these already and used them in his other works. It is even more surprising that he makes no mention of 'St. Dunstan's classbook from Glastonbury', which contains a portrait of Dunstan prostrate at the feet of Christ. This is certainly contemporary and may well have been penned by Dunstan himself, as a much later inscription on the same page declares. It is now MS. Auct. F.4.32 in the Bodleian Library at Oxford and perhaps the most interesting relic of Dunstan to survive.[18] An even more significant omission from William's *Life* is all mention of Glastonbury's claim to possess the body of Dunstan. This belief was very competently refuted by Eadmer when he wrote to Prior Nicholas of Worcester in *c.* 1120, yet it persisted throughout the Middle Ages, being only finally disproved in 1508, when Archbishop William Wareham opened the Canterbury tomb and forbade any further veneration of the Glastonbury relics. Two of the Archbishop's letters to the Abbot of Glastonbury and one from the abbot to him have survived. If William had supported Glastonbury's claim in this matter, he could not conscientiously have asserted himself that he was removing 'all filth of falsity' from his account.[19]

The work is divided, naturally enough, into two books: Dunstan's life before (Book I) and after (Book II) the accession of King Edgar in 959. This event marked the end of the uncertainty of Dunstan's early life, and was closely followed by his consecration as Bishop of Worcester, whence he was translated first to London and then to Canterbury. Dunstan was born at Baltonsborough, near Glastonbury, in 909 (not 925, as William and Stubbs declared) and was educated by English clerics and Irish *peregrini* at Glastonbury. William could not resist the temptation to say that the Irish still study the *quadrivium*, but that nowadays they don't know much Latin. Dunstan was a keen student, especially of Holy Scripture, and in his spare time used to play the harp; later in life he spread the use of the 'barbiton, now called the organ'. He went to live in the household of Athelm, Archbishop of Canterbury, who soon presented him to King Athelstan. Other courtiers were envious of him, accused him of witchcraft, dragged him off his horse and rolled him in the mud. After this experience he retired from court and went to live with Elphege, Bishop of Winchester. Recovering from a serious illness, Dunstan resolved to become a monk, was professed (presumably as a private commitment), and lived for a time as a hermit at Glastonbury. He was restored to favour under King Edmund, who with the lady Elfreda decided to restore Glastonbury as a full monastery with Dunstan as abbot, after a narrow escape from death while hunting in Cheddar Gorge. The new régime began in 940. Dunstan gathered disciples around him, among them Ethelwold, the future Abbot of Abingdon and Bishop of Winchester. Dunstan was in high favour with Kings Edmund and Edred, both of whom were buried at Glastonbury; but fell later into disgrace and was exiled to Mont Blandin, near Ghent, supposedly for his unwelcome reproof of King Edwy on his coronation day. Edwy had abandoned the company of the magnates of the kingdom in order to amuse himself with a young woman and her mother. This is most probably an oversimple account of the reality, but it was worked up by the biographers into a drama in which Edwy's perpetually unforgiving mother-in-law was cast as the villain of the piece. But Dunstan's exile did not last long: Mercia soon revolted against Edwy and chose Edgar, his brother, as king in his place. One of Edgar's first actions was to recall Dunstan from exile and have him consecrated as Bishop of Worcester in 957. When Edwy died two years later Edgar became King of Wessex also; thenceforward Dunstan's future was assured.

Of his life as Archbishop of Canterbury the biographers tell us little. Charter evidence, however, shows that Dunstan was in frequent attendance at court, even after Edgar's death. The biographers emphasize and perhaps exaggerate Dunstan's influence on Edgar: William says he was responsible for the foundation of a new monastery nearly every year and the absence of private robbers and common thieves all over the country. Again the monastic biographers emphasize his share in the monastic revival, but modern historians tend to think that, after his elevation to Canterbury, Dunstan was but the 'elder statesman' of the movement, whose active leadership had passed to Ethelwold and Oswald.

The only episode in William's *Life of Dunstan* which is really new is that of Alfwold, a rich young man who became a monk at Glastonbury but afterwards left the monastic life. He asked for his wealth to be returned; when the abbot demurred, Alfwold called in the help of the king. This was Ethelred the Unready, no friend of Dunstan, whose protégé had been Ethelred's murdered half-brother, Edward the Martyr. Ethelred sent his agents to Glastonbury, who demanded in the king's name whatever Alfwold wanted. They also did additional damage to the monastery's possessions. So the monks appealed to Dunstan, then very old. He answered: 'A Domini matre ultionem exigite; illum comedant vulpes.' Alfwold soon fell mortally ill, repented of his decision to leave Glastonbury, and asked to be buried there. As his funeral procession approached the monastery it was attacked by a large pack of foxes which scattered the mourners and savaged the body. William told the story as a dramatic and macabre cautionary tale, connected by prophecy to a famous saint; to us it is more interesting for the light it throws on medieval belief in the power of the patron saint to avenge despoilers of her property, and on the comparative impotence of one of England's most venerable abbeys during the reign of a king unfriendly to monks.[20]

William's account of Dunstan's last illness and death adds nothing to the other accounts, but his summary of Dunstan's daily life is worth quoting, because it is the nearest he got to making a portrait of Dunstan:

. . . pacifici salubritate sermonis jurgia sedare et turbulentos animorum motus in serenam quietem revocare, viduis et orphanis non solum patrocinium exhibens sed etiam dignanter eos juxta praeceptum Jacobi revisens. Omnibus postremo pauperibus saepe et opportune adesse, his victum, illis vestimentum largiri; aliquibus tectum, nonnullis nummum, cunctis auxilium. Aedificia labantia et vetera restituens, nova nec ignave aggrediens nec avare absolvens, provisioni monasteriorum curam suam in patria exponere, nec transmarina maximeque in Flandria negligere. Praedicationis ex eius ore manabat imber continuus: bonis lenis et profluus, malis ut fulmen et tonitrus.[21]

He would calm quarrels by salutary and peaceful words and restore ruffled tempers to tranquillity. He protected widows and children but also courteously visited them in accordance with James' teaching. Moreover he would call on poor people at suitable times and give food or clothing to some, shelter or money to others: help of some kind to one and all. He restored old and ruinous buildings and was not slothful or niggardly in undertaking or completing new ones. He made careful provision for monasteries in England, but did not neglect foreign ones, especially in Flanders. He was an assiduous preacher: his words were smooth and gentle for the good, but he thundered violently against the wicked.

Some details of the picture are general and based on no documentary evidence: it is interesting both as a sample of William's style and as an indication of how later writers needed good contemporary evidence to make a lively portrait.

William's *Life of Wulfstan* is a much more successful and important work. While his *Life of Dunstan* adds little to our knowledge, nearly everything we know of Wulfstan comes through him. This last of the Anglo-Saxon monk-bishops, whose episcopate straddled the Conquest, thoroughly deserved his contemporary biographer and deserves to be better known today. When William's *Life* can be checked, it is proved to be most reliable.[22]

This *Life* has survived complete in only one contemporary manuscript, but there are four copies of a medieval abridgement. It was written at Worcester during the priorate of Warin, sometime between 1124 and 1140. William took only six weeks over the task: he made considerable use of a *Life* written in Old English by the monk Coleman, chaplain to Wulfstan for several years until he became prior of Wulfstan's refounded monastery of Westbury-on-Trym in 1093. Coleman has left his signature on several manuscripts from Worcester; from his marginal additions there it may be reasonably supposed that he was at one time in charge of the Worcester scriptorium, from which survive a considerable number of manuscripts containing Anglo-Saxon. Coleman is also called by William *cancellarius* of the diocese; this may well be an anachronistic use of the word, although it is likely enough that Coleman would have written a certain number of documents for Wulfstan.[23]

Coleman's *Life of Wulfstan* has not survived. It is almost certainly to be identified with the Old English *Life* mentioned by Innocent III in his letter canonizing Wulfstan 14 May 1203.[24] We know of Coleman's *Life* only through William's, and opinions will probably always differ about how far William's *Life* is an original work, how far the credit for it should go to Coleman. Close study of William's methods in his other works like the *Commentary on Lamentations* and the abbreviation of Amalarius have convinced the present writer that even when he claimed to be copying or abridging he was in reality writing an original work. Even as a copyist of St. Anselm's *Letters* or of the Canterbury forgeries, William shows a disconcerting originality. And in the *Life of Wulfstan* he lists his own alterations. From his treatment of other writers it seems that the alterations are, if anything, more considerable than he states: in this case he was also writing in a different language from that of the original. William was probably too exuberant and impatient to sustain a long exercise in exact translation; it seems that his share in the *Life* is much more creative than has often been thought. His list of alterations may thus be summarized. He suppressed long passages of rhetoric, quotations from other saints' *Lives* and irrelevant verbiage about the episcopal office. He also added new material from Prior Nicholas, a disciple of Wulfstan and friend of William, who died in 1124. This material mostly concerned Wulfstan's daily life; its close contact with its subject makes it likely that William wrote this work earlier rather than later. Some episodes from it occur in the *Gesta Pontificum*, completed in 1125. But William's extreme freedom in the use of his sources make it impossible to say which was derived from which.[25]

While he generally followed Coleman's order of events, William divided the *Life* differently. Coleman ended his first book with Wulfstan's consecration. William, with an historian's sense of the importance of 1066, divided his *Life* there, adding a third book on Wulfstan's 'private' life.[26] This last element is more significant than

it seems. It has long been realized that William made use of Suetonius' *Lives of the Caesars* in his treatment of the reigns of William II
and Henry I. These occur in the fourth and fifth books of the *Gesta
Regum*. William has been criticized here for completely lacking
classical proportion and linking incongruous forms of narrative in
the same work.[27] The section on the 'private life' of Wulfstan seems
to be an importation of this Suetonian element into hagiography,
as is the description of Wulfstan's personal appearance. Hitherto
such descriptions had been reserved for *Lives* of secular rulers.[28]
The description of Wulfstan is based on a passage in Einhard's *Life
of Charlemagne*.[29] The section on 'private life' corresponds with that
on *mores* or character in Suetonius; it is perhaps significant that
William used the same word to introduce it. Another element of
technique borrowed by William from Suetonius was his frequent
use in all his works of *exempla*, vivid and sometimes unimportant
details, which gave verve to his character sketches. This practice
made for interesting reading, but it could degenerate into carica-
ture. Without it William might have been a more accurate writer
and would certainly have been a duller one. In the *Vita Wulfstani*
we can see the best use of this technique: the details are generally
significant and contribute to a coherent whole. Thanks to William,
using Coleman's indispensable memoirs, but pruned to proper pro-
portions, we know much more of the character of Wulfstan than of
Edward the Confessor or almost anyone of the same generation.

Wulfstan was born in Itchington (Warwickshire) in about 1008.
His name was compounded of those of his parents, Ælfstan and
Wulfgifu. He was educated at the abbeys of Evesham and Peterborough, although not then intending to become a monk. His
teacher at Peterborough was a monk named Erwin, a highly skilled
illuminator, two of whose splendid manuscripts were later given to
Wulfstan. But he was not only bookish. As a boy at home for the
holidays he carried off the prizes at the village sports and excited
feminine admiration there. A little later, perhaps as the result of
losing lands in the war between Cnut and Edmund Ironside
(William does not mention this), Wulfstan's parents separated and
entered monasteries in Worcester. Wulfstan then entered the household of Brihteah, Bishop of Worcester, at the age of about twenty-
five. Later he was ordained priest and offered the care of a richly
endowed church, but he refused it. Already he was outstanding for
his serious bearing and his consideration for others.

Adeo inedia et omni parsimonia corpus attenuare et animae vires dilatare curabat; adeo mente sobrius, sermone serius, reverendus aspectu, iocundus affectu, laicum vestibus, monachum moribus agebat . . . non asperum videri poterat, quod licet durum sonaret, intus caritatem redoleret.[30]

By fasting and temperance of all kinds he tried to reduce the demands of his body and increase the powers of his soul; with his sober outlook and grave speech, his reserved bearing and cheerful disposition he was already a monk in spirit although still wearing the clothes of a layman. His words could not sound harsh when, although they sounded stern, they really diffused love.

Instead of a career as a curial cleric, he chose the life of a monk in the cathedral monastery of Worcester. There he soon held in succession the offices of master of the boys, cantor, and sacristan. He was instant in prayer, especially at night. Once during his vigils he was assaulted by a rough countryman known to Coleman. The fight lasted a considerable time; Wulfstan was ultimately victorious at the cost of a painful sore on his foot; both the wound and combat were believed to be due to the Devil possessing, or masquerading in, the body of the countryman.[31]

He was soon chosen prior. By example more than by precept he won his community to a more fervent observance of the rule. He also restored the monastery finances, then in a parlous state; of this an important record survives, the Cartulary of Hemming. He was also zealous in preaching and in baptizing the children of the poor. Unlike certain other priests, he exacted no payment for this service. As a confessor he was both kind and firm, being both unshockable and compassionate.[32]

Such a gifted and attractive character was bound to win friends, among the rich as well as the poor. Earl Harold and Aldred, Bishop of Worcester, were among them; so was a rich and pious house-wife, who made unsuccessful advances towards him. In 1060 Aldred was promoted to the see of York, but hoped to retain the see of Worcester as well, as some of his predecessors had done. This arrangement had been due to the notable loss of property by the diocese of York during the Danish invasions. But Pope Nicholas II refused to renew this arrangement: he witheld the pallium until Aldred resigned Worcester, and sent cardinal legates with him back to England to help choose a successor and generally look into the state of the Church in England.[33] After staying at Worcester Cathedral Priory for Lent, they recommended that Wulfstan should be chosen for the vacant see. This met with general approval at the witan. On 8 September 1062 Aldred consecrated Wulfstan bishop at York, but managed to retain for his new diocese some of the lands which belonged to Worcester. Wulfstan recovered them only after Aldred's death.[34]

As a bishop Wulfstan was energetic and firm. He built several churches on his own lands and encouraged the lay lords to do the same. He decreed that stone altars should replace wooden ones in his diocese. He insisted on celibacy of the clergy: married priests were deprived if they would not relinquish their wives. He was the first English bishop known to visit his diocese systematically. Preceded by a visit from the archdeacon in the district, he would baptize and confirm children, consecrate churches and altars, and meet his people in large numbers. But in his own life contemplation, too, kept its rights. After Mass in his manors he would retire to a room apart, where he would pray and study undisturbed.[35]

Inevitably Wulfstan was caught up in the troubles of 1066. King Harold, who knew his worth before his short reign began, used him as an envoy to win the loyalty of the Northerners. But for the intervention of Tostig, his goodness and kindliness would have won them over to Harold before, instead of after, the Battle of Stamford Bridge. Like some other writers, including the Anglo-Saxon chronicler, William thought that the Conquest was a divinely appointed scourge and punishment for the sins and failures of the late Anglo-Saxon people. Modern historians tend to underline the achievements rather than the limitations of the same period, but the remarks of Wulfstan on the decadence of the people, symbolized by their wearing of long hair, show again that contemporaries shared the 'pessimistic' view of these events. Wulfstan's words strike an almost topical note when he said that young men who allowed their hair to grow long and made themselves like women with their flowing locks would be no better than women in defence of their country against overseas invaders. He used to keep a pocket-knife handy with which to 'cut away the wanton locks' should opportunity offer. He used the same knife to cut his nails and to scrape away blots from books.[36]

Realizing that the Battle of Hastings was decisive, 'as though all the strength of England had fallen with Harold', Wulfstan was one of the first bishops to recognize and submit to the Conqueror. He also took part, although Coleman and William did not mention it, in the suppression of the barons' revolts in 1074 and 1088, when the custody of Worcester Castle was committed to him by the king. A post-Conquest threat to the status of Worcester came not from the king, but from the new Archbishop of York, Thomas, who claimed that the see of Worcester belonged to him. Wulfstan, supported by Lanfranc, established his independence of York; Worcester was recognized as part of the province of Canterbury; at the council of Parret, Lanfranc also entrusted to Wulfstan the temporary care of the diocese of Chester. This mark of confidence, following the original choice of Wulfstan as bishop by the papal legates and the witan, not to speak of his own record as a bishop, should be amply sufficient to refute the oft-repeated assertion that Wulfstan was ignorant or incapable. It is based only on a late legend in Osbert's *Life of Edward the Confessor*.[37]

In the second book of the *Life of Wulfstan* there are several miracle stories of considerable interest, situated in well-known places and told of people known through other sources, but they cannot be discussed here. Specially worthy of mention is Wulfstan's successful bid to abolish the slave trade at Bristol. A story had circulated that sailors had successfully invoked Wulfstan's intercession during a storm on the Irish Sea when all seemed lost. Wulfstan (or rather, says William, his *effigies praestantissima*) was seen on the boat soon after,

> making fast the tackling and splicing the ropes, calling now on one man, now on the whole crew. 'Take heart,' he said, 'hoist the yards, belay the halliards and the sheets; by God's will and my aid you will soon reach the land.'[38]

No doubt William worked up the story somewhat and others may have done so before him, but the consequent repute of Wulfstan's miraculous power must have greatly increased his influence.

> At last he eliminated from them a long established custom, which was so rooted in their hearts that neither the love of God nor the fear of king William could eradicate it before. They used to buy men from all over England and carry them off to Ireland in hope of making large profits; they even offered for sale women whom they themselves had seduced and made pregnant. You would be heartbroken to see the rows of young men and women bound together

with rope, whose youth and beauty might move even the savages to pity, brought here to be corrupted and sold the same day . . . Little by little Wulfstan suppressed this ancient custom, passed on from father to son . . . He would stay in the neighbourhood for two or three months, coming to Bristol each Sunday, where by his preaching he sowed the good seed which bore such abundant fruit in due season that they not only abandoned this sin, but also became a good example to all the rest of England.[39]

This passage is of the utmost importance for the light it throws on the abolition of the Anglo-Saxon slave trade, too often forgotten. Even if he had done nothing more than this, Wulfstan would be most deserving of our veneration.

Another intervention of his was also concerned with charity and shows him as a peacemaker in the days of blood feuds and *wergild*. A man called William had killed another man unintentionally and by accident, but could obtain neither pardon nor friendship from the victim's relatives at any price. In particular, the dead man's five brothers 'breathed out such threats of slaughter as to terrify anyone'. When brought before Wulfstan, they utterly refused all pardon, even when the bishop prostrated himself before them in his pontifical vestments. At this Wulfstan said it was easy to distinguish the sons of God from the sons of the Devil: the former are peacemakers, the latter are not. As the consequence of a popular outcry against them, one of the five brothers was stricken with a (possibly epileptic) fit. Reconciliation with William shortly followed. The episode served as the occasion to report an abridged sermon of Wulfstan's on peace.

> Mortal man [he said] can hear of nothing sweeter, seek nothing more to be desired, find nothing more precious. Peace is the beginning and end of man's salvation, the final purpose of God's commandments. The angel choir chanted it at the Incarnation, the Lord gave it to his disciples before his crucifixion, and at his resurrection brought it back to them as a trophy of victory.[40]

At the beginning of the third book William says that the few miracles he has willingly described are sufficient as witness to Wulfstan's holiness; now he proposes to tell of his private life. He begins with a physical description of Wulfstan, very rare in saints' *Lives* at this time:

He was of middle height, smaller than some and taller than others, well proportioned in all his limbs. His calmness of mind matched the condition of his body, so that he won the reverence of everyone. He was always in good health: this was due in large measure to his frugality in food and sleep. In his choice of clothes, shoes and bedding he was neither lavish nor niggardly. He avoided display of either extreme, knowing that there can be vainglory in squalid or mournful clothes. He chose a simple standard of living, with no display on the one hand, yet no failure in the distinction befitting his rank on the other.[41]

He would eat with either his monks or his knights, listening to the books that were read and explaining them in English afterwards. His own food was fish, milk, vegetables, cheese and butter. He offered ale or mead to his guests; unknown to them, he drank only water, or in his later years watered ale or wine.[42] Even when travelling he would say Matins regularly in a church, rising early and going on foot through rain and mud. Other psalmody he would say on horseback. Each day he would hear two Masses and sing a third. In summer he would take a siesta after lunch, but could not go to sleep unless someone was reading to him *Lives* of the saints or other *scripturae edificatoriae*. But if the reader stopped, Wulfstan woke up at once.[43]

In an age when endless difficulties were beginning between bishops and their monastic chapters, Wulfstan combined with conspicuous success the offices of bishop of the diocese and abbot of the cathedral monastery. Every week-end was spent following the ordinary monastic routine of the house, and he would take his turn of singing the daily Mass and Office as *hebdomodarius*. A trait which must have contributed much to his popularity with his community was that, unlike many prelates, he was humble towards his monks, approachable and unpretentious, not afraid of the criticism that some of the simple services he rendered to others were beneath the dignity of a bishop. Two facts which contributed to Wulfstan's success in combining his two offices were his creative role in the growth of the community (its numbers had risen during his rule from twelve to fifty, not counting his foundation at Westbury), and the fact that Worcester was not a large nor a very important diocese. But above all was the fact that he was an 'imitator of Christ' in a total and heroic way. It was natural that he should venerate those countrymen of his who had passed before him on the same way of holiness. He dedicated at least one church to St. Bede; while awaiting the council which decided the fate of his diocese, he read the *Lives* of St. Dunstan and St. Oswald, his predecessors. He also rehoused the bones of Oswald in a splendid shrine, partly, perhaps, to make up for his destruction of part of Oswald's church to make room for his new cathedral. The whole idea of it reduced him to tears:

'Nos,' inquit, 'miseri sanctorum destruimus opera, pompatice putantes nos facere meliora. Quanto praestantius nobis sanctus Oswaldus, qui hanc fecit ecclesiam, quot sancti viri religiosi in ea Deo servierunt!'[44]

Nevertheless Wulfstan's cathedral was built; his crypt, somewhat mutilated, survives to this day.

One of the many ways in which Wulfstan resembled his predecessor Oswald was in his care of the poor. Every day in Lent it was his practice to wash their feet and give them an allowance of food. On Maundy Thursday in particular he would spend almost the whole day either at the church offices or in the relief of the poor. On that day he gave them not only food, but a change of clothing as well. But on the Maundy Thursday before his death his diligence in previous years was quite eclipsed by the scale and lavishness of the almsgiving.

He told each of his reeves to provide from each of his manors full raiment for one man, shoes for ten men and food for a hundred. He told his chamberlains to make similar provision, so that his household should supply what his estates could not find. Three times that day the great hall was filled with poor people, closely packed. . . .

The third time supplies ran out. But the situation was saved by the sudden arrival of messengers bringing money, a horse, and some oxen. The livestock were sold at once; together with the sum of money there was ample for all the poor who came that day. On Easter Day he filled his dining-hall with these poor men as his chosen guests.[45]

Like many old men of robust constitution, Wulfstan sank gradually towards death, declining steadily from Whitsun until January. He made his confession to Robert, Bishop of Hereford, 'a man of much worldly prudence and virtuous life', and died at the age of about 87. He had been bishop for thirty-four years. It was 19

January 1095. He was buried at Worcester and miracles were soon reported at his tomb.[46]

He had lived under ten kings and been bishop under three. With his passing went the last noteworthy survivor from a civilization that had passed. It is fitting that he be remembered at the ninth centenary of the Battle of Hastings as the only English bishop to play an important part after 1066. We should also recall that we would know extremely little about him were it not for the biography written by William of Malmesbury. We should be the poorer if it had not survived. For its abundance of authentic detail and sureness of judgement it should be ranked with the best *Lives* of medieval English saints.

NOTES

[1] John Milton, *Works* (Columbia, U.S.A.) X, p. 180; M. R. James, *Two Ancient English Scholars* (Glasgow, 1931), p. 33; V. H. Galbraith, *Historical Research in Medieval England* (1951), p. 17; L. D. Reynolds, *The Medieval Tradition of Seneca's Letters* (Oxford, 1965), pp. 120–4.

[2] Over and over again William has been shown to be wrong on points of detail. The latest attack on him, for his view of Robert of Gloucester in the Civil War, comes from R. B. Patterson, 'William of Malmesbury's Robert of Gloucester', *American Historical Review* lxx (1965), 983–97. William himself admitted that writing contemporary history was an almost impossible task; cf. *Gesta Regum*, prologue to Book IV (ed. W. Stubbs, *RS*, 1887–9), vol. II, p. 357.

[3] The principal study of William of Malmesbury is still that of W. Stubbs in his introduction to the Rolls Series edition of the *Gesta Regum*. For a shorter treatment see H. Farmer, 'William of Malmesbury's Life and Works', *Journal of Ecclesiastical History* XIII. (1962) 39–54.

[4] James, *op. cit.*, pp. 10–15.

[5] *Gesta Pontificum* (ed. N.E.S.A. Hamilton, *RS*, 1870), pp. 438–9. The whole of Book V of this work is an amplified biography of Aldhelm, which I hope to treat in detail elsewhere.

[6] *Gesta Regum*, prologue to Book II, p. 103.

[7] *Gesta Pontificum*, p. 407; *Memorials of St. Dunstan* (ed. W. Stubbs, *RS*, 1874), pp. 301–2.

[8] *Gesta Pontificum*, p. 431.

[9] It is interesting to note that some of England's more important saints had no early *Lives* written of them. Bede, Theodore, and Acca are obvious examples. Apparently no *Lives* of English saints were written in the ninth century.

[10] All the medieval *Lives* of Dunstan, together with other relevant documents, were printed by Stubbs in his *Memorials of St. Dunstan*.

[11] R. W. Southern, *St. Anselm and his Biographer* (Cambridge, 1963), p. 281.

[12] *Ibid.*, pp. 322–3.

[13] D. Whitelock, *Anglo-Saxon Wills* (1930), p. 45.

14 *Memorials of St. Dunstan*, pp. 69–71; 250.

15 *Ibid.*, pp. 250–3.

16 Cf. D. Knowles, *The Monastic Order in England* (Cambridge, 1940), pp. 32–36.

17 The MS. is now Rawlinson D. 263 in the Bodleian Library, Oxford, and contains Eadmer's *Miracles of St. Dunstan* after the *Life* by William. Book I is written in a late fifteenth-century hand; Book II and the *Miracles* in one of the first half of the sixteenth. Its existence may well be due to the revived interest in monasteries shortly before the Dissolution in Anglo-Saxon saints. This interest certainly existed at Canterbury, Durham, and Glastonbury, and may have been more general. At least sixteen MSS. of Osbern's Life of Dunstan survive.

18 Facsimile edition by R. W. Hunt, *St. Dunstan's Classbook from Glastonbury* (Leyden, 1963); see also M. T. D'Alverny, 'Le symbolisme de la Sagesse et le Christ de saint Dunstan', *Bodleian Library Record* V. (1956) 232–44.

19 *Memorials of St. Dunstan*, pp. 252, 426–39.

20 *Ibid.*, pp. 313–14.

21 *Ibid.*, pp. 314–15.

22 The Latin text of the *Vita Wulstani* was edited mainly from MS. Cotton Claudius A. V, probably a Peterborough book, with much supplementary matter by Professor R. R. Darlington for the Camden Series in 1928. An English translation was published by J. H. F. Peile (Oxford, 1934). The standard biography is by J. W. Lamb, *St Wulstan, Prelate and Patriot* (1933); for a good short account, see D. Knowles, *The Monastic Order in England*, pp. 74–78, 159–63.

23 N. R. Ker, *Catalogue of Manuscripts containing Anglo-Saxon* (Oxford, 1957), p. lvi. The manuscripts which contain notes by Coleman are of Bede's Ecclesiastical History (C.U.L. Kk, 3.18), Ælfric's Homilies (Cambridge, CCC 178), Directions for Confessors, etc. (Cambridge, CCC 265), and more Homilies (Oxford, Bodleian, MS. Hatton 113–14). See also N. R. Ker, 'Old English Notes signed Coleman', *Medium Ævum*, 1949.

24 Printed by Darlington, pp. 148–50.

25 William's collection of Anselm's Letters, written in his own hand (MS. Lambeth Palace 224), has marked eccentricities in the text. For his treatment of Paschasius, cf. H. Farmer, 'William of Malmesbury's Commentary on Lamentations', *Studia Monastica* IV. (1962) 283–311.

26 *Vita Wulfstani* (hereinafter abbreviated as *VW*) I. 16; III. 1.

27 For William's use of Suetonius, cf. M. Schutt, 'The Literary Form of William of Malmesbury's Gesta Regum', *EHR* xlvi. (1931) 255–60. The whole plan of William's treatment of Henry's reign is Suetonian, according to Schutt. Thus William's paragraphs 390–1 treat his *genus* and *educatio*: his father, place and date of birth, liberal education, and knighting. 392–3 are his *initia imperii*: his election to the throne, coronation, and marriage. 395–9 treat of *res internae*: wars against Robert and the restoration of order in England. 400–10 treat of *res externae*: Scotland, Wales, Brittany, Flanders, and France. 411 describes his *mores*, i.e. Henry as friend, foe, and judge. 412 describes his *propria corporis*, stature and appearance, and his *propria animi*, jocundity, wisdom, continence (!), eloquence, etc. etc.

[28] Southern, *op. cit.*, pp. 326–7.

[29] Southern, *op. cit.*, p. 327, n. 1: the reference to Einhard is ch. 22–24.

[30] *VW* I. 2 and Introduction, pp. xxii–xxiii.

[31] *VW* I. 4.

[32] *VW* I. 7–8; see N. R. Ker, 'Hemming's Cartulary' in *Studies in Medieval History presented to F. M. Powicke* (Oxford, 1948), pp. 49–75.

[33] *VW* I. 6, 9, 10.

[34] *VW* I. 12; II. 1.

[35] *VW* I. 14; III. 9–10.

[36] *VW* I. 16.

[37] *VW* II. 1; cf. M. Bloch, 'la Vie d'Edouard le Confesseur par Osbert de Clare', *Analecta Bollandiana* xli. (1923) 17–44. This legend made Lanfranc, at a non-existent 'council of Westminster', wish to depose Wulfstan, who placed his crozier at St. Edward's tomb. It could not be withdrawn by anyone except Wulfstan himself, who was promptly reinstated.

[38] *VW* II. 19 (Peile's translation, pp. 63–64).

[39] *VW* II. 20.

[40] *VW* II. 15.

[41] *VW* III. 1; William introduces the section thus: 'nunc interiorem eius vitam et mores aggrediar'.

[42] *VW*, p. 94: this passage is supplied from the abridged text, as a leaf is missing from the principal MS.

[43] *VW* II. 4–6.

[44] *VW* III. 10–13.

[45] *VW* III. 18–20.

[46] *VW* III. 21.

VIII

The Lives of St. Francis of Assisi

ROSALIND BROOKE

AMONG the innumerable biographies written in the Middle Ages it is comparatively rare to find one whose author was specially concerned to make his subject live as a human being. The peculiar interest of the *Lives* of St. Francis is that they all reveal an extraordinary personality, and that most of them were deliberately intended to do so. This may seem natural and obvious enough; but we have only to compare them with the *Lives* of St. Dunstan in the tenth century, or the *Lives* of Francis's own contemporary St. Dominic, to realize that powerful personalities could as easily be hidden as revealed by medieval biographers and hagiographers. The vivid personality of Francis was no doubt one cause for the human interest of his *Lives*; a second was his own concern that the impact of an intensely personal revelation of God's will for his Order should prevail, and so (in marked contrast to Dominic) he seems to have fostered what we should call a personality cult in his Order; and the third reason is that his *Lives* come at the end of a tradition of human, intimate biography, which flourished during the twelfth-century renaissance and the epoch of medieval humanism.

Francis was the son of a merchant of Assisi, and the small Umbrian city was the centre of all his activities; small wonder that several of his biographers, from the conciliatory St. Bonaventure in the 1260s to the romantic Sabatier in the 1890s, have gone back there to write his *Life*.[1] He was born in Assisi about 1181–2, and brought up to riches; but his dreams carried him beyond the walls of his father's house, first to a career of chivalry, then to a life of poverty and service. He abandoned his family in 1206, but it was not till 1209 that he found his final vocation, when years of reflection were summed up in the overwhelming impact of Jesus' instruction to the disciples: 'Wherever you go, preach, saying, "The

kingdom of heaven is at hand." Heal the sick . . . cleanse the
lepers, cast out devils. Freely you have received, freely give. Take
neither silver nor gold nor brass in your purses, neither scrip nor
two coats nor shoes nor staff, for the labourer is worthy of his
meat . . ." '2 Francis began to preach and to gather followers; and
after a few years the Order grew in numbers and fame and favour
with the Church's hierarchy. In his later years Francis abandoned
direct control and handed over the office of Minister General to
other men; but he always reckoned to be himself the ultimate
touchstone of the Order's nature, to have final authority to direct
it by example, inspiration, and if necessary by precept. At the end of
his life, in his own *Testament*, he summed up the basis of his authority thus: 'After the Lord had given me brothers, no man showed
me what I ought to do; but the Most High Himself revealed to me
that I ought to live according to the teachings of the Holy Gospel.
And I dictated a simple Rule in a few words, and the Lord Pope
confirmed it for me'.3 Francis's vocation, his method of work, if
such it can be called, had three marks: the well-known mark of
poverty, so absolute that the merchant's son would not let his
followers even touch a coin; of obedience equally total; and of
teaching, by the direct word and by example. 'Holy obedience . . .
makes a man subject to all the men of this world, and not only to
men but also to all beasts and wild animals, to do with him what
they will—so far as is granted them by the Lord on high.'4 In this
characteristically vivid, whimsical way, Francis revealed his attitude
to obedience—no negative virtue in his eyes, but a positive personal
submission; and a submission of all creatures to each other and to
God. It helps us to understand the paradox of the man who could
write in his *Testament*: 'I firmly purpose to obey the Minister
General of this brotherhood and any Guardian he is pleased to
appoint over me', and go on to say: 'I strictly enjoin all my brothers
. . . on obedience, not to add glosses to the Rule nor to these
words . . .'5

Francis was an exceptionally gifted preacher and teacher; he
taught by direct precept, by example, by acting and by mime; above
all, he taught by paradox and absurdity,6 so that his hearers did not
forget. His conception of authority was in keeping with this:
exciting but bewildering, it never let his followers subside into
passivity. Its very personal nature tended to emphasize Francis's
personal authority. Even after his death when any dispute arose

about how the Order should be run or should behave the protagon-
ists tended to turn to Francis's own words or actions for justification. This acted as a spur to those who knew him and cared for his
message to tell stories about him and ensure they were recorded;
and after the first generation of eyewitnesses had passed away, it
encouraged the warring groups in the Order to embellish or invent
stories to meet new situations, much as Mohammed's followers had
devised stories about the founder after his death to lend authority to
their views on situations never envisaged by the author of the Koran.
Brother Leo died *c.* 1272, and with him (to all intents and purposes)
memory of the living Francis died too. Authentic materials survived longer—and still survive—but the new Francis of legend,
especially of the legends fostered by the austere, sometimes fanati-
cal, Spiritual Franciscans, was born in the 1270s, and flourished in
the early fourteenth century, in the *Fioretti* (the Little Flowers of
St. Francis), and in Angelo Clareno's *Historia Septem Tribulationum*.[7]

The *Lives* of St. Francis represent the high summer, or perhaps
one should say the Indian summer, of the human biographies of the
age of medieval humanism. The rise of the genre has recently been
described by Professor R. W. Southern in *St. Anselm and his Biographer*.[8] The key moment in this story was the composition of
Eadmer's *Life of Anselm* at the turn of the eleventh and twelfth
centuries; here for the first time for many centuries was a man
capable of describing human personality in a clear and lifelike way,
interested to do so, and with a hero to inspire him. Eadmer was not
entirely original, and knew something of earlier models for his task.
In secular biography he shows no interest, even though Suetonius
served as a model for his contemporary and friend William of
Malmesbury. His account of Anselm's predecessor, Lanfranc, in his
Historia Novorum is reminiscent of the commemorative lives, like
the lives of the abbots of Cluny, 'which avowedly subordinate the
display of supernatural powers to the display of activity directed
towards a practical end'.[9] But devoted as Eadmer was to Canterbury
and its cathedral, the personality of Anselm overshadows all such
interests in his *Life* of the saint. This was partly due to Eadmer's
personal feelings, partly to the purpose of his work. It was intended to justify the hero's canonization, an event which never, in
fact, took place,[10] and was based inevitably on a type of biography
which Southern has classified as the heroic, the main characteristic
of which 'may briefly be described as an overwhelming concern

with the impact of supernatural power on the natural world'. Almost every medieval hagiographer knew Sulpicius Severus' *Life of St. Martin of Tours*; many quoted from him. Such authors lifted stories from earlier lives to improve their own unvarnished tales as freely as Einhard took excerpts from Suetonius or the monk of Caen from Einhard. This model could inspire *Lives* in which the human element scarcely entered: an extreme in this direction was marked by the *Lives* of the Welsh saints written in Eadmer's own day, which are full of folklore and miracle, but probably retain no trace of the genuine human physiognomy of the Celtic saints. In a similar way Gregory the Great had preserved St. Benedict's memory only in the form of miracle stories; and the popularity of Gregory's *Dialogues* was one of the reasons for the growth of this type of literature in the twelfth and thirteenth centuries. The early Dominicans are known to us mainly from the *Vitae Fratrum* by Gerard of Fracheto, an honest retailer of improbable stories, which are not *Lives* in any true sense.[11] But the 'heroic tradition' did allow some infiltration of human events and human situations, and to that extent gave scope to Eadmer's purposes. At least it provided him with the framework, even though the miraculous is less apparent, the human more, than in almost any other saint's *Life* before the *Legend of the Three Companions*.[12]

Anselm was a noted talker, and Eadmer's *Life* is full of his talk. Here Southern detects another influence, that of the *Lives* of the fathers of the Deserts, especially as transmitted in the *Conferences* of Cassian; and what he says of the relationship of these to Eadmer is so entirely appropriate to their relation to the lives and legends of Francis that I quote it in full:

> The words of the Desert Fathers convey the sense of spiritual crisis and illustrate the role of friendship and discussion in the formation of an ideal. These elements can never have been absent from monastic life [we could also say 'from the religious life'], and they are conspicuous in the lives of Anselm and his friends. But it was in the nature of this influence that it should be difficult to detect. In Anselm a few sayings, a few principles, can be traced back to Cassian. It is a slender thread. In Eadmer the influence is even less obvious, but he may have found in this literature an inspiration for the kind of biography he wished to write. Though far removed in time and circumstance, it provided his nearest and best model.[13]

That Francis was directly influenced by Cassian is unlikely. If so,

he seems to have hidden it; for in his own writings he presents himself to us as a simple, comparatively unlettered man, who could only
write the plainest Latin. In some sense, he deceives us; the simplicity of his Latin is something deliberate, the effect in part of art. But
there is no reason to suppose that he was widely read or in any
sense a man of learning. Many of his followers were, in spite of his
uncompromising rejection of learning for them as a source of pride
and as a barrier between the friars and the simple folk among whom
they mainly worked. The Spiritual Franciscans revealed the direct
influence of the Desert Fathers in their heremitical tendency and
their spiritual extravagances. Among Francis's early biographers,
one finds in different measure the concern to reveal a great preacher
and teacher through his talk and his teaching.

II

To the historian and the student of Latin literature alike the most
interesting memorials of St. Francis written by his followers are the
First Life by Thomas of Celano and the collection of stories written
down by Brother Leo and other companions of the saint, which record
his sayings and doings in a series of vivid but disconnected vignettes.

The most usual type of medieval biography has been described
by Southern as the heroic, and it is to this category that Thomas of
Celano's *Vita Prima S. Francisci* belongs.[14] It contains all 'the essential
and invariable features' of his classification: the portents at birth,
the miracles and prophecies during life, the deathbed with attendant
signs and the continuation of miraculous intervention after death.
Yet the *Vita Prima* is more interesting and valuable a biography
than this summary of its contents might suggest.

Francis had been venerated as a saint while he still lived; soldiers
guarded him in his fatal illness lest his precious body be stolen: and
the movement for his canonization began the moment he had
breathed his last. That very night (3 October 1226) Brother Elias
wrote letters announcing to the whole Order the sad news of his
death and the unheard-of miracle of the stigmata which proclaimed
his sanctity. Eighteen months later Elias had already secured a site
and was preparing to build the great Basilica which should house his
relics. In July 1228 Pope Gregory IX himself laid the foundation
stone and commissioned Celano to write. The sequence is unusual.
Even though the process of formal canonization was still comparatively new, it would seem to have been more normal to write a *Life*

first, for use as evidence. Eadmer's *Vita Anselmi*, Jordan of Saxony's *De Principiis Ordinis Praedicatorum*, the *Vita Prima* of St. Bernard of Clairvaux, and some of the *Lives* of Becket, for example, were written at least partly to further a canonization process. But in this case the Pope knew the candidate well. Yet, though not a working brief, the *Life* was written with a definite purpose, and this determined its tone, scope, and who was chosen to write it. It catered for readers whose interests and expectations were different from ours and answers to questions we might like to ask may not be given simply because they were not considered relevant. Francis's acts were thought worthy to be recorded to the praise and glory of Almighty God, and those who read about them and him might hope to be edified and moved to thanksgiving. He had a circle of close friends who knew him intimately and loved him, but it was not one of them the Pope asked to write the official life.

Thomas of Celano was probably received into the Order by St. Francis *c.* 1215: he may have seen, even spoken to him occasionally during the next few years; after two years spent in Germany (1221–3) he was again in Italy and may have had opportunity to gain first-hand knowledge. But he did not know Francis well. His qualifications were those of a writer. His style and his presentation of his material were inspired by the literary models that were the normal equipment of learned men of his generation. His knowledge of the Bible was extensive and he quotes from it on every page.[15] He makes frequent use of the two standard models, Gregory the Great's *Dialogues* and the *Life of St. Martin* by Sulpicius Severus, and of the more recent *First Life* of St. Bernard.[16] In citing these authorities Celano was following a normal convention, but his reliance on them inevitably raises doubts as to his accuracy and reliability. He did not incorporate stories about other saints that took his fancy and attach them heedlessly to his hero, as was often done, but this does not settle the issue. Any biographer must select. Were his criteria governed by a desire to portray Francis's essential characteristics or did literary authorities dominate his selection? His description of Francis's physical appearance may be taken as an illustration of this problem. Celano had actually seen St. Francis on at least three occasions, probably more, and could describe him from personal knowledge and observation. A pen portrait from him could be extremely illuminating and the inclusion of a pen portrait of any sort in a medieval saint's life can by no means be taken for granted; all too often any attempt at personal description was omitted as irrelevant. The earliest painting of St. Francis (that we know of) is indeed attributed to 1228; but it does not purport to be a portrait drawn from life.[17] But when we examine Celano's attempt it is clear that he shared the difficulty, noted by Southern, that medieval hagiographers apparently had in achieving a physical description without a model.[18] He has used a model: the *First Life* of St. Bernard. But is his description therefore invalid? In secular biography the descriptions of Suetonius and Sidonius Apollinaris were used as models, and when Einhard described Charlemagne's appearance he used Suetonius' framework and borrowed all he could, but altered and adapted where his model was inapplicable, so that the finished product, though mostly couched in borrowed language, was yet a vivid and revealing portrait of Charles and not a literary reconstruction of a composite Caesar.[19] It would seem that Celano has done likewise. He has adapted the detail from St. Bernard's *Life* to fit St. Francis and added further details so that what he says is probably true as far as it goes. This is not to deny that he might have given us a more lifelike impression had he trusted his own inspiration. The display of erudition, though it probably did not result in actual falsification, could impede and inhibit revelation of the truth.

This conventional approach makes it all the more important to ascertain and assess what other sources he used. He assures us in his preface of the high value he attached to historical accuracy and that he has therefore supplemented his own knowledge with information gained from faithful and approved witnesses; but such statements were common form in prefaces and need to be checked. The book took him only six months to write. It is unlikely that he could have spared much time for collecting material. A few informants could be quickly consulted, and they would tell him so much and were of such standing, that it would have been unnecessary for him to prolong his inquiries.[20] The Pope himself talked of St. Francis and of his own relations with him when he commissioned Celano to write, and his testimony which can be discerned in several passages is at one point specifically acknowledged.[21] Brother Elias, to whom St. Francis had entrusted administrative control of the Order during the last five years of his life, was at Assisi, and eager to put at Celano's disposal all that he knew about the close friend he was actively engaged in glorifying. Elias's reputation was tarnished later, but his subsequent disgrace and notoriety do not alter the fact that St. Francis loved and trusted him.[22] As a witness to the saint's life and character the only criticism that could be levelled against Elias would be that he was partial, that he admired and loved him so much that he would be unable to say anything to his discredit. And that indeed could be said of all Celano's informants, the Pope included. Francis had many friends, not all in the Order, but towards the end of his life he had gathered round him a small group of companions who tended him in his sickness and were in continual close contact with him. They formed the habit of authenticating their reminiscences with the hall-mark 'nos qui cum ipso fuimus'. Celano renders this 'qui cum illo conversati sunt fratres';[23] and he gathered much information from them, particularly for his account of Francis's last two years. These few faithful and approved witnesses could have provided the bulk if not the whole of what Celano needed to discover orally.

He also used a few written sources which the Order already possessed. His account of Francis's death is partly based on Elias's letter, written immediately after that event,[24] and the final section on his miracles is condensed from the actual list of miracles read out by Octavian, one of the Pope's subdeacons, at the ceremony of canonization. Finally, he recognized and used what was after all the most important source: the saint's own writings. The references to and quotations from the two redactions of the Rule, the *Regula Prima* and the *Regula Bullata*, Francis's letters, admonitions, prayers and praises, and his *Testament* occur even more frequently than do literary sources. Celano used the *Testament* just before it became a controversial document. Only a year later Gregory IX was to decide, in the bull *Quo elongati*,[25] that it was not legally binding on the friars; but it provided Celano with a framework and a touchstone he welcomed. It was largely autobiographical and it emphasized what Francis himself considered most vital and significant in his experience. His use of the *Testament* and his quotations from the letters and admonitions enable us to affirm that Celano faithfully recorded the saint's own priorities, and the sense and intention of his teaching. Fidelity is a marked characteristic of I Celano; though in its brevity it leaves much unsaid or only implied, it is in complete harmony with the emphases of other good sources.

The *Vita Prima* is divided into three unequal parts. The first covers some eighteen years, taking the story of Francis from the age of about 25 to 43. It does not contain a great many facts, and gives no dates. But the essentials are there, mapped out by the *Testament* and in harmony with what we can learn from other more detailed sources; the process of conversion with its reversal of previously held values, his faith in churches and in priests, his desire for martyrdom, his preaching, his concern for the poor and for animals. The contrast with Jordan of Saxony's account of Dominic is very striking. Jordan's *Libellus* is in form a life of the saint, in content a history of the foundation of his Order.[26] It may be deliberately ambiguous in scope. In any event, the stages in the formation of the Order of Preachers are clearly defined in its pages. In Celano after the first gathering of disciples in 1209, the visit to the Pope in 1210, and the return to the neighbourhood of Assisi, the development of the Order is largely ignored. The author was concerned with the personality and attributes of Francis, not with the government of the Order or the writing of the Rules; and as Francis progressively abandoned day-to-day direction, so the Order, in Celano's narrative, recedes farther into the background. Celano perceived that Francis was the kind of man most clearly revealed in anecdotes, and several of the best stories about him are included in this first part of the *Vita Prima*. To this section we owe the earliest version of the famous story of how Francis preached to the birds on the road to Bevagna, and how they flapped their wings in response to his preaching, but did not fly away;[27] also of how he showed his delight in God's love by dancing before Pope and cardinals, to the intense, though unnecessary, embarrassment of his friend and protector, Cardinal Hugolino; 'pedes quasi saliendo movebat, non ut lasciviens, sed ut igne divini amoris ardens, non ad risum movens sed planctum doloris extorquens', as Celano characteristically expresses it.[28] The section concludes with the Christmas scene at Greccio, when Francis collected a real ox and ass around a Christmas crib, a part of the process by which he added a new dimension to contemporary appreciation of the humanity of Jesus.[29]

The second section opens with a statement of the date of Francis's death; it then tells in brief compass, but with more precise details of place and time than in the first section, the story of Francis's last two years: his illnesses, the stigmata, his final return to Assisi, his blessing of the friars, and his death and burial. Here the human Francis is already being obscured by the saint. The third section completes the story with his canonization and an appendix of miracles. For once the external events are described in some detail and the continuous narrative of the Pope's flight from Rome, his visit to Assisi, the many discussions of the cardinals on the canonization, and the process itself, emphasize that Celano is describing recent events at some of which he was present. He gives an account of the Pope's sermon, of the reading of the miracles by the papal subdeacon Octavian, of how they moved Pope and cardinals to tears. 'Plorat denique populus cunctus et desiderabili exspectatione suspensus, vehementius fatigatur'.[30]

Celano's first *Life* has jarred on some readers because of the polished, rhetorical Latin in which it is written. He was one of the leading stylists of his age, and his Latin is heavily charged with Biblical phrases and other echoes; he loved the fashionable rhythmic clausulae of the cursus and the rather windy metaphors of his age.[31] Occasionally his prose style comes close to poetry (as in I Celano, c. 115), reminding us that he has been supposed the author of the *Dies Irae*. He succeeded in giving in short compass the essence of the story and the man, and his narrative has been the frame of every *Life* written since. The technique of story-telling helps to bring Francis alive; undoubtedly this is more effective in the later collections which give more scope for dialogue and multiply the anecdotes further than Celano felt inclined or permitted to do. Celano was in any case chosen for his capacity as a writer, not for his personal knowledge or affection for the saint. His account of Francis's illnesses and treatment, and of the rejoicing in Assisi that he came home to die[32]—that his relics would be preserved there—do not suggest that Celano's personal affections were involved. Gregory IX doubtless wanted an elegant, brief, authentic, and yet edifying statement of his friend's life, personality, and sanctity: and with this purpose in mind the *First Life* must be pronounced a notable success. The saint's friends were likely to feel, however, as time passed, that too much was missing—that many of their best stories had passed untold; and that not enough indication had been given of the saint's intentions or outlook on crucial problems of life and discipline. The modern student is bound to add: not enough is told of the events of his life, or how his Order grew, or his attitude to its development. For a clear narrative of events we ask in vain; only occasional incidents can be dated, such as his visit to Syria and his preaching to the Sultan (1219–20); this is also one of the rare occasions when an external event (in this case, the Fifth

Crusade) is referred to.[33] The first Rule was verbally approved by Innocent III in 1210, but never confirmed in writing; yet Francis escaped the prohibition on new Orders (or new Rules, as it was interpreted) of the Lateran Council of 1215.[34] Of how this was done no early source gives the slightest hint. In I Celano there is no mention at all of St. Dominic; one story about the meeting of the saints has been given a place in II Celano—though Dominic was later skilfully excised from this story by St. Bonaventure.[35]

The comparative poverty in anecdote and comment was, however, substantially cured about fifteen years after the writing of I Celano. In 1244 the General Chapter issued an appeal for new material to be written down and collected while men who had known the saint personally still lived. The most substantial collection (so it seems) was completed in 1246; and the task of editing the stories was again allotted to Celano, who submitted his *Second Life* (II Celano) to the Minister General in the course of 1247.[36] To his sources we shall return anon. His own book is larger and less orderly than the first; the author writes not in his own person but as the mouthpiece of the saints' companions; but in style it is identical with the earlier work. Celano was not entirely successful in anecdote, and sometimes shortened his stories so much as to make them jejune. Since it was written as a supplement to his earlier book, it lacks unity and a central theme. The first part is an addendum to his earlier account of Francis's early life; the second, and far more substantial, is a collection of stories arranged under qualities and themes: 'De Spiritu prophetiae; De paupertate; De paupertate domorum; De pauperate utensilium' and so forth. The arrangement is tolerably clear, yet it is impossible to discern any genuine pattern. It is based on stories which, like their hero, were often inconsequent and unpredictable, and Celano's comparatively orderly and somewhat platitudinous cast of mind found them intractable material. These seem to be the reasons why II Celano is notably less successful than I Celano. But it must be confessed that in the eyes of modern readers the book suffers from the fact that many of the stories the author used survive in an earlier, simpler, less rhetorical or abbreviated form; and that their earlier guise is more to our taste.

One notable feature of most saints' lives is almost entirely lacking in II Celano: there are hardly any miracles, and Francis is represented as a man of exceptional sanctity, indeed, but as a recognizable human personality. His qualities are arranged to provide a commentary on the qualities required of a Friar Minor, and in particular of a Minister General;[37] there is far more comment on how the Order should be run, or friars arrange their life, than in I Celano. The practical aim is clear. But miracles are notably scarce; and the friars did not let Celano finally rest until he had supplemented his two *Lives* with the *Tractatus de Miraculis*, probably written between 1250 and 1253.[38]

III

The next *Life* of any substance is the so-called *Legend of the Three Companions*.[39] At first reading this appears to be a fresh and coherent account, singularly free from miraculous or legendary features, which suddenly takes wings a year or two after the foundation of the Order, and having described Francis's early years more fully than any other *Life*, dispatches his last years, death, canonization, and translation in a brief and perfunctory summary. Its arrangement, authorship, and date all pose problems. It opens with an introductory letter written by three of the closest companions of the saint's last years, Leo, Rufino, and Angelo, at the hermitage of Greccio in 1246. But what follows conforms neither in content nor arrangement to the haphazard collection of anecdotes promised in the letter. There are no stories about Francis's later years and the narrative proceeds chronologically. The *Legend of the Three Companions* is misnamed. The letter refers to a bundle of reminiscences that were the main source of II Celano. The Legend is a pastiche of I and II Celano and of II Celano's sources. The perfunctory nature of the conclusion suggests haste in its completion, and yet it is after a fashion a complete and even, for much of the way, elaborate work. It is possible that the explanation of these peculiarities is that it represents an attempt by someone working in Assisi *c.* 1260 to produce a large compendium of the known sources, who learned before the task was completed that a new official life was on the way, finished the work in haste, and made it available to the official biographer, so as not to seem a competitor.

The official biographer was no less than St. Bonaventure himself.[40] The great scholastic, the second founder of the Order, was faced as Minister General with a diplomatic problem of much complexity: how to preserve the true spirit of the Order (as he understood it) while keeping the factions and divergent inspirations within it at peace. He started by codifying and remodelling the constitutions of the Order, and his new edition was promulgated at Narbonne in 1260. Then he set to work, or was set to work, to write a new life of the founder. This was a logical step; an attempt to subdue disputation by removing the cause of offence. When the *Life* was completed, the General Chapter accepted it, and made it official, and subsequently ordered the suppression of all earlier legends. This extraordinary measure tells its own story; and it hardly comes as a surprise to find that Bonaventure's *Life* is little more than an elegant pastiche of earlier *Lives*. The author tells us that he went to Assisi to write it, and consulted those who survived who had known the saint. This we may believe; but when he sat down to write he produced what is for the most part an abbreviated, rewritten amalgam of Celano's two lives, with controversial items, especially the saint's own prophecies of future trouble or comments on the qualities of Ministers General, suppressed. There is neat surgery here and there; and if it were the only *Life* to survive, we should still know much about Francis, for Bonaventure renders good sources with tolerable fidelity. But if the decree of 1266 had been fulfilled to the letter, much of our insight into Franciscan origins would have perished, and the edge would have been taken off their study.

The effect of the decree is curious and interesting. I Celano had evidently circulated widely already and eleven manuscripts have survived destruction and neglect, a small number compared with the dozens of Bonaventure's known, but high when compared with II Celano, of which only two substantial copies, neither quite complete, are known.[41] One of the manuscripts of II Celano is still at Assisi, and seems very likely to have been a copy made at the Order's headquarters in the fourteenth century from an early and authoritative text. It may seem surprising that such should have been preserved at the Portiuncula or the Sacro Convento, but there are very clear indications that one deliberate exception to the decree of 1266 was made, and a virtually complete set of earlier material preserved in Assisi itself—no doubt safely under lock and key. And there it stayed, unread so far as we can tell, for over forty years.

Rumour and oral tradition, meanwhile, became all the busier because the suppression of the old legends in the 1260s was shortly followed by the death of the last of St. Francis's companions in the early 1270s. Oral tradition became particularly active among the dissident groups, the 'Spirituals', which were formed in the last quarter of the thirteenth century. Many stories were recorded in the fourteenth century as coming from this or that brother of the Marches, who had it from Brother Conrad of Offida, the Spiritual leader, who had it from brother Leo, companion of St. Francis. And rumour had it that Leo had left not only oral traditions but written materials in Assisi, though most of these were feared lost. In 1305 the Spiritual Ubertino da Casale notes with sorrow that most of Leo's *rotuli*, his notebooks, have disappeared;[42] the way lay open to the growth of oral legend which culminated in the *Fioretti*, the charming but legendary stories most familiar of all Franciscan literature to modern readers.

Yet the writings of Brother Leo had not perished.[43] By 1311 Ubertino had found access to them, to his great joy, and had even acquired possession of a small collection of stories which he believed to be written in Leo's own hand. In the same year the Spiritual leader was preparing his brief for the great argument between his dissident followers and the officials of the Order before the Pope at the Council of Vienne in 1312. If Ubertino could see this dangerous material, so naturally could the officials; and it seems that they briefed themselves against Ubertino's onslaught by putting together a collection of the official documents of the Order, the Rule and the papal bulls confirming and interpreting and amplifying the Rule, and a copy of Leo's precious stories and of Bonaventure's life. This collection survives, and it is perhaps the most exciting of all Franciscan manuscripts apart from the slender memorials from the saint's own hand. It is now in the Biblioteca Augusta Communale at Perugia; but it is almost certain that it was written in Assisi, highly probable that it was written in 1311–12, and possible at least that it was written for the Minister General's brief for the Council of Vienne.

The writings of Brother Leo were preserved in their primitive form (probably drafts in loose quires) for some years longer, and were copied again; above all they were used as the basis for the *Speculum Perfectionis*, a collection of stories which was compiled in the Portiuncula at Assisi in 1318. Soon after 1318 Leo's book seems to have disappeared. But the materials based on it had a wide circulation, especially in circles interested in preserving the memory of the primitive ideal, the circles that is from which the later Observants were to spring. In manuscript after manuscript of the mid-fourteenth century and later one finds the *Speculum Perfectionis* combined with that other Assisi book, the *Legend of the Three Companions*, and the treasure store of Spiritual legend, the *Actus beati Francisci et Sociorum eius*, the Latin source of the Fioretti.[44] Here history and legend are nicely mingled, and we may be sure that the proportion of legend would be far higher in these manuscripts but for the happy survival and rediscovery of Brother Leo's book in Assisi in the early fourteenth century.

IV

How can we be so confident that what Ubertino saw in 1311, the material which lay behind the Perugia manuscript and the *Speculum*, was Brother Leo's? Certainty in such matters one can never expect to have; but this is the conclusion so far, it seems to me, to a detective story which has occupied the attention of many Franciscan scholars since 1893. In that year the French Protestant, romantic scholar, Renan's pupil, Paul Sabatier, published his *Vie de S. Francois d'Assise*—still the most inspired successor to Celano's *Vita Prima*. Sabatier had observed in a late source of no evident authority a substantial group of stories about Francis which seemed to him to have a primitive air. This was not only based on the reports of his sensitive antennae, but on claims made in some stories to have been written by eyewitnesses, to be the work of 'nos qui cum ipso fuimus' or the like. Such claims can be invented, but Sabatier sensed that in this case they were genuine. When his book was published he toured Europe in pursuit of manuscripts, and he found numerous books in which very much the same group of stories appeared in a less unsatisfactory context, in manuscripts going back to the early fourteenth century. He had at first supposed that he was searching for the lost sources of II Celano. But when he found a manuscript which claimed that the work was written at the Portiuncula in 1227, he reckoned to have received an uncovenanted mercy: a collection of stories about St. Francis, written, as he supposed, by Brother Leo himself, within months of the saint's death, earlier even than I Celano.[45]

It is an ironical story, for Sabatier had been led in his search by a genuine insight of great brilliance, and a scribe's carelessness landed him in serious error. Other copies of the same book were soon found in which the date 1227 became 1318, and no serious scholar now doubts that that is the true date of the *Speculum Perfectionis*, the work Sabatier had discovered. A few years after Sabatier had published the *Speculum*, a German Franciscan, Father Lemmens, published the text of what he claimed to be an earlier version from a manuscript in the Collegio San Isidoro in Rome. Soon after, the English scholar Dr. A. G. Little published an account of a closely related manuscript then in his possession; and finally, in 1922, the French Franciscan Père Delorme announced the discovery of the manuscript in Perugia. Although Sabatier lived to see all these discoveries, he never quite reconciled himself to the idea that they represented an earlier version of the stories than his own; and one must in justice concede that the differences between the versions are not profound. But it is now generally recognized that these three manuscripts give us the story in a version more primitive than that of the *Speculum*, and recent study has shown that the Perugia manuscript was composed in Assisi and is probably a direct copy from the loose quires left behind by Brother Leo.

That these loose quires were written in his hand, as Ubertino supposed, is far from certain; and one may be tolerably sure that the stories were not all told by Leo. It has long been recognized that the letter now attached to the *Legend of the Three Companions* was originally the preface to the collection of stories associated with Brother Leo; and this letter shows that it was not the work of one man, but of three, Leo, Angelo, and Rufino, acting as the scribes for a wider circle of Francis's surviving friends and associates, sending in their contribution to the common stock in 1246, to form a substantial nucleus of the material remodelled by Thomas of Celano in his *Vita Secunda*.

Two examples[46] will serve to reveal the quality of this collection.

. . . When he was keeping Lent on Monte La Verna, his companion one day, when it was time for the meal, was lighting the fire in the cell where they ate; when it was lit he came to St. Francis in the cell where he prayed and slept, as it was his custom to read to him the portion of the Gospel which was recited at mass that day. When St. Francis could not hear mass, he always wanted to hear the Gospel for the day before he ate. When he came to eat in the cell where the fire had been lit the flames of the fire had reached the gable of the cell and were burning it. His companion began to put it out as best he could but he could not manage alone. St. Francis did not want to help him, but picked up a skin, with which he covered himself at night, and went out into the wood. The brothers of the place, although they lived far away from the cell, as the cell was a long way from the friary, when they sensed that the cell was on fire, came and put the fire out. St. Francis afterwards returned to eat. After the meal he said to his companion: 'I do not want to have this skin over me any more, since through my avarice I did not want brother fire to eat it.'

Once, when it was getting near the time the friars' chapter was due to be held at the church of St. Mary of the Portiuncula, St. Francis said to his companion:

'It does not seem to me that I am a Friar Minor unless I am in the state which I am going to describe to you. Imagine that the brothers come to me with great devotion and reverence and invite me to the chapter, and moved with devotion towards them I go with them to the chapter. When they are gathered together they ask me to announce to them the word of God, and I rise and preach to them as the Holy Spirit teaches me. At the end of the sermon it is put to them, what do you think of it? and they say against me: "We do not want you to rule over us for you are not eloquent and are too simple and we are too ashamed to have so simple and despicable a superior over us; so from now on do not presume to call yourself our superior!" Thus they cast me out with insults. It does not seem to me that I am a Friar Minor if I do not rejoice in the same way when they revile me and cast me out with shame, not wishing that I be their superior, as when they honour and revere me, if their profit in each situation is equal. For if I am glad at their progress and devotion when they exalt and honour me, where danger to the soul is possible, it is more suitable that I should be glad and happy at my profit and the salvation of my soul when they revile me, casting me out with shame, in which there is profit to the soul.'

These stories are in a variable, but distinctive form. Each opens with a slight reference to time or place or both; each is related to a theme—the giving of alms, devotion to brother fire, and animals, and all nature, his sympathetic insight and compassion; each centres in or ends with a memorable saying, acted parable, or moral. Some are clearly told partly for the moral: one must seek alms cheerfully, show reverence to God's creatures, take no thought for the morrow, and so forth; and the stories which relate to poverty or simplicity often reveal a direct concern with the world in which they are written: they are intended as propaganda to the friars of the 1240s and later. But the form and selection of the story in all but a handful is palpably due to a real concern to keep Francis alive as a person; and in some, such as the absurd story of his reluctance to hurt brother fire, this motive almost excludes all others. One could say that, in general, medieval hagiography was full of anecdotes, and that this only differs from other collections of stories, or from the stories in I Celano, in degree. Yet this would seem to be a superficial view of the case. It is clear that Francis lent himself to this genre; that he was naturally recalled in stories with their centre in some notable saying or paradoxical action; and it may be, too, that the life of the Franciscans gave special opportunities to the older friars—Leo, Angelo, and Rufino among them—to reminisce in this form and fashion. As in the Gospels, the constant repetition of certain formal patterns in the surviving narratives compels the question: Were there other models for such tales; do they reflect in some special way the historical character at their centre, or the manner in which tradition passed from mouth to mouth? In both cases the personality seems stamped on the form of the stories; and with the Franciscan stories one may surely say this with particular firmness, since there is every reason to suppose that most of them were set down by eyewitnesses.

This is not to say, however, that all the stories are precisely true, still less that all the conversations are precisely recorded. Direct speech is a familiar element in serious historical writings from Thucydides to the eighteenth century, and in spiritual writings in the Cassian tradition. Cassian made no attempt to reproduce actual conversations, but represented in his own words the characteristic manner and teaching of the desert fathers, adapted to the needs of Western monks.[47] The same applies to most conversations in historical literature. They were sometimes intended to represent the sort of thing that was said, or ought to have been said, on the occasion; perhaps more often a speech was a rhetorical exercise or an opportunity for the author to comment. It is rare in ancient or medieval historians to find any concession made to the actual occasion, or any serious attempt to reproduce actual conversations. To this there are some notable exceptions. Among Latin lives of the central Middle Ages, the most remarkable are Eadmer's *Vita Anselmi* and *Historia Novorum* and the collection of stories now under inspection. All three try to convey the natural effect of their heroes' conversation. One should not suppose even in these cases that exact speeches have been recorded; in Eadmer one can see signs of patchwork, of the making of effects, of elaboration of what may originally have been terse and simple; Brother Leo and his associates seem also to have enlarged on what could be clearly remembered; their lengthy harangue on the technique of founding a new convent,[48] for instance, seems to be a set piece made up from the memories of Francis's principles as much as from his actual conversation. And we have only to compare these stories with their rendering in II Celano to see that contemporaries were far from regarding Francis's words, as recorded by his companions, as in any way sacrosanct. They are abbreviated, embellished with Biblical quotations, their rhetoric improved; sometimes they are just altered. Yet Celano succeeds, even so, in rendering the message with considerable fidelity; and we need not doubt that the companions commonly give us the tone as well as the message of Francis's utterances.

V

The unusual simplicity and directness of these stories are evident enough at first reading. A swift glance at the early lives of St. Dominic makes the quality of all the early legends of Francis stand out in bold relief. Dominic is by no means exceptionally obscure for a thirteenth-century saint. Of the founder of the Carmelites we know far less; of St. Edmund of Abingdon we have several lives which tell us more while revealing less than Jordan of Saxony's account of Dominic.[49] Biography and intimate hagiography were to languish until the Renaissance. The art was dying with the passing of medieval humanism. The comparison with St. Dominic underlines how much the biographies of Francis owed to the saint himself. Dominic, it seems, deliberately tried to avoid the growth of any personality cult in his Order: it was to be directed and governed, under God and the Pope, by the collective wisdom of an Order of responsible men. The Franciscans were founded by a man who could, almost in the same breath, promise obedience to the Minister General he had set up to run the Order, and give him firm and strict instructions.[50] Francis was an obedient son of Pope and Church; but he claimed that the inspiration for his Order came direct from God; his own sense of inspiration, and his inspired quality as a teacher, made him (for all his humility) actively foster an interest in his own sayings and doings. Thus it is no coincidence that his life should have been recorded in I Celano, the last of the distinguished human saints' *Lives* of the age of medieval humanism, and in the writings of Brother Leo and the other companions, a collection of stories revealing the humanity of a medieval saint unique in quality and interest.

NOTES

[1] Bonaventure, *Legenda maior*, in *Analecta Franciscana* X (Quaracchi, 1926–41), c. 4; A. G. Little, *Franciscan Papers, Lists and Documents* (Manchester, 1943), p. 181 (on Sabatier). For general discussions of the *Lives* of St. Francis, see especially P. Sabatier, *Vie de S. François d'Assise* (Paris, 1894 (1893)), pp. xxxvi ff; F. C. Burkitt, in Burkitt, H. E. Goad, and A. G. Little, *Franciscan Essays* II (British Society of Franciscan Studies, Manchester, 1932), ch. II—an especially illuminating study; J. R. H. Moorman, *Sources for the Life of St. Francis of Assisi* (Manchester, 1940), with useful bibliography; R. B. Brooke, *Early Franciscan Government* (Cambridge, 1959), ch. I.

[2] *Legenda trium sociorum*, c. 25, in *Acta Sanctorum*, Oct. II. 730; Matt. X. 7 ff, the Gospel for St. Matthias' day in missals probably used at this time.

[3] *Testament*, in *Opuscula S. Francisci Assisiensis* (2nd ed., Quaracchi, 1941), p. 79.

[4] *Salutatio virtutum, Opuscula*, p. 21.

[5] *Testament, Opuscula*, p. 82.

[6] See below, pp. 192–4, for an example.

[7] On the Spiritual Franciscans, see D. Douie, *The Nature and Effect of the Heresy of the Fraticelli* (Manchester, 1932), ch. I–V; on Leo, the introduction to my edition of the *Scripta Leonis* (forthcoming).

[8] Cambridge, 1963, pp. 320 ff, to which my discussion is much indebted.

[9] Southern, *op. cit.*, p. 323.

[10] Southern, *op. cit.*, pp. 336–43: the cult was formally approved, however, in the eighteenth century.

[11] Ed. B. M. Reichert, *Monumenta Ordinis Praedicatorum Historica* I (Louvain, 1896).

[12] See below, p. 188.

[13] Southern, *op. cit.*, p. 328.

[14] Southern, *op. cit.*, pp. 320 ff; the best edition of the *Vita Prima* is in *Analecta Franciscana* X.

[15] Cf. Burkitt in *Franciscan Essays* II. 28.

[16] See *Analecta Franciscana* X. p. ix.

[17] Reproduced in L. von Matt and W. Hauser, *St. Francis of Assisi: a Pictorial Biography* (Eng. trans., 1956), pl. 173; cf. pl. 174–6 and jacket for other early 'portraits'.

[18] Southern, *op. cit.*, pp. 326–7.

[19] See above, pp. 101–4.

[20] Moorman, *Sources for the Life of St. Francis*, p. 67, favoured a later date, allowing more time for the collection and arrangement of the material. This

seems unnecessary and improbable, as has been argued by M. Bihl in *Archivum Franciscanum Historicum* XXXIX. (1946–8) 21 ff.

[21] *Vita Prima*, c. 101.

[22] See Brooke, *Early Franciscan Government*.

[23] Moorman, *op. cit.*, p. 99; *Vita Prima*, c. 115.

[24] See Brooke, *op. cit.*, p. 12 and n.

[25] *Bullarium Franciscanum* I, ed. J. H. Sbaralea (Rome, 1759), pp. 68–70.

[26] Ed. H. C. Scheeben, *Monumenta Ordinis Fratrum Praedicatorum Historica* XVI (Rome, 1935); cf. C. N. L. Brooke in *Trans. Royal Historical Soc.*, 5th Series, XVII (1967), forthcoming.

[27] *First Life* (henceforth *I Celano*), c. 58.

[28] c. 73.

[29] cc. 84–87.

[30] c. 125.

[31] On this see Moorman, *op. cit.*, pp. 70 ff; corrected by Bihl, *Archivum Franciscanum Historicum* XXXIX. (1946–8) 14 ff.

[32] c. 112.

[33] c. 57—'tertio decimo anno conversionis suae'; for the date cf. note to c. 57 in ed. cit.

[34] On this see the penetrating discussion in H. Grundmann, *Religiöse Bewegungen im Mittelalter*, 2nd ed. (Stuttgart, 1961), pp. 142 ff.

[35] See C. N. L. Brooke, art. cit.

[36] Ed. *Analecta Franciscana* X; for the circumstances see R. B. Brooke, *Early Franciscan Government*, p. 251 and n. 4.

[37] cc. 184–6.

[38] Also ed. in *Analecta Franciscana* X; for the date see pp. xxxvii–xxxviii.

[39] The most available edition is still that in *Acta Sanctorum*, Oct. II. 723–42. For critical comment see especially F. Van Ortroy in *Analecta Bollandiana* XIX. (1900) 119–97; Moorman, *op. cit.*, pp. 68 ff. Van Ortroy believed it to be a pastiche of no original interest; Moorman argues that it was actually the source of Celano's first and second *Lives*. Neither view seems entirely acceptable; for a critique of Moorman's argument, see M. Bihl in *Archivum Franciscanum Historicum* XXXIX. (1946–8) 4 ff.

[40] The *Legenda maior* is in *Analecta Franciscana* X. 555–652; pp. 653–78 contain the abbreviated version in lection form, the *Legenda minor*. On the former, the *Life* here discussed, see *ibid.*, pp. lxii ff.; Moorman, *op. cit.*, ch. VII.

[41] For the MSS. of Celano and Bonaventure's works, see the introduction to *Analecta Franciscana* X, and references there cited.

[42] Ubertino da Casale, *Arbor Vitae Crucifixae*, quoted by Sabatier, *Speculum Perfectionis* (ed. of 1898), pp. cxliii–cxliv; Moorman, *op. cit.*, p. 97. On the Spirituals, see above, pp. 179, 181.

[43] For what follows, see the introduction to my forthcoming edition of the *Scripta Leonis* in Oxford Medieval Texts, based on a fresh study of the manuscript evidence. Current views are summarized and developed in Moorman, ch. V.

[44] Many of these MSS. are described in Sabatier's introductions to the *Speculum* (eds. of 1898 and 1928–31) and *Actus* (Paris, 1902); for those which include the *Legenda trium sociorum*, see Van Ortroy, *Analecta Bollandiana* XIX.

(1900) 119 ff. On the *Actus* and its famous Italian counterpart, the *Fioretti*, see Moorman, *op. cit.*, ch. VIII.

[45] The story is splendidly told by Sabatier in the introduction to *Speculum*, 1st ed. (1898); see also above, notes 43–44; and A. G. Little's memoir of Sabatier, in *Franciscan Papers, Lists and Documents* (Manchester, 1943), ch. xi. The manuscripts discussed below are now Collegio San Isidoro 1/73; Oxford, Bodl. Lat. th. d. 23; Perugia, Bibl. Augusta, 1046.

[46] My own translation from cc. 50, 83 in the edition of F. Delorme, *La 'Legenda antiqua S. Francisci'* (Paris, 1926). The second story is characteristically rendered in II Celano, c. 145.

[47] See O. Chadwick, *John Cassian* (Cambridge, 1950), pp. 26–33.

[48] cc. 14–16.

[49] D. Knowles, *Religious Orders in England* I (Cambridge, 1948), pp. 195 ff; C. H. Lawrence, *St. Edmund of Abingdon* (Oxford, 1960).

[50] In the *Testament* (see note 3).

p. 117, *Ael.* 1.1. 'who have held imperial rank in that position which you maintain'.

Ibid. 'have been addressed by the title of Caesar, but have never become emperors or Augusti or in any other way gained the reputation or the hope of being emperor'.

p. 118, *Av. Cass.* 3.3 'who legally or illegally have held the imperial title, . . . in order that you, Augustus, may learn about all those who have worn the purple'.

p. 118, *Ant. Heliog* 35.6. 'To these must be added Licinius, Severus, Alexander and Maxentius, whose power, in each case, passed into your hands—but without detracting from their merits, for I do not intend to follow the example of the majority of writers and disparage those who have been defeated, since I understand that it will increase your glory if I give a full and true account about all of the noble qualities they possessed.'

p. 119, *Ael.* 2.2 'in more or less the same way as in your time Maximianus and Constantius were given the title of Caesar by Your Clemency, as if they were the sons of emperors, marked out by their merits as heirs to your August Majesty'.

p. 119, '*Gord.* 34.5 'It is said that Licinius overthrew this inscription at the time when he obtained the sovereignty, since he wished to appear to have derived his origin from the Philippi.'

p. 119, *tyr. trig.* 22.12 'Therefore your relation, Herennius Celsus, ought to know, when he desires the consulship, that what he wants is not lawful.'

p. 120, *Aurel.* 1.1 'At the feast of the Hilaria, at which, as we know, everything should be said or done in a holiday mood, after the conclusion of the ceremonies I was invited into his carriage, that is, into his official coach, by the prefect of the city, Julius Tiberianus, a man of great distinction who should be mentioned in terms of great respect.'

Ibid. 1.5 'the most famous ruler and most upright emperor, by whom the whole world was brought once more under the sway of Rome'.

Ibid. 2.2 ' "Write as you wish," he said. "You will say whatever you wish quite safely, for you will have as your fellow liars those writers whom we admire for their historical style." '

p. 121, *Pesc. Nig.* 1.1 'It is an unusual and difficult task to write fairly about men who were made usurpers by other men's victories, and as a result not all the facts are fully recorded about such people in our records and histories.'

p. 122, *Aurel.* 12.3 'from the books of Acholius, who was Chamberlain in the reign of Valerian, in the ninth book of his account'.

p. 124, *Amm. Marcellinus* XXVIII. 4.14 'Some, detesting serious thought like poison, read Juvenal and Marius Maximus with quite careful attention, gazing in their deep leisure at no other volumes besides these—for what reason, it is not for me to judge.'

p. 126, *Aurel* 42.5–6 'For Valerian, excellent man though he was, is separated from all the rest by his evil fortune. See then how few are the good emperors, so that in the time of this same man, Claudius, a stage comedian made the very shrewd point that the names and portraits of the good emperors could be engraved upon a signet ring. But on the other hand, what a long list of bad emperors there is! For to leave out people like Vitellius, Caligula, and Nero, who could put up with people like Maximinus, Philip, and all the dregs of that crude mob? Although I ought to make an exception for the Decii, whose life and death alike should be compared to men of olden times'.

p. 126, *Tac.* 19.1 'Autronius Tiberianus sends greetings to his father, Autronius Justus. Now it is fitting, most noble father, for you to be a member of our distinguished Senate and to deliver speeches before that body, now that the authority of that distinguished house has grown so great that, with the State restored to its old position, it is we who appoint princes, it is we who create emperors, it is we, finally, who proclaim them Augusti.'

p. 127, *tyr. trig.* 33.8 'I do not think I have given any guarantee of style but only of facts, since these booklets which I have composed about the lives of emperors I do not write but dictate, and I dictate at a speed which (whether I myself have promised it or you have requested it) you urge on so keenly that I do not have a chance to get my breath.'

p. 128, *Carus* 21.2–3 'Here, my friend, is my gift which, as I have said, I have produced not for the sake of its style but as a piece of learned investigation. My special purpose has been that, if any stylist should wish to disclose the exploits of our emperors, he might not fall short of raw material, since he would have my booklets as handmaids to his style. So please be content, and take the point of view that I had the wish to write well, but not the power.'

p. 128, *Tac.* 8.1–2 'In case anyone should think that I lightly trusted in some Greek or Latin writer, there is to be found in the Ulpian Library, in the sixth bookcase, a volume of ivory in which this decree of the Senate has been written out, and is signed by Tacitus with his own hand; since for a long time those decrees of the Senate which concerned the Emperors were written out in volumes of ivory.'

p. 128, *Probus* 2.1–2 'Likewise too from the Palace of Tiberius, using also the lists of the clerks of the Portico of Porphyry, and also the transactions of the Senate and People; and since in compiling exploits of this great man I have derived great assistance from the diary of Turdulius Gallicanus, an upright and noble gentleman, I do not think it right to leave unacknowledged the kindness of my aged friend.'

p. 128, *Clod. Alb.* 5.10 'Whoever wants to learn about them should read Aelius Cordus, who describes all the petty details connected with omens of this kind.'

p. 128, *Maximini* 28.10 'in case anyone who reads Cordus might think that I had overlooked something connected with my subject'.

p. 129, *Gord.* 21.3–4 'For we do not think that we ought to mention the foolish and stupid stories found in Junius Cordus, about his personal pleasures and other matters of no importance. Whoever would like to hear about them should read Cordus himself, for Cordus tells us the names of the slaves and the friends of each individual emperor, and how many overcoats he possessed, and how many cloaks, facts which are just not worth knowing.'

p. 129, *Av. Cass.* 5.1 'who has given an account of the usurpers from ancient times to the present day'.

p. 129, *Severus* 5.5 'when already the armies of Illyria and Gaul had been compelled by their leader to swear allegiance'.

p. 130, *quad. tyr.* 1.2 'a most long-winded individual, who involved himself in bogus works of history'.

p. 131, *tyr. trig.* 21.1 'he was given the title of Thessalicus. He was a man of the greatest righteousness, and in his own day he was called Frugi, and was said to trace his descent back to that branch of the Pisos with which Cicero had formed a marriage alliance for the purpose of joining the aristocracy.'

p. 131, *Claud.* 17.5 'two bowls studded with jewels, three pounds in weight; two golden cups studded with jewels; a silver plate with an ivory motif of twenty pounds weight; a silver dish with a pattern of vine leaves, thirty pounds in weight'.

p. 134, *Probus* 2.8 'For I am one of those engaged in research, urged on, a thing I cannot deny, by you, who, however much you know, still desire to know much more.'

Index of Names

Abdalonymus, 27
Achilles, 152
Acholius, 122
Adelard, 160
Aelfstan, 167
Aelius Caesar, 117, 119, 121
Aemilius Parthenianus, 129
Aemilius Paulus, 49, 53
Aeneas, 152, 153
Agamemnon, 152
Agesilaus, 3, 4, 8, 12, 58, 61, 81
Agis IV, 47, 62, 65
Agis (Macedonian), 19
Agricola, 50, 51, 58, 81, 84
Agrippina (Minor), 83
Alcibiades, 7, 11, 53, 54, 56, 58,
    61, 65
Alcuin, 98
Aldhelm, 158, 159
Aldred, 168, 169
Alexander, 18–43, 53, 58, 62,
    67, 70
Alfred, King, 162
Alfred, Atheling, 148
Alfwold, 164
Amalarius, 166
Amazons, 27, 34
Ambrose, St., 97
Ammianus Marcellinus, 113, 124
Ammon, 27, 36
Ammonius, 45
Amyntas, 18, 27, 30
Amyot, 67

Angelo, Brother, 188, 192, 194
Annius Cornicula, 129
Anselm, 154, 166, 179, 180,
    194
Antigonus of Carystus, 4
Antoninus Pius, 113, 117, 130
Antony, Mark, 9, 10, 24, 67
Aratus, 47, 49, 51, 70
Archilochus, 60
Aristander, 19
Aristides, 7, 59, 61, 65, 68, 70
Aristobulus, 21, 34
Aristophanes, 51, 60
Aristotle, 3, 57
Aristoxenus, 4
Arrian, 20, 34–37, 39
Artaxerxes II, 47, 48, 70
Asser, 159
Athelm, 163
Athelstan, King, 159, 163
Atherianus, Julius, 129
Atticus, 2, 5, 6, 8, 9, 12
Auerbach, E., 104, 105
Aufidius Bassus, 84
Augustine, St., 144
Augustus, 9, 10, 24, 25, 33, 58,
    66, 71, 83, 85, 87, 89–91, 99,
    101–3, 107, 152
Aurelian, 118, 120–2, 125, 131
Aurelius Victor, 97, 114, 123,
    124
Aureolus, 131
Avidius Cassius, 117, 121